How Russia Learned to Write

PUBLICATIONS OF THE WISCONSIN CENTER
FOR PUSHKIN STUDIES

David M. Bethea

SERIES EDITOR

HOW RUSSIA LEARNED TO WRITE

Literature and
the Imperial Table of Ranks

Irina Reyfman

THE UNIVERSITY OF WISCONSIN PRESS

Publication of this volume has been made possible, in part, through support from the Wisconsin Center for Pushkin Studies in the Department of Slavic Languages at the University of Wisconsin–Madison and from the Harriman Institute, Columbia University.

Studies of the Harriman Institute
Columbia University

The Harriman Institute, Columbia University, sponsors the Studies of the Harriman Institute in the belief that their publication contributes to scholarly research and public understanding. In this way the Institute, while not necessarily endorsing their conclusions, is pleased to make available the results of some of the research conducted under its auspices.

The University of Wisconsin Press
1930 Monroe Street, 3rd Floor
Madison, Wisconsin 53711-2059
uwpress.wisc.edu

3 Henrietta Street, Covent Garden
London WC2E 8LU, United Kingdom
eurospanbookstore.com

Printed in the United States of America

This book may be available in a digital edition.

Library of Congress Cataloging-in-Publication Data

Names: Reyfman, Irina, author.
Title: How Russia learned to write: literature and the Imperial Table of Ranks / Irina Reyfman.
Other titles: Publications of the Wisconsin Center for Pushkin Studies.
Description: Madison, Wisconsin: The University of Wisconsin Press, [2016] | ©2016
| Series: Publications of the Wisconsin Center for Pushkin Studies |
Includes bibliographical references and index.
Identifiers: LCCN 2015039995 | ISBN 9780299308308 (cloth: alk. paper)
Subjects: LCSH: Pushkin, Aleksandr Sergeevich, 1799-1837—Criticism and interpretation.
| Russian literature—18th century—History and criticism.
| Russian literature—19th century—History and criticism.
| Russian literature—18th century—Social aspects. | Russian literature—19th century—
Social aspects. | Nobility—Russia. | Literature and state—Russia.
| Authors, Russian—18th century. | Authors, Russian—19th century. | Russia—History.
Classification: LCC PG2975 .R49 2016 | DDC 891.709/358—dc23
LC record available at http://lccn.loc.gov/2015039995

Contents

Acknowledgments

I am grateful to the many colleagues, too numerous to name, who have given me much-appreciated feedback at all stages of this book. My special thanks go to Deborah Martinsen for her unwavering willingness to offer moral, conceptual, and editorial support. Andrew Kahn's sense of humor and readiness to help with matters large and small sustained me throughout my writing. William Mills Todd III, Richard Wortman, and David Bethea read the introduction at its various stages and offered excellent commentary. My editor, Nancy Workman, has done her usual magic on my manuscript. My anonymous readers for the University of Wisconsin Press offered invaluable advice for improving my manuscript. I am greatly beholden to Gwen Walker, Matthew Cosby, and Sheila McMahon of the University of Wisconsin Press for guiding me through the publication process. My sincere thanks go to Marlyn Miller for masterful copyediting and Trudi Gershinov for designing a beautiful book cover. All the volume's shortcomings are my own.

I would like to acknowledge the generosity of the Harriman Institute, whose support made this publication possible. Its Faculty Research Small Grant (Summer 2015), PepsiCo Travel Grant (Summer 2013), and Faculty Seed Grant (Summer 2010) helped me in both the early and finishing stages.

I thank the following publishers for their permission to republish my work in revised form. Chapter 1 is partly based on "Writing, Ranks and the Eighteenth-Century Russian Gentry Experience," in *Representing Private Lives of the Enlightenment*, ed. Andrew Kahn, SVEC 11 (Oxford: Voltaire Foundation, 2010), 149–66, and is reprinted by permission of the Voltaire Foundation, University of Oxford. Academic Studies Press graciously granted me permission to reprint, in revised form, the following chapters from my collection *Rank and Style: Russians in State Service, Life, and Literature* (Boston: ASP, 2012): "Writing, Ranks, and the Eighteenth-Century Russian Gentry Experience" became part of chapter 1; and "Writing and the Anxiety of Rank: Pushkin's Prose

Fiction," "Pushkin the Kammerherr: On Pushkin's Social Reputation in the 1830s," and "Kammerjunker in 'Notes of a Madman': Gogol's View of Pushkin" were incorporated into chapter 2. I also thank those publishers who assign copyright to authors or do not require special permission for republishing.

To my steadily growing family, near and far, my love. To Simon, my thanks for everything.

Note on Transliteration and Translation

I use a modified Library of Congress system of transliteration in the text, adopting -y for names ending in *ii*. I use the standard spelling of first and last names adopted in the West (e.g., Alexander Pushkin, Alexander Herzen, Leo Tolstoy, Nikolai Gogol). I retain the original Danish for Vladimir Dahl.

All translations are mine, unless otherwise indicated.

How Russia Learned to Write

Introduction

Russian Writers and State Service, 1750s–1850s

For every lover of Russian literature, Alexander Pushkin is first of all a great writer, the author of *Eugene Onegin, Boris Godunov, The Bronze Horseman*, and some of the most celebrated lyric poetry in the language. For many, he is the creator of modern Russian literature, a culture hero who continues to speak to readers of different historical epochs. Accordingly, much scholarship has focused on his work, life, and cultural significance. This study, however, will place Pushkin in a hitherto unexamined context and view him with other members of Russia's service nobility who were also writers.

As a nobleman, Pushkin was expected to engage in state service, and so was defined in part by his rank. In 1833 he also received the court title of *kammerjunker* (junior chamberlain), the lesser of two honorary court titles. While to contemporary readers and even scholars Pushkin's service may seem the least important aspect of his life, it was not so for Pushkin himself or for his contemporaries, who all knew that Pushkin had never achieved success in service. Furthermore, many were amused by his title of *kammerjunker*, and some gloated over his receiving it instead of the greater one, *kammerherr* (chamberlain), deeming it inappropriate for a man of his age and status as a paterfamilias. Significantly, Pushkin's participation in the service hierarchy is reflected in his literary works, which demonstrate Pushkin's uneasiness about his undistinguished service career: along with his famous cockiness, his poetry and prose reveal a lack of social confidence about his low service rank.

3

Pushkin's works also demonstrate his uncertainty about the status of the writer in contemporary Russia. Throughout his life as a writer, he kept considering the writer's status in different contexts, including state service and the system of ranks.

Pushkin was not unique in having to balance the identities of writer and state servitor. For about a hundred years, between the mid-eighteenth and mid-nineteenth centuries, the main producers of literature in Russia were members of the nobility (*dvoriane*). In the eighteenth century, state service was a particularly strong presence in their lives, and writers from Aleksandr Sumarokov to Nikolai Karamzin used a variety of strategies to deal with their double-edged situation, putting different emphases on service and writing: they might present writing as a form of service, regard service as an impediment to their literary pursuits, or engage in both but keep their service separate from their writing. Until at least the mid-nineteenth century, state service continued to loom large in the lives of Russian writers. Pushkin's younger contemporary Nikolai Gogol is well known for portraying state servitors in his works. At the same time, he was curiously equivocal about service itself: an utterly unsuccessful low-ranking clerk, at times he expressed great service ambitions, while at others he wrote contemptuously about service as a worthless occupation that interfered with his writerly aspirations. Though his literary portrayal of state servitors now seems unproblematic, it turns out to be just as surprising as his personal attitude: he represents the Table of Ranks quite creatively, distorting the value of ranks as he sees fit. Furthermore, in Gogol's works the rank system serves not merely as subject matter, but as a structural principle that he (perhaps jokingly) uses to explain his artistic choices.

While many writing nobles began their service in the military, most chose to abandon it in favor of civil service or retirement. Three poets, Denis Davydov, Aleksandr Polezhaev, and Mikhail Lermontov, spent their entire service careers in the military, which to a large degree determined their lives. All three suffered to various degrees from their subjection to military discipline, but the extent of their suffering, and especially their attitudes toward it, were quite different, ranging from Davydov's emphatic (if perhaps insincere) nonchalance, to Polezhaev's and Lermontov's self-destructive behavior, which cut their lives tragically short. Each poet's work reflects his experience as a military man in a different way. Fedor Dostoevsky also spent his two service stints in the military. He felt no enthusiasm for it and no obligation to continue serving, both times resigning his commission as soon as possible.

Nonetheless, Dostoevsky consistently thematized state service, particularly civil service. His portrayals of servitors, however, depended not on first-hand experience, but on literary tradition: in his treatment of the hierarchy of ranks, Dostoevsky was continually in dialogue with Gogol. Dostoevsky both developed and rewrote Gogol's legacy by complicating and deconstructing Gogol's characters, portraying them as both more human and less sympathetic. In doing so, he was not so much acknowledging his indebtedness to Gogol as freeing himself of his predecessor's powerful influence, enabling himself to use Gogol's legacy for his own artistic objectives.

While eighteenth-century Russians were beginning to emulate European cultural models, the situation of writers in Russia differed greatly from those in Europe. In Europe, members of the privileged upper classes rarely dominated the literary scene, whereas in Russia they did. This fact raises many questions about the status of writing nobles in Russia. How did compulsory service or after 1762 the strong expectation that nobles participate in state service affect Russian writers, particularly their self-images as writers? How did the service and rank system influence their literary standing and, how, conversely, did their writing affect their position in the service hierarchy? How were the complexities of the service hierarchy reflected in their literary production? While the answers to these questions vary for individual writers, one important consequence of the competition between service and writing obtained: it impeded the rise of professionalism in the Russian literary sphere. Several factors worked against nobles' becoming professional writers— that is, writers for whom writing was not only their main or most important occupation but also their chief source of income. Most importantly, noble writers were reluctant to abandon service in favor of full-time gainful literary work even after they acquired the legal right not to serve. Being in service defined them as noblemen, whereas writing, while often seen as a necessary accomplishment for a true gentleman, was not ennobling in and of itself and for many was acceptable only as a personal pursuit.

The term "nobility" requires a brief elucidation. Students of Russian history and culture of the Imperial period face a difficulty when choosing the appropriate term for this group. Not only are all of the possible translations of *dvoriane* or the collective term *dvorianstvo* into English ("aristocracy," "nobility," "gentry") misleading to various degrees (as Marc Raeff argues in his seminal study of the eighteenth-century Russian nobility), but even in Russian the term competes with other designations, such as *aristokratiia* (aristocracy) or *znat'* (notables). For this reason, many contemporary historians prefer to use, often alongside *dvorianstvo*, the neutral terms "elite" and "elites" (*elita* and *elity*), as neither existed at the time discussed and are therefore "unburdened" by contemporary connotations.[1] However, these terms are too vague to be used without a qualifier, such as "service," "cultural," "intellectual," or "economic," all of which intersect only partially with the terms *dvoriane* and *dvorianstvo*, with the degree of intersection changing over time. The more traditional if imperfect terms "nobles" and "nobility" are thus preferable.

This linguistic uncertainty reflects an uncertainty about the composition of the group itself. For all practical purposes, the post-Petrine *shliakhetstvo* (or *dvorianstvo*, as it came to be called later in the eighteenth century) was a newly formed estate.[2] The eighteenth-century *dvorianstvo* incorporated not only all kinds of pre-Petrine elite groups (such as the upper echelons of Muscovite nobility—boyars—as well as both middle and upper serving classes, *deti boiarskie* and *dvoriane*) but also commoners who were able to enter the noble class thanks either to successful service or to *sluchái,* imperial favor.[3] The boundaries of the group, particularly in the early eighteenth century, were thus uncertain and shifting. As Raeff points out, one thing that this rather motley group "had in common—and which had no equivalent in the West— was that they held a specified rank in the Table of Ranks."[4] The Table of Ranks, a list of positions in the military, civil, and court services introduced by Peter the Great in 1722, allowed Peter to replace the Muscovite service elite with a new class of servitors. It also forcefully reconfirmed every nobleman's obligation to serve the emperor and the state. According to Peter's law, service was to begin at age fifteen and continue indefinitely. In the late 1730s, the duration was limited to twenty-five years.[5] Only in 1762 did his grandson Peter III abolish compulsory service for nobles. Some serving nobles retired at this point, but others remained in service, which continued to define a nobleman's place in society for at least another century and even beyond.[6]

The Table of Ranks thus seems a useful tool for defining who was a nobleman. Divided into fourteen grades or classes, from the first (the highest) to the fourteenth (the lowest), it clearly indicated the status of every servitor and his position vis-à-vis his peers. Yet not everyone who held a rank according to the Table was necessarily a nobleman: anyone serving in civil or court service below the eighth class could be (and often was) a commoner. At the same time, by making it possible for commoners to be ennobled through ascending the hierarchy of ranks, the Table of Ranks preserved and prolonged the uncertainty about who was truly noble. The conspicuous lack of homogeneity in the newly formed noble estate was a source of considerable tension.[7] Those members of the noble class who viewed themselves as the heirs of the pre-Petrine service elite resented the newcomers. Imperial favorites integrated faster and more easily than those working their way up the ladder of ranks, but the traditional nobility perceived both groups as intruders well into the nineteenth century. Commoners entering the noble class via civil service had particular difficulties integrating, because civil service was given a lesser status and to gain hereditary nobility they had to rise to the eighth class, whereas in the military, until 1845, it was granted beginning with the fourteenth (that is, the lowest) class. Finally, many of the so-called new aristocracy (the term coined to designate families that acquired their high status thanks to imperial favor) became far more powerful than some of the families with a pre-Petrine lineage, which added a particular edge to the latter's resentment. Noblemen engaged in literary pursuits came from all the groups discussed above, and their diverse provenance needs to be taken into account when their particular modes of writerly behavior are considered.

Orderly as it was, the Table of Ranks not only failed to ease the tensions existing between the different groups that comprised the emerging noble class, but it also introduced new ones, adding to the nobility's heterogeneity and creating internal disagreements. One of the most divisive issues for the eighteenth-century Russian nobility as well as for the newly emerging Russian writing community was the noblemen's attitude toward state service. The established nobility accepted service as a duty—mostly honorable and desirable, but often unwelcome.[8] Some members of the established nobility viewed participation in the civil service, especially its entry-level positions, as a chore beneath their dignity, to be avoided if possible.[9] Aleksandr Sumarokov, for example, fought passionately to retain his military status even after 1756, when he was appointed director (manager) of the first Russian public theater. Though no longer engaged in military duties, he insisted that he had the right to remain in the military and be promoted to the next military rank. For commoners, in contrast, the civil service was particularly valued, as it provided a way—though difficult and time-consuming—to enter the noble estate by climbing the ladder of ranks. Mikhail Chulkov (1743 or 1744–92), a prolific writer and the author of the first novel set in Russia, *The Comely Cook* (*Prigozhaia povarikha*, 1770), for example, was born a commoner and ennobled through civil service.

Another divisive issue was cultural: members of the established nobility considered former commoners to be lacking in education and polish. Ironically, however, these allegedly illiterate upstarts were predominantly bureaucrats, whose primary occupation was writing and who had historically been the earliest producers of secular literature in Russia. Furthermore, as a rule, commoners ennobled through service came from the historically literate estates, most often from the clergy. Nonetheless, the new producers of culture, the eighteenth-century nobility, dismissed the newcomers' contributions and portrayed them as illiterate, unkempt, and ill-mannered. Sumarokov, for example, considered clerks (*pod'iachie*) the epitomes of illiteracy. He ends his essay addressed to typesetters with the following instruction on correct spelling and usage: "And don't conclude about clerks that they are more skillful than you are because [. . .][10] they are richer than you are: every day [you can] note that illiterate people are always richer than literate ones. And they are called scribes [*pistsy*] ironically, because [in fact] they don't know how to write, and this is not their [true] occupation: their occupation is fleecing [*obirat'*]."[11] This kind of skepticism about the education and breeding of writing non-nobles survived well into the nineteenth century and can be seen, for example, in Pushkin's famous mistreatment of the journalist Nikolai Nadezhdin, the son of a priest. In one of his *Table-Talk* sketches, Pushkin writes: "I met Nadezhdin at Pogodin's. He seemed to me very low-class [*prostonarodnyi*], *vulgar* [Pushkin uses English word here], dull, arrogant, and without any manners."[12] Written in the mid-1850s, Nikolai Nekrasov's *How Great I Am!* (*Kak ia velik!*) is another, even more striking, example: this vicious lampoon of Dostoevsky—who owed his nobility to his father's service rank—presents him as an ill-mannered upstart.[13]

While eighteenth-century clerks could perhaps be suspected of having an archaic writing style that was not up to the modern tastes advocated by Sumarokov, Nadezhdin was a highly educated professional writer, critic, and historian, and Dostoevsky's prominence as a writer needs no documentation.[14] It seems that, while the established nobility considered writing well to be every nobleman's inalienable quality, possessing this skill did not necessarily make a non-noble person an equal. Moreover, noble status, even if it was hereditary (as in Dostoevsky's case), did not guarantee a person's full integration into the noble estate, especially if it was of recent origin and received due to one's father's or grandfather's service success. The tensions created by the historical heterogeneity of the Russian nobility and exacerbated by the Table of Ranks survived long into the nineteenth century and affected relations within the community of writers, sometimes regardless of their level of education or writing ability.

The eighteenth-century nobility's active participation in the production of literature was a new phenomenon for post-Petrine Russia: from the Kievan period to the end of the Muscovite period, writers from the upper secular classes were few and far between. In the eighteenth century the nobility came to dominate in this area, competing with the previous producers of literature: state bureaucrats and clergymen. State bureaucrats—historically the oldest secularly educated group in Russia—were also the first writers of modern literature. It was the so-called *prikaznaia shkola* (that is, seventeenth-century bureaucrats, from *prikazy*, offices or ministries) that created the first examples of Russian secular poetry.[15] They were also the first translators of secular books, particularly fiction, into Russian.[16] Furthermore, it is likely that early native examples of fiction, adventure tales (*gistorii*), and other types of entertainment literature were also generated chiefly by this group. The clergy, the dominant literati of the medieval period, had also begun transitioning to modern literary forms, particularly poetry and drama. These new trends arrived from Ukraine and Poland. Simeon of Polotsk—a town that was under Polish rule in the seventeenth century—and his Muscovite followers, such as Sil'vestr Medvedev and Karion Istomin, led the way.[17]

In the early eighteenth century there were still few writers outside of these two groups. Not only was writing not perceived as a prestigious occupation by the Muscovite secular elites, but even their level of literacy was uncertain. It is difficult to establish reliable estimates of literacy rates in seventeenth-century Muscovy, save to assess the literacy of different social groups, including the upper secular classes.[18] It is safe to assume, however, that Muscovite secular elites were less literate than their European counterparts. As Lindsey Hughes points out, in pre-Petrine Russia, education was "left to the discretion of parents, only a handful of whom (mainly those who had been exposed to other cultures by travel abroad or association with foreigners) educated their sons beyond basic literacy, if that."[19] Education for the English nobility, by contrast, became necessary around the mid-sixteenth century.[20] For the French nobility the transition came about one and a half to two centuries later; in Domna Stanton's formulation, in France, "the seventeenth century was bent on intellectualizing or civilizing the noble."[21] In his book *Aristocratic Experience and the Origins of Modern Culture*, Jonathan Dewald emphasizes the particular importance that writing acquired for the seventeenth-century French nobility: "Nobles turned to writing in a variety of surprising circumstances, as a part of both public and intimate life. They wrote political reflections and love letters; many began assessing their lives in written form, producing memoirs for their own amusement or the instruction of their families. They closely followed contemporary poetry, and they participated intently in contemporary discussions of linguistic purity. Most striking, in the course of the seventeenth century good writing came to be closely associated with nobility itself."[22] It is clear from this observation that for European nobles challenged by changes in the idea of what makes an aristocrat, writing became a new tool of public and private self-fashioning.

In Russia, this process of "civilizing the noble" dates from the early eighteenth century. Raeff rightly argues that an important goal of the Petrine reforms was to educate the nobility.[23] Peter's various educational initiatives directed at nobles are well known, and, despite a certain resistance on the nobles' part, these initiatives eventually bore fruit.[24] Like their European counterparts, newly literate Russian nobles turned to writing in search of modern modes of existence. Beginning with Peter's reign, diary and memoir writing emerges and grows steadily. Tables 1 and 2 in Andrei Tartakovsky's *Russian Memoirs in the Eighteenth and the First Half of the Nineteenth Centuries* show that noblemen predominated among eighteenth-century memoir- and, particularly, diary-writers.[25] By turning to autobiographical genres, the Russian nobility, like the seventeenth-century French nobility, could separate "themselves from their surroundings, establishing themselves as individuals and freeing themselves from a variety of constraints."[26] In fact, individuation may have been even more important for the Russians than for their European counterparts, since, as Hughes emphasizes, Peter's new policies severely limited nobles' freedoms in virtually all areas of their lives.[27]

Some of Peter's initiatives in the cultural sphere, however, facilitated the nobility's developing interest in literary pursuits. Peter strongly discouraged the traditional monastic devotion to writing. At the same time, he expected state bureaucrats to be engaged in a useful, practical kind of writing: legal, pedagogical, political, or scientific. He left literature proper unregulated and thus allowed it to become a private occupation.[28] Among the newly emerging group of amateur writers of poetry, fiction, and drama were members of the nobility, and even though they remained an anonymous minority for a while, eventually their numbers grew and their desire to remain anonymous diminished.

One prominent example of a noble openly embracing literature was Antiokh Kantemir, the son of Peter's supporter Dimitry Kantemir, prince of Moldavia, who had fled to Russia and entered the Russian service when his principality was conquered by the Turks in 1711. His son Antiokh received the best possible education, among other places at the Slavo-Greco-Latin Academy in Moscow, where writing in various genres was part of the curriculum. His literary career in Russia was short but prolific: he wrote most of his satires (for which he is best known) between 1729 and 1732, when, at the age of twenty-three, he was appointed as an envoy to London. He was never to return to Russia, dying in Paris in 1744. His literary works, well known to contemporaries in manuscript copies, were first published in Russia long after his death, in 1762. Despite the fact that the major part of Kantemir's life as a writer took place abroad, and his role in shaping contemporary Russian literary life was thus likely to be limited, his literary debut was strong and influential: he left a significant mark on the early development of modern Russian literature, serving as a model for writers of noble status who followed in his footsteps.

In post-Petrine Russia, as in France a century earlier, being able to write—and to write well—gradually became one of a Russian noble-man's necessary skills.[29] Perhaps in response to this new expectation, the curriculum at the first educational institution for children of the nobility, the Noble Infantry Cadet Corps, established in 1732, was pre-dominantly humanistic. The cadets also often occupied their leisure time with literary pursuits.[30] According to some sources, the corps even boasted a literary society and, later, a theater. Several important eighteenth-century writers, beginning with Aleksandr Sumarokov, were educated at the corps. The cadets' interest in belles-lettres indicated that Russian nobles were on their way to becoming active producers of literature. By the last third of the eighteenth century, they began to dominate the literary sphere. In contrast, in arts other than literature (painting, sculpture, music, and theater), nobles did not participate overtly in any significant numbers until the second half of the nine-teenth century. Thus literature was the only art nobles did not consider beneath their dignity to acknowledge as their predominant occupation.[31]

The swiftness with which the nobility appropriated the literary field is the more noteworthy in that it happened under the patronage system that prevailed in eighteenth-century Russia.[32] For a nobleman, seeking patronage from a fellow nobleman could obviously be awkward, and writers of noble status employed different strategies to deal with this problem: some ignored the patronage system; some resisted it; others turned the tables on their patrons, insisting that it was their poetic dedications that immortalized their patrons' names; yet others participated in it partially or fully, using it to their advantage.

One needs to take into account the fact that the patronage system in eighteenth-century Russia was of the type Raymond Williams calls "protection and support," meaning that it was "concerned less with the direct retaining and commissioning of artists than with the provision of some kind of social protection and recognition."[33] It was different from the situation in seventeenth-century France described by Alain Viala as having two types of supportive relations: clientage and patronage. Clientage, widely accepted in the higher echelons of society, was similar to "protection and support" practiced in Russia: it constituted various kinds of practical help, including assistance with obtaining employment and profitable administrative positions, provided in return for some kind of service. Patronage, by contrast, presupposed material support of artists and writers by socially prominent people. Notably, in France it presumed more equal and mutually respectful relations, and therefore a writer of noble status could receive a reward from his patron without violating the norms of noble behavior.[34] It is significant that Russian writers of noble status, while accepting "protection and support," were much more ambivalent about receiving material rewards from their fellow nobles than French writers were.

In eighteenth-century Russia, the patronage system coexisted and blended with the vestiges of court culture, and writers had to define their position vis-à-vis the monarch and the court. For writers of common descent, such as Vasily Trediakovsky, Mikhail Lomonosov, or Vasily Ruban, receiving imperial favors in return for their literary tributes was less complicated than it was for writers of noble status. For them imperial patronage became especially uncomfortable toward the end of the eighteenth century and even more so in the early nineteenth century, when many began to see the emperor not as a divine creature but merely as the first among equals.[35] Such an attitude made writers with connections to the court feel that they had to be especially careful lest they be seen as playing the role of court poet. This circumstance needs to be taken into account when examining the self-presentations of such literary figures as Gavrila Derzhavin, Mikhail Murav'ev, Nikolai Karamzin, Vasily Zhukovsky, or Alexander Pushkin—all of whom had different types of connections to the court.[36]

Russian nobles were also concerned about—and often repulsed by— the idea of becoming professional writers. While there are various markers of literary professionalism in a given society—a sense of calling or collegiality, the emergence of various institutions (such as literary societies or copyright), or the ability to make a living from publishing—most scholars agree that only the last makes an individual writer truly professional.[37] Eighteenth-century Russian writers of noble origin accepted the first two ways of being professional, were open to the third, but found the fourth seriously problematic. Sumarokov, for example, viewed writing as a calling, an occupation central to his existence. He was also the head of what can be considered the first "literary school" in Russia.[38] Yet Sumarokov rejected the possibility of earning his living through the commercial publication of his works. Even though he was free to abandon service in favor of full-time literary work, he was more than reluctant to do so—he simply could not imagine himself not serving. Having a rank defined him as a nobleman, whereas writing did not. His contemporaries of noble status fully shared his sentiment: they loathed the idea of writing for a living.

Professionalism as commerce presupposes the existence of a book market, where writers not only can but also are willing to sell the fruits of their writerly labor. Even though a book market arose in Russia somewhat later than in the West, it did exist by the second half of the eighteenth century.[39] Its overall size was defined primarily by the rate of literacy, which was low; accordingly, the overall readership was small. Furthermore, this readership was split into two unequal parts. A larger group consisted mostly of lower-class readers of traditional entertainment literature (such as popular woodcut prints [lubki], romances, adventure tales, and—later in the century—novels) and sustained a substantial book market.[40] A much smaller group, made up predominantly of nobles contemptuous of the "bad taste" of lower-class readers and interested in works by writers who adopted contemporary European literary norms, was too small to support a book market for the writers of noble status—even if the latter had wanted to commercialize their writing activities. Furthermore, the bustling market for entertainment literature repulsed the high-minded Russian nobles to a far larger degree and for much longer than the similar activities of Grub Street displeased serious English writers. Many of them, including John Milton, Jonathan Swift, Alexander Pope, and Samuel Johnson, began their careers on or near Grub Street, which allowed them to participate in the book market early, making the road to professionalization considerably shorter.[41] Russian nobles' elitist view of entertainment literature and of commerce in general prevented them both from attempting to participate in the existing book market and from creating their own.

In Russia, nobles' works were usually printed in facilities supported by state institutions, such as presses owned by the Academy of Sciences and Moscow University. Moreover, these publications often remained unsold.[42] During the short period when the state officially allowed private ownership of printing presses (1783–96), some noblemen, especially Freemasons, attempted to use them to publish and sell a wide range of books, from novels to philosophical treatises to esoteric Masonic works. Nikolai Novikov, the most successful among these publishers, was arrested and persecuted in 1792, after Catherine the Great became outright hostile toward Freemasonry.[43] The Russian government's distrust of the free press following the French Revolution eventually led to the banning of most privately owned publishing houses and the establishment of censorship. Private presses continued to exist in the provinces, but few were owned or used by noblemen.

The patronage system, real or imagined vassalage to the court, and the specter of literature's commercialization exacerbated the ambivalence eighteenth-century writers of noble rank felt about their literary pursuits, especially about publishing.[44] This ambivalence persisted at least to the end of the eighteenth century and perhaps longer. Although it did not seriously hinder noblemen from taking part in the production of literature, it did result in later professionalization. The few attempts by writers of noble origin to become professionals in the first half of the nineteenth century were either abandoned (Karamzin) or unsuccessful (Pushkin), and even in the second half, the first truly professional writers, such as Dostoevsky, still had a difficult time establishing literature as a profitable occupation in an atmosphere traditionally hostile to the very idea of writing for profit.

The late rise of professionalism contributed to the elevated prestige writers acquired in Russia. High-minded and ostensibly financially disinterested (their lack of business sense was frequently linked to their presumed high-mindedness), writers of noble status remained above the fray and thus unpolluted by association with their supposedly greedy and unscrupulous market-oriented contemporaries. Pushkin, who died penniless (despite his relatively high honoraria), or Gogol, who kept burning his purportedly artistically unsuccessful works in manuscript instead of publishing them for profit, made better culture heroes than the supposedly greedy, financially successful, and thoroughly professional Faddei Bulgarin. Consequently, the process that began in the eighteenth century, with noblemen who both served and wrote trying on different behavioral models, resulted, about a century later, in a reading public that expected from literature answers to all sorts of non-literary questions—moral, philosophical, religious—and writers who did not shy away from providing them.

At the same time, being a writer made the situation of a nobleman in service more complex, and this complexity gives rise to many questions. Did service and the system of rank significantly affect nobles' status as writers and, conversely, did their being writers complicate their position in the service hierarchy? If either is the case, could such considerations have influenced Derzhavin's decision to treat his service career separately from his career as a writer, devoting his memoir almost exclusively to the former and his "Notes on the Works of Derzhavin" and "Explanations of the Works of Derzhavin" to the latter? Did success with the reading public take precedence over a writer's place in the service hierarchy? Was rank important at all for those who tried to achieve the status of professional writer? More concretely, was Pushkin's failure to thrive in his service career important to him and his contemporaries? Finally, was the rank system uniformly essential throughout the Imperial period, or did the emergence of the liberal professions undermine its relevance among the writing community?

Broadly speaking, the relative significance of service for individual writers varied, but it was always a factor in the eighteenth and the first half of the nineteenth centuries. The lingering sense of its importance is reflected in the curious fact that to this day, entries in Russian dictionaries of literary biography not only regularly include information on a particular writer's service status but also surprisingly frequently on that of his (and, less consistently, her) father. For example, the entry on Sumarokov in *The Dictionary of Russian Writers of the Eighteenth Century* lists both his father's highest military rank, colonel, and the rank with which he retired, actual state councilor.[45] The entry on Mikhail Lermontov in *Russian Writers, 1800–1917: A Biographical Dictionary* states that he was the son of "an army captain," despite the fact that his father not only died young but was almost entirely absent from the young poet's life.[46] The same dictionary informs us that Nekrasov's father was "a retired major"—even though Nekrasov left home at age seventeen, severing connections with his depraved and cruel father.[47]

The editors of *Russian Writers, 1800–1917* describe the gradual changes in the importance of service in the supplement to volume 2, "State Service in the Russian Empire": "In the first two-thirds of the nineteenth century, for the educated classes of Russian society, military or civil service was almost mandatory, even if only for the short time that was necessary to earn [the first six ranks, from fourteenth class to ninth]; in the decades after, [state service still] remained one of the most common occupations."[48] For writers, however, a service career seemed to diminish in importance more rapidly as the nineteenth century progressed, due not only to the slow but steady weakening of the general expectation that every nobleman serve but also to the surge in the number of non-nobles taking up writing and succeeding at it. The community of writers was increasingly mixed with regard both to their noble or non-noble status and to their participation in state service. The two collaborators in the radical journal *The Contemporary* (*Sovremennik*), Nikolai Nekrasov (one of the editors) and Nikolai Chernyshevsky (the leading critic from 1854 until his arrest in 1862), provide a good example: Nekrasov was a noble who, having repeatedly failed the university entrance examinations, did not receive the education necessary to enter service and therefore never served, whereas Chernyshevsky was a priest's son and university graduate who spent several years in service (first as a teacher in the Saratov Gymnasium and later in the Second Cadet Corps in Saint Petersburg). Chernyshevsky's and Nekrasov's different origins and career experiences did not impede their collaboration or their sharing of both literary and political views.

Another factor that undermined the importance of the Table of Ranks among writers was the emergence of a new hierarchy: the hierarchy of financial success, most evident in the size of the honoraria writers received from publishers and journal editors. Differential pay for writers with different professional reputations and the ensuing competition both among writers and among publishers and journals clearly signaled the professionalization of literature, thereby rendering state service far less attractive.

These changes in the significance and value of state service for a writing noble define the chronological boundaries of this inquiry: it begins in the mid-eighteenth century with Aleksandr Sumarokov, the first Russian writer of noble lineage to make literature central to his life without, however, diminishing his regard for service, and it stops about a hundred years later, when far fewer writers served with enthusiasm. Signs that a cultural shift had occurred abound. The young Leo Tolstoy, for example, worried about his service status until he achieved renown as a writer. Contemporaries' puzzlement over Ivan Goncharov's and Mikhail Saltykov-Shchedrin's dedication to their service obligations (both served until the late 1860s) signals the end of the writing nobility's acceptance of service as an honorable and unavoidable duty. Afanasy Fet's friends and acquaintances were flabbergasted by his continued efforts to gain the title of *kammerherr* and his joy upon finally receiving it in 1889. By the early twentieth century, writers who served were rare, no matter what their origins, and those few who actually served did so purely to support themselves, often regarding the work as a hardship. Over the course of a century, the competition between serving and writing thus ceased to be a factor in Russian writers' self-fashioning.

This study also raises questions about the representation of the system of ranks in literature. The system of ranks was pervasive and extremely important in the lives of the upper classes, but did it find its way into their writings? If yes, did the frequency and manner of representation of service in literature change with time? It seems it did: eighteenth-century writers almost completely ignored service as a literary topic; early nineteenth-century writers engaged with it vigorously and often on a personal level; and mid-nineteenth-century writers, Dostoevsky in particular, regarded it as a nearly indispensable theme in their works. To put it differently, from a fact of life state service changed into a topic of biographical significance and then into a literary topos.

Eighteenth-century writers were mostly concerned with finding ways to balance—reconcile or separate—service and writing in real life. Even Sumarokov, for whom writing was service to the state, refrained from making service a subject matter in his literary works. Ranks and service positions are mentioned with some regularity only in late eighteenth-century comedies (such as Denis Fonvizin's 1769 *Brigadier*), particularly the ones satirizing bureaucracy and bribe-taking (Vasily Kapnist's 1798 *Chicanery* is the best example). Comedy as genre notably keeps the implied author at the greatest possible distance from his characters; the ranks in eighteenth-century comedies were needed to add verisimilitude to criticism of corrupt bureaucrats, not to form the authors' identity vis-à-vis state service. Descriptions of service in literature did not thus echo service in life, as it would for the next generation of writing nobles. The chapter on the eighteenth century therefore concentrates on writers' negotiating the relations between service and writing, citing their literary production only rarely.

The Pushkin chapter emphasizes his service career more than his literary one, for the simple reason that the former has received far less scholarly attention than the latter. Nonetheless, it also examines his prose, which oftentimes betrays his anxieties about his status as a state servitor. This is particularly evident in "The Shot," but also in "The Station Master," in *Dubrovsky*, and in "A History of the Village of Goriukhino." Pushkin's prose also preserves his concern about the status of the writer in Russia of his time, particularly as a professional, a subject he explores in the unfinished *Egyptian Nights*.

The chapter on Gogol likewise begins with the discussion of his service career, a subject that has not been examined before. It then turns to Gogol's portrayal of the Table of Ranks in his prose and drama, focusing on the equivocal and whimsical representation of the hierarchy of ranks in his so-called Petersburg Tales ("Nevsky Prospect," "The Nose," "The Overcoat," and "Notes of a Madman") and *The Inspector General*—the representation that Gogol succeeded to pass for a realistic portrayal of servitors that is still accepted as such even today.

The chapter on poets in the military focuses on three individuals: Denis Davydov, Aleksandr Polezhaev, and Mikhail Lermontov. For all three, service was extremely important both as a life experience and as a subject for their poetry. It was especially true for Davydov—who created a poetic image of himself as a carousing happy-go-lucky hussar; and for Polezhaev—who served against his will and whose poetry often expressed an extreme unhappiness with this situation. Lermontov's engagement with the military thematic was more sophisticated than Davydov's and, especially, Polezhaev's. He used it to work out a universal and poetically powerful persona, rooted in his military experience but detached from his biographical self.

Dostoevsky was a reluctant and sporadic servitor, who relied on the literary tradition to portray the Table of Ranks. Gogol was his main interlocutor: Dostoevsky challenged his predecessor's one-dimensional presentation of civil servants, underscoring their humanity, both good and bad, and making their behavior far less defined by their rank than Gogol makes it in his work.

Russian writers continued to depict state servitors, although less vigorously and often less vividly, until the end of the Imperial period. Consequently, any reader of literature produced during this time is bound to meet the entire Table of Ranks on the pages of books he or she reads. What do contemporary readers miss? How does being unversed in the significance and value of the various ranks and unsure about the status of different types of service affect their reading experience? Some readers may remember that the Table of Ranks had only fourteen classes and thus see the joke in the title of Anton Delvig's and Evgeny Baratynsky's 1822 poem "Singers of the Fifteenth Class," which criticizes their literary opponents.[49] But other questions might be more difficult to answer. Was the rank of titular councilor as low as Gogol leads us to believe in both "Notes of a Madman" and "The Overcoat"? If not, why did Gogol try to convince us that it was? What does Pushkin mean when, in his story "The Station Master," he claims that narrative ability is inversely proportional to rank? Why, in Tolstoy's *Anna Karenina*, does Stiva Oblonsky hesitate before taking a private job as opposed to a position in state service, even though his dismal financial situation obviously makes the former a wiser choice?

Historians of Russian literature have paid little attention to these questions. Only a few scholars (such as Iury Lotman, William Mills Todd III, W. Gareth Jones, Joachim Klein, and Andrei Kostin) have touched on the problems addressed in this study. Yet it is crucial to take into account the full spectrum of life circumstances affecting the leading writers of the period under investigation. It is equally crucial to keep these circumstances in mind when we read the literature that they produced; the revised perspective on cultural context that this study offers allows us to appreciate one powerful, often overlooked force that contributed to the development of classic Russian literature. The enduring questions of identity, ethics, and individual and collective responsibility that were live issues for Russian writers during the period under discussion became woven into the fabric of the literary masterpieces that they created and that we read today.

1

To Serve or to Write?

Noble Writers in the Eighteenth and Early Nineteenth Centuries

In the eighteenth century, Russian literature was in the final stages of a transition from medieval forms of writing to modern ones, based on European models. Both institutions of literary life (such as the Russian Academy, established in 1783 on Ekaterina Dashkova's initiative to emulate the Académie Française; according to its bylaws, its main purpose was to standardize the Russian language and compile a dictionary) and literary institutions (such as the new system of versification, the syllabo-tonic; and the new system of genres) emerged in the course of that century.[1] Most importantly, a new, modern concept of authorship was developing: instead of medieval producers of written works, including anonymous, often collective authors/editors/copyists as well as authors who positioned themselves as conveyers of divine wisdom, individual authors appeared. Authors' relation to the text changed accordingly: they obtained firmer control over their writings, and began to edit them, generating several redactions of the same work.[2] These changes affected writers of all groups—lowbrow producers of entertainment literature; learned commoners like Trediakovsky and Lomonosov, who were among the first writers to emulate European models; and the writers of noble status who are at the center of this inquiry.

While all three groups shared the modern understanding of authorship, there were important differences among them. Writers of entertainment literature were the earliest to professionalize, selling their literary production in the book market that emerged in the eighteenth century; they flourished after private ownership of publishing presses was allowed. The second group was the best educated: they knew modern and ancient languages (including Old Church Slavonic), philosophy, history, and linguistics, as well as, in the case of Lomonosov, fields outside literature, such as geology, geography, chemistry, and mathematics. They were salaried employees of the Academy of Sciences (founded by Peter the Great in 1724), through which they generally published; thus they were not professionals in the commercial sense of the word. The third group was, of course, in state service. Their education was both different from that of the second group (they rarely knew ancient Greek or Latin, and though they were certainly familiar with Old Church Slavonic, their knowledge was usually superficial) and sometimes downright deficient, despite all the efforts by the state to encourage and even demand some level of learning from its servitors. In fact, obligatory and, later, expected service could interfere with young nobles' education. Such was the case with Derzhavin, who initially received only the meager education his widowed mother could provide for him at home (uncharacteristically for an eighteenth-century nobleman, he did not know French but knew German, because a cheap German teacher happened to be available in Kazan guberniya whereas a French one was not). He was then accepted to Kazan Gymnasium, where he did very well until he had to leave to begin his service. He was thus an autodidact, and his better-educated friends felt responsible for checking his poetry for grammatical mistakes. Apparently, Derzhavin's situation was not unique, and as late as 1802, in his essay "Why Is There So Little Writing Talent in Russia?," Nikolai Karamzin still blamed the nobility's service obligations for the lack of educated writers: "Now I ask: who among us would do battle with a great obstacle to become a good author, if even the most happy endowment possesses a hard crust which can only be rubbed smooth by constant labor? [. . .] In Russia, nobles study more than others; but for how long? Until fifteen years of age: then it is time to enter the service, time to seek rank, the most trustworthy way to obtain respect."[3] Indeed, even after 1762, when Peter III abolished compulsory service for the nobility, the majority of nobles—or at least the upper echelon of this group—continued to serve, at least briefly, to receive a presentable rank and retire as respectable members of the service class.

As a group, writers of noble status also differed from the producers of entertainment literature and academicians in yet another important way: while they wrote, often prolifically, they sometimes felt uneasy about publishing their literary production.[4] Not everyone had such scruples (Sumarokov did not), but many had. This reluctance could be explained by the fear some nobles had that publishing would bring them too close to the book market and thus literary professionalism, whereas a true noble, in their view, could only be a dilettante.[5] Furthermore, assuming the role of dilettantes allowed noble writers to separate themselves from the "servile" behavior encouraged by the patronage system and court culture.[6]

This chapter explores different models of writerly behavior that eighteenth-century Russian writers of noble status worked out to deal with the described circumstances. Their methods of balancing writing and service ran the gamut from insisting that writing is a type of service to considering writing inconsistent with service, with various intermediary positions in between. Whether they acknowledged their writing publicly (and thus published their literary works) or preferred to keep it private (and thus did not publish or published anonymously) often depended on their particular view of the relationship between service and writing.

A short discussion of the notions of private life as opposed to public life as they were understood in eighteenth-century Russia is in order. It is commonly held that in Russia the former concept was underdeveloped in comparison to the Western tradition or, at least, understood differently; and the latter was dominated by the state.[7] According to Max von Vasmer's etymological dictionary, however, the word *privatnyi* (meaning *chastnyi*, private or individual) was first used in 1702; the word *publichnyi* (meaning *obshchestvennyi*, public or social) dates from 1704.[8] The words thus existed, and their meaning corresponded roughly to their modern usage. Furthermore, private (*chastnaia*) life also existed, in the forms of home and family life, individual interests and emotions, and, importantly for this inquiry, private pursuit of the arts, including writing. It is the notion of privacy (the right to lead private life without interference either from the state or other individuals) that seemed to be if not entirely lacking, then certainly not fully developed in Russia. Privacy rights were not universally guaranteed by law until late in the Imperial period, if then.[9] Moreover, there was no word in Russian to designate the notion of privacy, and it is hard to determine whether it exists even today: the calque *privatnost'* not only sounds artificial but, as defined in dictionaries, seems to designate "private life" rather than "privacy."[10]

Although the absence of the notion of privacy in eighteenth-century Russia should be duly noted, this study is more concerned with the forms of private life developed by noblemen to accommodate their desire to write. Peter III's 1762 edict freeing nobles of service obligations created opportunities for them to experiment more easily with the forms of private life and with ways of creating private space. At least one of the writers discussed further in this chapter, Andrei Bolotov, attempted to do so. Most importantly, he did so using writing as his main tool. The reluctance of Bolotov and some other noblemen to publish their literary works also indicates that they assigned literature to the private sphere.

In eighteenth-century Russia, literature was extensively used in the public sphere, most obviously in the form of laudatory poetry (such as ceremonial odes and inscriptions describing public events, like fireworks, masquerades, or coronations) and drama—that is, genres that served the state. More interesting was the use of literature to create an intimate public space, so to speak—friendly circles, whose members shared literary views and came together to read their poetry or prose to each other. One of the most prominent circles of this type was the group that included Derzhavin and Nikolai L'vov, among several other writers. The private and public spheres were thus not always mutually exclusive, and, as Andreas Schönle puts it, "fantasies of privacy reveal a longing for sociability, perhaps not for the broad public sphere, but for a narrower elective circle."[11] Literature thus allowed nobles to create public spaces independent of the state. This kind of social life, based on friendships that brought together nobles interested in writing, flourished in the early nineteenth century, fostering further separation between the nobility and the autocracy later in the century.

It is logical to begin the discussion of eighteenth-century modes of writerly behavior with Sumarokov, the first writer of noble origin in the modern Russian literary tradition who considered writing to be his most important occupation. Pushkin, though he generally disliked Sumarokov's poetry and drama, recognized his devotion to literature, calling him a man "passionate towards his art."[12] Some even consider Sumarokov to be the first professional writer in Russia, and whether one agrees with this view or not (Sumarokov never sold his literary works directly to publishers and felt uneasy about the very idea), he undoubtedly saw writing as his calling.[13]

Aleksandr Sumarokov (1717–77), the well-educated scion of a respectable family of servitors that became prominent in seventeenth-century Muscovy, was in many ways representative of the new post-Petrine nobility. His father, a supporter of Peter the Great's reforms, had a long and successful service career, retiring in 1762 in the rank of actual privy councilor (second class). In 1740 Sumarokov graduated from the newly established Noble Infantry Cadet Corps, the first educational institution for children of the nobility, and began his service as a member of the staffs of several important statesmen, including Aleksei Razumovsky (1709–71), Empress Elizabeth's favorite and the head of the Life-Guards, the guards regiment that helped Elizabeth ascend the throne in 1741. In his capacity as Razumovsky's aide-de-camp, Sumarokov ran the regiment's affairs. In 1755 he was promoted to the rank of brigadier (fifth class).

Parallel to fulfilling his military duties, Sumarokov built up a formidable literary career, actively producing in all genres and vying for the place of Russia's foremost author with two prominent contemporaries, Trediakovsky and Lomonosov. Despite his success as a writer, the idea of leaving the service never occurred to Sumarokov. Moreover, even after he was appointed director of the first Russian public theater (which officially became a court theater in 1759), he retained his military rank as brigadier.

Given Sumarokov's success in the literary and theatrical spheres, it is surprising to observe how much importance he gave to his place in the state service hierarchy. When his service career came to a halt following his appointment as theater director, he complained bitterly and repeatedly that he was being "passed over" for promotion (*menia obkhodiat*). In a letter of November 15, 1759, to Ivan Shuvalov (Elizabeth's favorite at the time and the overseer of several Russian cultural institutions, including the theater), Sumarokov writes: "I never took part in a war and perhaps never will, but I labor as much in time of peace as I would have in time of war, but they pass me over." The labor he has in mind is managing the theater and writing plays and poems. Furthermore, Sumarokov believes that this labor qualifies him for a military rank. Asking in the same letter to be appointed to the Academy of Sciences, he insists that as a member of the Academy he would have the right to remain in the military service: "I don't want a civil rank, since I am a senior brigadier, and I am not inclined to take off voluntarily the military uniform I have worn for twenty-eight years; and nothing prevents me from being in both the Academy Chancellery and the Conference."[14]

Sumarokov was "relieved of his duties" (*uvolen*) as theater director by Elizabeth's decree of June 13, 1761. In anticipation of this event, he vigorously campaigned for promotion ("My memory tells me that upon retirement everyone gets promoted, even if he has been in his current rank for only a year. And I have been senior brigadier and a most unhappy man for six years," 91); or, at least, for keeping his military rank. In his letter to Shuvalov of April 24, 1761, he writes, obviously not quite sincere in his expressed desire to accept the rank of captain (ninth class): "Have mercy on me [. . .] and dismiss me. I just don't want a civil rank, since, having worn a military uniform and boots all my life, it will not be easy for me to learn to wear shoes. After all, I am retiring, not going into the civil service, and I would rather be a captain [ninth class] than receive a higher civil rank" (92).

When, in September 1762, the newly enthroned Catherine conferred on Sumarokov the civil rank of actual state councilor (fourth class), following his request for promotion and as a sign of her benevolence, Sumarokov was not satisfied in the least: he felt that he had not gained anything, rightly arguing that a military rank was in fact equivalent not to the civil rank with which it shared a line on the Table of Ranks but to the civil rank one or two slots above it. Having been promoted from the military rank of fifth class to the civil rank of fourth class meant, effectively, that he had not actually risen in the hierarchy of ranks at all. Sumarokov summarizes his grievances in his letter to the empress of May 3, 1764: "After the general promotion that took place before the [1756–63 Seven Years'] War, I was second or third brigadier, and not only have all brigadiers [fifth class], colonels [sixth class], and lieutenant-colonels [seventh class] overtaken me, but many of those below the seventh class; and now even those who in the time of Your Majesty's reign were promoted from lieutenant-colonel are my seniors in military rank, and I was never in civilian service" (96).[15] Rejecting the rank conferred on him by the empress, Sumarokov concludes his letter with a plea: "I ask only to learn what I am: am I in service, and [if so], which one am I in? Otherwise, retire me properly, as all good people are retired, with a proper rank" (97). He is asking for what, in his view, is his due: to be promoted to the next rank upon retirement, as a servitor in good standing. His requests were never satisfied: he died in 1777 in the rank of actual state councilor.

It is possible that service was Sumarokov's main source of income, the way he supported himself and his family, and thus his interest in being promoted was primarily financial. Indeed, his requests for promotion were often accompanied by requests for money, usually back pay. However, these requests were for the most part satisfied, even if not always immediately, and other sources of income, divorced from the question of promotion, were also available to him. For example, after Sumarokov's retirement from the position of theater director, an arrangement was made to continue to pay him his allowances both as brigadier and as theater director.[16] Once she was in power, Catherine in her turn forgave his considerable debts to the Academy of Sciences press and granted him the "lifetime privilege of having all his works printed at her cost."[17] Even in the 1770s, when Catherine's benevolence faded (and Sumarokov's financial situation drastically worsened, owing to a 1767 family quarrel that deprived him of much of his inheritance), the empress occasionally granted the writer monetary support. All this suggests that, for Sumarokov, anxiety over rank was a separate issue from anxiety over his financial situation.

Furthermore, the option of publishing for money was available to Sumarokov, and he threatened, if only half-heartedly, to take it, as is evident from his letter to Catherine of January 13, 1773: "Perhaps, having worked for fame, I should undertake the writing of novels, which could bring me a good income, because Moscow likes this kind of writing. Now, is it really becoming for me to write novels, especially in the reign of the wise Catherine, who, I am sure, doesn't have a single novel in her entire library? When Augustus rules, then Virgils and Ovids write, and *Aeneids* are held in respect, not 'Bovas the King's Sons.'[18] I, however, wouldn't dishonor myself even if I wrote a 'Bova,' although I wouldn't gain much honor either" (163). What is remarkable in this passage is the mixture of contradictory views of himself as a writer. Sumarokov sees himself as a client writing to laud a powerful patron (Virgil lauds Augustus, and Sumarokov, Catherine), as a producer of saleable goods (an identity that Sumarokov tries on reluctantly), and as a nobleman serving the state by producing literary works (evident in Sumarokov's use of the vocabulary of honor).[19]

Sumarokov's seeing himself above all as a servitor to the state caused him to resist the patronage system. Even though at times he accepted the role of a client of powerful patrons, such as Shuvalov and, later, Catherine's favorites Grigory Orlov and Grigory Potemkin, for the most part he attempted to reject it.[20] He writes in a letter to Shuvalov of

June 10, 1758: "In all truth, I haven't asked for a present, which I have never done and will never do, but requested from your cabinet a loan for the theater, and it was not any kind of political game on my part. I would sooner become a beggar and be exposed to various misfortunes than be among those who seek patrons in order to profit from them" (79). His view of his writing as a fulfillment of service duties helped him justify his protestations.

Sumarokov consistently presents his writing as a form of service. In October 1758 he complains to Elizabeth that he has not been paid for nine months and lists his managing the theater and his writing as service: "I [. . .] must live on what I have thanks to my rank and my labors, laboring as hard as I can in versification and the theater" (83). He goes on to compare his literary efforts to his service as Razumovsky's aide-de-camp. Arguing that he deserves promotion (in his letter to Shuvalov of November 15, 1759), Sumarokov again insists that his writing is comparable in importance to other types of service: "My [literary] exercises do not have the slightest similarity to either court or civil duties, and therefore I don't impede anyone's progress, but my labors are no smaller that anyone else's, and they are of some use, if literature is considered useful in this world" (86). Continuing his fight for promotion in a letter to Shuvalov of April 24, 1761, Sumarokov directly labels his achievements in literature as service to the state and the empress: "I have served exactly thirty years, and tomorrow it will be twenty years that I have served h[er] m[ajesty] [that is, Elizabeth]" (92).

Sumarokov uses the same argument in his letters to Catherine. In August 1762 he writes again that he has been "passed over": "And I am offended more than anyone, because, without any fault on my part, having labored both in fulfillment of my duties as well as beyond them in literature, I have been left behind everyone, not only behind my peers, but also behind those who were much junior to me in rank" (94). According to Sumarokov's reasoning, writing was additional service on his part and should have particularly qualified him for promotion. Sumarokov ends up asserting the superiority of literary activity over other types of service. In his letter to Catherine of March 4, 1770, he declares: "Sophocles, the first among tragic poets, was also the Athenian general and the comrade of Pericles, but still is better known as a poet than a general" (139; original in French). Thus, gradually, Sumarokov comes to see his literary activities as not just comparable but superior to the types of service legitimized by Peter in the Table of Ranks. What is astonishing in his position is the trouble he had assigning value to himself as a writer outside the rank system. He needed a rank to confirm the significance of his writing activities, in both the eyes of the public and his own. This explains Sumarokov's reluctance to retire and his insistence on his right to be promoted.[21]

While interpreting his writing as service to the state, Sumarokov sometimes mentions the Muses. Curiously, these references are consistently connected with the idea of service. At least once Sumarokov directly calls his relations with the Muses "service" (91). On another occasion, he reports to Catherine about a rare period of harmony in his life as a playwright: "The Muses, the local governor-general, the chief of the police, the impresarios, and the actors are in total agreement with me" (125). Characteristically, Sumarokov never complains that his service to the state interferes with his service to the Muses, but does explain his failure to advance in his service career by his devotion to them: "The main reason for all of this is my love for poetry, because, having relied on it and literature, I cared not so much for rank and possessions as for my Muse" (174).

Notably, the idea of literature as a private pursuit is absent from Sumarokov's view of himself as a writer. Only once does Sumarokov seem to express a desire for a "Parnassian refuge" (*parnasskoe ubezhishche*, 118), but even then he justifies his wish for a retreat by his eagerness to be useful to the state. He writes to Catherine in February 1769: "In my letter to the count [Grigory Orlov], I also asked for a small humble estate. I need only have a Parnassian refuge there, and it would bring more profit in the form of verses and other compositions than it gives grain to the state treasury" (118; cf. 116). Once he received the desired "Parnassian refuge," it did not figure in his representations of his authorial pursuits at all. Clearly, Sumarokov viewed writing as a fulfillment of his service duty to the state and the monarch, its success to be reflected by his place in the system of ranks. Even though Sumarokov did not quite succeed in placing his literary activities in the context of state service during his lifetime, his attempt proved essential for the eventual construction of the image of the Russian writer as an influential public figure.[22]

Certain expressions in Sumarokov's letters suggest that for him rank not only indicated his place in the service hierarchy but defined who he was as a human being. This is clearly evident in his question to Catherine in his letter of May 3, 1764: "What am I?" (*chto ia?*). The expression also crops up earlier in the same letter, with similarly anguished overtones: "I, by the way, don't have a place or position. I am not in the military, not in the civil service, not at court, not in the Academy, and not retired. I dare to submit my request to Your Imperial Majesty, so that something might be done with me in order that I might know what I am" (96).[23] Sumarokov obviously had trouble conceiving himself outside the service hierarchy, and his writing (which, as Lomonosov caustically claimed in his letter to Ivan Shuvalov of January 19, 1761, Sumarokov put "above all human knowledge") was not quite enough for him to define his identity.[24] It is noteworthy that when Sumarokov wants to claim his status as poet, he does so by using the formula "an officer and a gentleman" and adding a third component, "a poet," to it. He does it twice in his correspondence, in Russian ("Dvorianin i ofitser, i stikhotvorets sverkh togo," that is, "[I am] a gentleman and an officer, and a poet to boot," 73) and in French ("poète, gentilhomme, et officier," 78).

In contrast to Sumarokov, Andrei Bolotov (1738–1833), arguably the most prolific Russian writer ever, viewed service as inimical to writing, which was for him an activity of private self-fashioning. As a teenager, he amused and educated himself by copying his favorite books, both translations of European fiction and traditional Russian literature, such as saints' lives. As a young officer stationed in Königsberg during the Seven Years' War, he discovered "the pleasures of letter writing," initiating a correspondence with the navy officer N. E. Tulub'ev.[25] In 1789, when Bolotov began his formidable writing enterprise, the memoir *The Life and Adventures of Andrei Bolotov, Depicted by Himself for His Descendants*, he adopted an epistolary form, addressing entries to an imaginary "dear friend." In addition to the *Life and Adventures* (on which he worked until the late 1820s, eventually penning thirty-seven manuscript volumes that covered his life from the year he was born to the early nineteenth century), Bolotov also kept several diaries and various kinds of journals, minutely documenting his life. He also wrote prolifically in other genres, including poetry, drama, literary criticism, books for children, and treatises on economy, agriculture, philosophy, and religion. Bolotov continued writing well into his eighties, eventually producing, in Thomas Newlin's estimation, "the equivalent of some 350 volumes of written material."[26] The purpose of Bolotov's lifelong writing activity was, in significant part, to create a model of Russian private gentry experience that lacked precedent in the life of the eighteenth-century service-bound nobility.[27]

Like every eighteenth-century Russian nobleman before 1762, Bolotov was obliged to serve: at the age of ten he was enlisted in the regiment of which his father was commander. Even though his service was

nominal, and his time mostly occupied with schooling and partly spent
away from the regiment, he was promoted twice, first to corporal, and
then to sergeant. Bolotov began actual service at the age of seventeen,
still in the rank of sergeant, and was made a commissioned officer in
1757.

Bolotov's career shaped up reasonably well, but he disliked service,
viewing it as a hindrance to his writing (which, like Sumarokov, he
often calls "exercises"). His resentment of his service duties is often
mentioned in his memoir. In "letter" 61, for example, he complains that
his clerical duties as an officer stationed in Königsberg were difficult
and boring and describes how he rejoiced when, having cleared up a
backlog of paperwork, he was able to free himself for more interesting
occupations:

> Now, continuing my story, I will tell you that as this life was
> for me at the beginning somewhat difficult and boring, so after-
> wards it became pleasant and merry. [. . .] When I finished up
> this difficult work, there was much less writing left for me to do,
> and finally there was so little that I had hardly one page a day to
> write. Therefore I could finish this small task in half an hour,
> and not only did I not have to go to the office in the afternoon,
> but sometimes even in the morning I didn't have any work and
> could, with the permission of my little old man, absent myself
> and sometimes even spend the entire day at home. This circum-
> stance, which allowed me more leisure and free time [. . .],
> pleased me, because I could devote a longer time to my exercises
> and live as I wished, without any concern that I would be sent to
> perform some company duties or appointed to guard detail.[28]

Later, when Bolotov's knowledge of German landed him a job in the
governor's chancellery as a translator and interpreter, he was again
upset by the large volume of boring paperwork. Even the governor's
benevolence did not quite console him: "But when, on the other hand, I
recalled the difficult and tedious translations that bored me silly in a
single day, when I pictured how I would be obliged to go to the chancellery every day and to spend the entire day toiling incessantly over them
and be deprived completely of all the freedom so pleasant to me, these
thoughts diminished my delight [at being accepted in the governor's
house] and concerned me indescribably. Most of all I grieved that I

would be tied down [by my duties] and would not have a minute, so to speak, of free time for myself, time that I could use for my own interesting exercises."[29] Only in retrospect does Bolotov acknowledge that his busyness kept him out of trouble, crediting his duties and his association with colleagues in the chancellery as good for his education.[30]

Describing his subsequent service in Saint Petersburg, Bolotov continues to complain that it was a tedious hindrance to his private occupations. He therefore chose to retire as soon as he could, right after Peter III granted the Russian nobility freedom from obligatory service with his edict of 1762. Bolotov writes in his memoir how ecstatic he felt on the day his retirement became official: "Finally, said date of June 14, the most memorable day in my life, arrived, and I received my so passionately desired dismissal. [. . .] Thus on that day my fourteen-year military service came to an end, and, having received my dismissal, I became a free and independent man forever."[31] Having retired at the age of twenty-three with the rank of army captain (ninth class), Bolotov returned to civil service between 1774 and 1797 and eventually retired with the rank of collegiate assessor (sixth class). He took great care, however, not to let his service interfere with his private pursuits.

Bolotov arrived on his estate in September 1762. When the autumn weather put a stop to urgently needed improvements (that is, planting his first garden), he turned to reading and writing in order to fill his lonely leisure.[32] Soon he realized that it was precisely these occupations that made his life in the country meaningful and pleasurable: "In a word, the effect my learned exercises produced was that, instead of boredom, I was beginning even then to perceive all the pleasure of country life, free and independent, unconstrained and tranquil; and I was not burdened in the least either by [free] time, or by my solitude."[33] Intellectual pursuits were so important for Bolotov that, in looking for a bride, he sought a partner with similar interests. Unfortunately, soon after the wedding, he realized that he had not succeeded: "I didn't find and could not notice in her even the slightest inclination toward reading books or to anything concerning learning."[34] He hoped that with time his young wife would develop these interests, so central to his own existence, but, to his disappointment, this never happened. However, he was lucky enough to find a kindred soul in his mother-in-law. His ideal of a private existence suitable for a nobleman was thus complete: he had his independence, plenty of time to read and write, and a person with whom to share his intellectual interests. Later, his son Pavel became his "best friend and dear comrade and interlocutor."[35] It is noteworthy that, while shaping his private existence, Bolotov also longed for a measure of sociability, albeit within his family.

Bolotov's literary pursuits were largely private: he published almost exclusively in non-literary and non-autobiographical genres, such as pedagogy, philosophy, science, gardening, and economics, the one exception being his drama *The Unfortunate Orphans*. Neither his poetry nor his memoirs and diaries went to print in his lifetime. It was not for the public that he wrote in these genres, but to give shape to his pastoral existence in the privacy of his estate. In this, he followed a literary tradition that imagined life in the country as necessarily including intellectual activities, such as reading and writing.[36] Based on Horace's Second Epode, this pastoral ideal was first formulated for Russians by Antiokh Kantemir in his satire "On True Happiness" (1738) and survived at least until 1834, when Pushkin sketched his unfinished poem "It's time, my friend, it's time," and perhaps longer, shaping the presentation of life on the estate in nineteenth-century Russian novels. It is crucial, however, that Bolotov not only wrote prolifically about a life in the country that was independent and full of intellectual pursuits but also succeeded in implementing this literary topos in real life.

Bolotov's experiment remained without consequence in his own time, at least in part because his authorial reticence kept his literary pursuits private. It is safe to assume that it did not affect the public view of writers in any significant way. Furthermore, it is not even clear whether Russians, who during the nineteenth century grew to expect a writer to be a public figure, would have approved of this kind of love of privacy in a writer. Even after the publication of Bolotov's *Life and Adventures* in the 1870s, Russian readers, while acknowledging the importance of his memoirs, did not warm to the writerly existence he led. Perhaps it was not public enough and thus not useful enough for the Russian taste. Early in the twentieth century, Aleksandr Blok, the preeminent Symbolist poet, devoted his undergraduate thesis to comparing Bolotov and Novikov. His essay confirms the durability of this attitude: Blok hails Novikov, a highly visible public figure, and presents Bolotov, with his subdued authorial aspirations and love of privacy, as a philistine, a man without "public interests" (*obshchestv[ennykh] interesov*).[37]

If Bolotov retired from service to pursue writing in the privacy of his estate, Aleksei Rzhevsky (1737-1804) did the opposite, abandoning literature "to devote most of his adult life to career advancement."[38] He began his service at the court at the age of twelve (most likely, as a page).[39] Rzhevsky then served in the prestigious Semenovsky Regiment, retiring from it in 1761 in the rank of second lieutenant of the guards (*gvardii podporuchik*, tenth class) and entering the civil service. In 1761–62 Rzhevsky participated both in the preparations for the coronation of Catherine the Great in Moscow and in the ceremonies themselves. He returned to Saint Petersburg in the mid-1760s.

In 1767 Rzhevsky's career truly took off: he was made a *kammerjunker* and engaged in Catherine's Legislative Commission as a deputy from the town of Vorotynsk (Moscow guberniya). Between 1768 and his retirement in 1800, he served in an array of increasingly important positions, such as vice-director—and, for two years, acting director—of the Academy of Sciences, president of the Medical College, and senator. At the same time, he steadily ascended the ladder of ranks, advancing in both court and civil services: he was made *kammerherr* in 1773 and privy councilor in 1783, and received his highest civil rank, that of actual privy councilor (second class), in 1797. He retired in this rank in 1800.[40]

As Rzhevsky's service career blossomed, his participation in literary activities steadily waned.[41] He made his debut as a poet in 1759 with an elegy published in Sumarokov's journal *The Industrious Bee* (*Trudoliubivaia pchela*), and was most active from 1761 to 1763 (when he published 225 poems in two journals edited by Sumarokov's follower Mikhail Kheraskov; he also produced a few solemn odes for Catherine), after which his literary works can be counted on the fingers on one hand: one poem in 1764, two tragedies, *A Charming One* (*Prelesta*, 1765) and *The False Smerdius* (*Podlozhnyi Smerdii*, first staged in 1769), and two solemn odes, one for Catherine, in 1767, and another for Alexander, in 1801.[42] Rzhevsky's concentration on his service career caused his literary production—quite interesting, even unique in many ways—to be thoroughly forgotten for a century and a half, until Grigory Gukovsky rediscovered it in the 1920s.[43]

Abandoning active writing, Rzhevsky nonetheless continued to participate in contemporary literary life: not only did he help Ippolit Bogdanovich (1743-1802) to publish his most successful work, the narrative poem *Psyche* (*Dushen'ka*), by financing the publication and supplying it with a foreword, but he also assisted Bogdanovich in constructing his writerly persona as a dilettante poet composing in his spare time, exclusively for his own pleasure, and not particularly interested in publishing the fruits of his leisure. Bogdanovich became the first Russian writer to present himself in this way. Remarkably, he wrote his *Psyche* during a time in his service career that was filled with uncertainty as well as activity. First, his civil service career faltered: in March 1779 he was transferred from the Foreign College, where he served as a translator in the rank of collegiate assessor (eighth class), to the Office of Heraldry, but the new appointment was without pay. Bogdanovich could not afford to serve without compensation and had to resign. He was able to return to service (to the newly established State Archive) only in October 1780. Bogdanovich also experienced difficulties in his parallel career as editor of several state-sponsored periodicals published by the Academy of Sciences, including the official newspaper *Saint Petersburg News* (*Sankt-Peterburgskie vedomosti*). In July 1782 the Academy Conference accused him of printing articles in *Saint Petersburg News* that were "poorly chosen and often childish."[44] In August, more accusations followed. As a result, in December 1782 Bogdanovich was forced to resign from his position as editor, and Catherine was informed of his alleged blunders. No doubt, in the late 1770s and the early 1780s, Bogdanovich must have been both overwhelmed by the volume of his duties and distressed by bad luck in his service career.

Bogdanovich's constructed biography completely omits any reference to his service woes. *Psyche*, which was composed during roughly the same years that Bogdanovich's career was unraveling (canto 1 appeared in print in 1778 and the entire poem in 1783), fostered in the minds of both his contemporaries and posterity a very different image of its author: not that of a busy, impecunious servitor whose career was being threatened, but that of "a carefree Bohemian" writing in his (seemingly abundant) spare time. Indeed, the first sentence in Bogdanovich's introduction to the 1783 edition reads: "To entertain myself in hours of leisure was my only motivation when I began writing *Psyche*." He goes on to claim that he did not even plan to publish it until the praise of his friends compelled him to do so. Bogdanovich concludes his introduction with an assertion of his dilettante status as a writer: "I am [. . .] not from among the established writers."[45] Rzhevsky's foreword to the same edition tells a similar story: "This poem was composed by Ippolit Fedorovich Bogdanovich, who, being my old friend, showed it to me [. . .] as a composition that he was writing from time to time for his own entertainment in his hours of leisure, without intending to publish it."[46]

Psyche was hugely successful. Most importantly, it gained Bogdanovich Catherine's patronage: in March 1783 the entire print run of the poem was acquired by the Academy of Sciences and, in November

1783, the poet was elected to the Russian Academy. The empress herself encouraged Bogdanovich in his literary pursuits, and he produced several plays for the Hermitage Theater, beginning with the 1786 adaptation of *Psyche* for the stage. His labors as a court playwright were rewarded with substantial sums of money and a diamond ring. More importantly, the poem also allowed Bogdanovich to relaunch his service career. In March 1784 he was promoted to the rank of court councilor (seventh class); in 1788 he received the rank of collegiate councilor (sixth class) and became the head of the State Archive. His literary activities gradually came to an end after this appointment. He retired in 1795.[47]

Bogdanovich's persona as a dilettante, however, not only survived but also grew to eclipse his real biography.[48] The image of Bogdanovich as an idle and carefree poet creating his *Dushen'ka* in the privacy of his home to amuse himself in his spare time was amplified and consolidated by Nikolai Karamzin in his 1803 article "On Bogdanovich and His Works." Claiming that the image of the author can be discerned from the poem itself, Karamzin writes: "He lived at the time on Vasilevsky Island, in a quiet, isolated little home, devoting his time to music and verse in happy insouciance and freedom; [. . .] he loved to go out on occasion, but he loved even more to return to where the Muse awaited him with new ideas and colors."[49]

The legend of Bogdanovich as the carefree creator of the charming *Dushen'ka* not only ignored the realities of his early struggles as a poorly paid bureaucrat but also completely disregarded his destitute and unhappy post-retirement life. It also overlooked his desperate and unsuccessful attempts to return both to service and to the literary scene in the early 1800s. In June 1801 Bogdanovich petitioned the Russian Academy for help in publishing his collected works and his ode on the coronation of Alexander I, but his petition was rejected. On several occasions in 1802 he sent his works to the Academy for publication, but they were rejected as well. In his accompanying letters Bogdanovich wrote of his utter poverty, which had forced him to sell his library. It is noteworthy that in his letters this self-proclaimed dilettante also begged for an opportunity to return to service or at least to be rewarded "either with a rank, or with a cross, or with any other state decoration, but not with [. . .] a small one-time monetary allowance, which humiliates the spirit and extinguishes zeal in a nobleman."[50] These requests were also ignored, and Bogdanovich died soon thereafter.

In contrast to Sumarokov, Bolotov, Rzhevsky, and Bogdanovich, who held extreme positions in dealing with service and writing, many writers of noble status felt that they could engage in both service and writing and balance these two activities. In doing so, they used various strategies to position themselves as writers and put different emphases on service and writing. For some, service was their principal activity; a few others attempted to make writing their main occupation, even abandoning service for long periods (as Karamzin did between 1784 and 1803).

Those who chose to create their public images with an emphasis on service sometimes managed this so successfully that their literary contributions were all but forgotten. While very successful in his service career, Nikolai L'vov (1753–1803), unlike Rzhevsky, never abandoned literature. However, he made it his private occupation, publishing little and, for the most part, anonymously. His literary production was well known only to his closest friends, such as Vasily Kapnist, Ivan Khemnitser, and Derzhavin, all of whom not only valued his poetry but also considered him "the genius of taste," solicited his advice, and even allowed him to correct their own poetry.[51]

More importantly, L'vov's literary production remained mostly unknown to the writers who succeeded him. Pushkin, for example, directly refers to L'vov's poetry only once, in the rough draft for his *Journey to Arzrum*, where he quotes, somewhat incorrectly, two lines from L'vov's epic *Dobrynia* (unfinished; published in 1804).[52] Pushkin's apparent disregard for (or ignorance of) L'vov's poetic heritage is particularly striking, because it was L'vov who first experimented, in the 1770s and 1780s, with poetry addressed to a small circle of close friends.[53] It seems probable, however, that Pushkin's and his friends' experiments with familiar genres and intimate public space were independent of L'vov's, or that his influence was indirect; in any case, L'vov's role as innovator was never acknowledged. The only possible reference to L'vov's writerly behavior in Pushkin's oeuvre is, perhaps, the character of Charsky in *Egyptian Nights* (1835): like L'vov, Charsky writes poetry and shares it with his friends, but does not publish it. It is significant that at the time *Egyptian Nights* was written Pushkin himself was on the verge of assuming a similar approach: of the poems he wrote in 1836, he did not publish a single one. This tacit acknowledgment by Pushkin of his predecessor's idiosyncratic writerly behavior was, however, an exception, and the majority of writers, critics, and literary historians ignored L'vov's literary legacy until late in the twentieth century, when the first collection of the poet's works was finally published.

It is curious, in this context, that Bogdanovich was the only one among his contemporaries not only to assume a constructed dilettante persona but also to announce it, as he did in the introduction to *Dushen'ka*. It is likely that he was influenced by Rzhevsky in doing so, and it is noteworthy that Rzhevsky helped create a dilettante persona for someone who belonged to the lower echelons of the nobility (Bogdanovich came from the impoverished Ukrainian nobility, while Rzhevsky's own family claimed its origin from the mythic Varangian Rurik, the founder of the Kievan dynasty), someone who was below him in the hierarchy of ranks, and whom he essentially patronized, despite claiming to be his friend. In contrast to Bogdanovich, non-publishing nobles of higher ancestry, including L'vov (whose family was of ancient pre-Petrine lineage), refrained from announcing their dilettante status.

It is significant that at the turn of the nineteenth century this group of writing nobles began to use service as a tool to assert their independence from the state and the monarch. Notably, the degree of service success achieved by many writing nobles at that time is nothing short of amazing. Not only L'vov and Rzhevsky rose to the rank of actual privy councilor (second class), but both Derzhavin and Ivan Dmitriev (despite their rather complicated and not always smooth career paths) also achieved this rank. Likewise, at the time of his unexpected death, Murav'ev was in the rank of privy councilor (third class); and even Karamzin (who between 1790 and 1803 attempted to lead the life of an independent writer and journalist) ended up receiving, in his position as court historiographer, the rank of actual state councilor (fourth class). At least part of the reason writers pursued success in service at the turn of the nineteenth century must have been their desire for independence. This strategy apparently did not work as well as they had hoped it would: not only did success in service not result in actual independence, but even achieving service success eventually became difficult. Consider the service careers of the next generation of Russian writers of noble origin, of whom, as far as is known, only Vasily Zhukovsky ended up in the rank of privy councilor (Petr Viazemsky also achieved considerable service success, but this happened under Alexander II—that is, in a different time and under different circumstances). Consequently, writing nobles of the 1830s and 1840s were far less enthusiastic about serving the state than their predecessors had been at the turn of the nineteenth century.

Service ambitions did not always compel successful eighteenth-century servitors to keep their writing private. Unlike L'vov, many of them (Derzhavin, Dmitriev, and Murav'ev, to name the most obvious cases) attempted to lead parallel public lives both in service and in literature—that is, simultaneously attending to their service obligations

and publishing their literary works under their own names. The ways
they did so varied, however. Most significantly, they each assigned a
different value to these two occupations.

There is no doubt that Derzhavin was very serious about his service
career and proud of his achievements. Furthermore, it may be argued
that at least occasionally he used his poetry to advance his service career:
the Felitsa cycle, addressed to Catherine, is a primary example. He did
worry about accusations of flattery and protected himself by either not
publishing certain poems (such as his early ode "To Catherine II"
["Ekaterine II"]) or, later, by using the "amusing style" (*zabavnyi slog*)
in his Felitsa cycle to remove the distance between the poet and the
monarch to whom he sings praises, thus reducing the sycophantic ring
of the poems.[54]

Toward the end of his life, however, Derzhavin came to resent what
he perceived as pressure from Catherine to continue praising her in
poetry. A small poem, written in 1792–93, illustrates his sentiment:

Поймали птичку голосисту
И ну сжимать ее рукой.
Пищит бедняжка вместо свисту,
А ей твердят: «Пой, птичка, пой.»

[They caught a songbird and began to clutch it tight. Instead of
warbling, it squeaks, but they keep telling it: "Sing, birdie,
sing."]

This jocular quatrain may signal Derzhavin's realization that it was
after all poetry that would be his greatest achievement and make his
name immortal. Such poems as "Monument" ("Pamiatnik," 1795) and
"Swan" ("Lebed'," 1804) also testify to this sentiment, but it is most
prominent in the concluding stanzas of "To Evgeny: Life at Zvanka"
("Evgeniiu: Zhizn' Zvanskaia," 1807), written after Derzhavin's dismissal from service by Alexander I.[55] Indeed, in the last line of the poem
he beseeches his interlocutor, the high-ranking cleric and historian of
literature Evgeny (Bolkhovitinov), to remember him as "the singer of
God and Felitsa," referring to the Felitsa cycle and to his poem "God"
("Bog," 1784), that is, as a poet, not a successful servitor.[56]

It is also telling that when, in the early nineteenth century, Derzhavin
turned to discussing his achievements, he chose to address his literary
accomplishments and his service success separately. Moreover, he

chose to comment on his poetry first, in "Remarks on Derzhavin's Oeuvre" ("Primechaniia na sochineniia Derzhavina," 1805) and "Explanations of Derzhavin's Oeuvre" ("Ob"iasneniia na sochineniia Derzhavina," 1809–10); only afterward did he address the history of his service, in his autobiographical *Notes* (*Zapiski*, 1812–13). This privileging of his literary achievements suggests that, whatever the particulars of Derzhavin's balancing of his two main occupations were throughout his life, in the final analysis, the poetry trumped the service. Furthermore, it is probable that, like Sumarokov, the poet began to see his writing as "superior to other kinds of service."[57]

Dmitriev, whose devotion to poetry is indubitable, nonetheless presents it as not particularly significant and certainly less important than his service. Sending the story of his life to the historian Dmitry Bantysh-Kamensky (through A. F. Merzliakov), he first reports on his service achievements: "[I] was Captain of the Guards, then Chief Procurator of the Senate; in this rank I had the honor of receiving the order of Saint Anna, 2nd class. Now I am in civil service, in the rank of privy councilor." He then adds almost dismissively that he also "published three little volumes [*tomika*] of some [*koi-kakikh*] poems"; he concludes, as if in disbelief: "and became, I don't know how, a member of the Russian Academy and an honorary member of Moscow University."[58] Dmitriev also downplays the importance and quality of his poetry in his memoir *A View of My Life* (1825). Blaming his service obligations for his inability to work on his poetry more diligently and patiently, he writes: "Therefore, perhaps, in my poems there can be seen, even by myself, a poverty [*skudnost'*] of ideas, more vivacity and ornamentation than deep thinking [*glubokomyslie*] and power. Therefore it also follows that none of my best poems has a broad foundation [*obshirnaia osnova*]."[59] Perhaps Dmitriev's emphatic undervaluing of his poetry should be seen as a modesty topos, but even so, it is significant that Dmitriev put his service above his poetry, at least publicly.

Similarly, Murav'ev, a diligent and successful if not always enthusiastic servitor, nonetheless devoted as much time to writing as he could, from the time he was a non-commissioned officer in a guard regiment to his death in the rank of privy councilor. Even though his literary production diminished as he rose in rank and received important appointments (his last appointment was as deputy minister of education and curator of Moscow University), his influence on Russian literature was considerable throughout his literary career. Yet Murav'ev presented his role as a poet as modest and his writing as no more than a private diversion.

Like Dmitriev, he describes his poetry as lacking power and failing to move its readers:

> Мои стихи, мой друг,—осенние листы:
> Родятся блеклые, без живости и цвету,
> И, восхищаемы дыханий злых усты,
> Пренебрегаемы разносятся по свету,
> Не чтомые никем. Но дух во мне кипит,
> И слезы зависти катятся по ланитам,
> Что, указуемый гражданами пиит,
> Не достигаю я в сообщество к пиитам,
> Биющим верные удары во сердца,
> Со воздыханьями влекущим слезы сладки.[60]

[My poems, my friend, are autumn leaves: they are born withered, without vividness and color, and, transported by the breath of evil lips, are scattered over the world, scorned and not read by anyone. But my spirit seethes, and tears of envy roll down my cheeks, because, recognized by compatriots as a poet, I cannot join the community of poets who strike the heart with precise blows, inspiring sweet tears and sighs.]

Murav'ev describes his muse as "lazy" (*lenivaia*), and concludes his 1803 poem "Looking Back at Myself" ("Oborot na sebia") as follows:

> Хотя Карамзину, Державину неравен,
> Но в обществе певцов Российских не безславен.
> Еще последую во тайные пути
> За собеседником Вергилья, Мецената.
> И в важных прениях Сената
> Я забавляюся стихи свои плести.[61]

[Even though I am not equal to Karamzin and Derzhavin, I am not without renown in the community of Russian singers. I will still follow the interlocutor of Virgil and Maecenas down secret paths. Even during important debates in the Senate I entertain myself by weaving my poems.]

His poetic composition takes place during important debates in which the poet is obliged to participate as part of his service in the Senate, and the process of writing is presented as a pleasant diversion, almost child's play. The verb for "writing, composing" that Murav'ev chooses, *plesti*, which in Old Church Slavonic denoted sophisticated writing (*pletenie sloves*, word weaving), had a negative figurative meaning in eighteenth-century Russian (to babble, talk nonsense, even to lie). While the title of the poem can also mean "A Parody of Myself" (*oborot* means "turn," and synonyms of "parody" in Russian include such words as *perevernut'* and *vyvernut' naiznanku*, that is, "to turn over," "turn inside out"), the meaning of the joke is clear: service is more important, but writing poetry, even if it lacks particular value, is irresistible.

Karamzin stands apart from the cases of his contemporaries and friends. His participation in establishing Bogdanovich's posthumous reputation as a dilettante poet demonstrates that he was thinking about possible self-representation as a dilettante. At the same time, the experimental nature of this enterprise is obvious: in the end Karamzin followed an entirely different path and instead constructed a public image as a professional writer. In his youth, a service career did not interest him much: he retired at the age of eighteen in the rank of lieutenant of the guards (ninth class). Karamzin remained in retirement until 1803, when he sought to return to service in order to gain the emperor's financial support for writing the *History of the Russian State*. That year he was appointed official court historiographer, with the rank of court councilor (seventh class), which, in addition to a yearly stipend of 2,000 rubles, brought him access to the state archives. When the first several volumes of his *History* were published in 1816, he was rewarded with the rank of state councilor (fifth class). What is most important, however, is that for almost twenty years, between 1784 and 1803, Karamzin led a life that, from the state's point of view, was that of a private person, not a useful state servitor. Until 1791—that is, his return from his European tour—Karamzin was an active Freemason, and his various literary enterprises were inspired and financed by the Novikov circle. However, upon his return to Russia, Karamzin parted ways with the Freemasons and for the next twelve years worked independently as a journalist, publisher, and translator; wrote and published the majority of his prose and poetry; and was extraordinarily active as a literary critic and historian of literature. In a word, he led the life of a professional writer: all his enterprises during these years (until he took up the writing of the *History of the Russian State*) were private affairs—not sponsored by the state or a wealthy individual. It is not clear whether Karamzin's numerous endeavors in the 1790s (such as publishing and editing *The*

Moscow Journal [*Moskovskii zhurnal*], issuing the almanacs *Aglaia* and *The Aonides*, and compiling the *Pantheon of Russian Writers* [*Panteon rossiiskikh avtorov*], to name but a few) brought him sufficient income to live on. However, at least one of his enterprises earned him a substantial sum: I. V. Popov, the publisher of *Messenger of Europe* (*Vestnik Evropy*), which Karamzin edited in 1802-3, paid him 3,000 rubles a year, "a salary three to four times that of the average government functionary."[62]

At the time Karamzin was receiving monetary compensation for editing *Messenger of Europe* as well as contributing to it, the only other commercially oriented writers were the despicable (in the view of the high-minded writers and readers) creators of entertainment literature. Editors thus were the first among highbrow literati to receive honoraria for their work.[63] Karamzin seemed to be aware of this awkward situation: in the "Letter to the Publisher" that opens the first issue of the journal, while laying out the rules and principles he planned to follow as a critic, he mentions one of the most popular works of entertainment literature, Matvei Komarov's novel *A Tale about the Adventure of the English Milord George*.[64] Though well aware of the novel's reputation, Karamzin nonetheless chooses not only to mention it but to treat its author with lenience: "I don't know what others think, but I wouldn't want to cause pain to anyone even for [writing] *Milord George* and getting it printed five or six times.[65] A silly book is a small evil in this world. Besides, we have so few authors that it is not worth our while to scare them.—But if something good comes out, why not praise it? The most moderate praise is often a great encouragement for a young talent.— Such are my rules!"[66] Karamzin wisely tries to play down the difference between the authors of entertainment literature and himself: now both they and he write for pay. The concept of receiving an honorarium, so frightening to Sumarokov, does not seem to trouble Karamzin at all.

Karamzin experimented with two different images of the Russian writer: that of the dilettante poet, which he helped construct for Bogda-novich, and that of the professional writer, which he created for himself. He eventually ended his own experiment and turned to a third writerly persona: the author as imperial client, receiving direct financial support from the tsar. According to Karamzin's letter to Murav'ev of November 3, 1803, he would not have been able to compose his *History* without this support; in this letter he thanks Murav'ev for arranging it.[67] The fact that Karamzin considered three different models of writerly behavior, of which he used two, clearly demonstrates that, at the turn of the nineteenth century, writers of noble status were still deciding which path to follow and how to present themselves publicly. Furthermore, the different modes of writerly behavior they tried on constituted a useful legacy for the writers who came after them.

Largely illiterate until the eighteenth century, Russian nobles took to writing with a vengeance in the post-Petrine era. Like their European counterparts, some used writing to define their private sphere of existence or to formulate an authorial position that made them, at least nominally, independent of the state and its hierarchies. At the same time, obligatory or, later in the century, expected service to the state made any non-service activity suspect, forcing Russian noblemen to balance service and writing, and they did so in a variety of ways. The presented picture is inevitably incomplete: not every eighteenth-century writer of noble status fits it neatly, and not every possible method of being a writer while in service has been considered.[68] Nonetheless, this picture is useful as a lens to identify some models of writerly behavior used by eighteenth- and early nineteenth-century nobles, whose participation in the service hierarchy was not only strongly expected by others, including but not limited to the state, but often avidly desired by the writers themselves. The examination of the situation of noble writers who also served exposes possible conflicts between the two occupations and shows some of the ways nobles attempted to resolve them. This schematic picture also facilitates investigation into the subsequent period, the so-called Golden Age of Russian poetry. Writers of this period inherited from their predecessors diverse patterns of conduct to emulate—or modify in response to new circumstances.

2

Pushkin as Bureaucrat, Courtier, and Writer

Alexander Pushkin is undoubtedly the most important poet of the Golden Age and, while his fame waned somewhat in the mid-nineteenth century, after the Pushkin celebration of 1880 it flourished again, and he continues to dominate the Russian Parnassus to the present day, speaking in a different voice to each new generation and always saying what that generation wants to hear.[1] For Russians, his significance as a writer has never been eclipsed by anyone else, even Tolstoy or Dostoevsky. At the same time, hardly anybody remembers that Pushkin also had a service career, and that it was quite unsuccessful: not only did his first stint in service end in dismissal, but he also never advanced beyond the rank of titular councilor. Though Pushkin's service career is sometimes acknowledged in passing in his scholarly biographies, his service record has never been the subject of special inquiry.

The question arises, what causes this apparent reluctance to engage with the topic of Pushkin's service? Is it avoided simply because, to contemporary scholars and readers, only his literary production is important, and service seems to be secondary, almost beside the point? Or is it ambivalence about Russia's greatest poet participating in the infamous imperial bureaucracy that puts students off? Could it be that Pushkin's serving the state, at times with enthusiasm, interferes with his admirers' desire to focus on his conflicts with that state and its rulers, which can be interpreted as heroic? Or do Pushkin scholars perhaps ignore his service career because it was rather unsuccessful?

To answer these questions, a brief overview of Pushkin's civil service career is in order. It is also necessary to examine some common opinions about his career—opinions that are, in some cases, debatable. Most importantly, certain established interpretations of Pushkin's biography interfere with an impartial examination of Pushkin's service career and with a consideration of its significance for him and people around him. Pushkin's contemporaries were not indifferent to it. Not only did many of them judge him by his low civil service rank, ignoring his reputation as a writer, but they were particularly captivated by the story of his receiving the court title of *kammerjunker* and his apparent displeasure at it. The general public reacted to this event with mirth, as did some of his friends. Furthermore, at least two writers, Osip Senkovsky (Józef Sękowski) and Nikolai Gogol, mocked Pushkin's service career in their works. This chapter concludes with a discussion of how Pushkin's participation in the service hierarchy is reflected in his prose, which has been less thoroughly examined from this point of view than his poetry. Pushkin's anxieties about his social status, particularly his service rank, are clearly evident in his prose fiction.

Pushkin the Titular Councilor

In comparison with the multitudes of volumes dedicated to Pushkin's literary works and other aspects of his life, his service has been surprisingly neglected.[2] A good example of such neglect by Soviet scholars is the 1931 *Guide to Pushkin*, a dictionary of names and subjects that comments on all aspects of Pushkin's life and works but nonetheless lacks entries explaining the ranks he held, collegiate secretary and titular councilor, whereas some other ranks are explained.[3] In twenty-first-century Russia the attitude has not changed much: volume 5 of the 2007 biographical dictionary *Russian Writers, 1800–1917* devotes to Pushkin's service career only one and one-third out of roughly sixty-four columns of text (excluding illustrations).[4] Western scholars follow suit: the entry on Pushkin in Victor Terras's *Handbook of Russian Literature*, while mentioning Pushkin's "status on the margin of two social and cultural positions—'gentleman' and 'author,'" does not address the question of whether his service rank played a role in this marginality.[5] To be sure, publications documenting Pushkin's service career do exist, but, with few exceptions, they concentrate on presenting facts, not interpreting them.

If biographies of Pushkin refer to his service career at all, as a rule they pay different amounts of attention to its different stages. His entering the College (or Ministry) of Foreign Affairs after graduation from the Lyceum is usually mentioned, although not examined in any serious way.[6] Pushkin's return to service in the early 1830s receives far less attention: it is either disregarded or briefly explained by his need to have access to the imperial archives in order to work on his history of Peter the Great.[7] The only episode of Pushkin's late service that is commonly commented on is his investiture with the title of *kammerjunker*— apparently both because Pushkin himself repeatedly wrote about this event in his diary and letters, and because it conveniently lends itself to interpretation as an offensive action by the tsar against the great poet.[8]

When putting together a record of Pushkin's service career, the first thing that becomes apparent is that it is short and not particularly glamorous. He served in 1817–24 and then again in 1831–37. Upon graduating from the Imperial Lyceum fourth from the bottom of his class (fourteenth out of seventeen graduates), Pushkin received the rank of collegiate secretary (tenth class). In comparison, his classmates whose class standing was higher received the rank of titular councilor (ninth class). Both ranks were high, given the age of the recipients, and opened paths to good service careers. The difference was felt by some, however: Fedor Matiushkin, Pushkin's fellow collegiate secretary, wrote to a friend: "I have been graduated with the rank of collegiate secretary. You certainly will congratulate me on a felicitous beginning of service. Without having done anything, to be of the tenth class, is, of course, a lot. But we judge by comparison: some of us have been graduated as titular councilors."[9]

Pushkin did not complain about his rank, but reportedly he was not overjoyed to be appointed to the civil service: he wanted to join the military. However, his father was not willing to pay for his equipment as was required, and Pushkin joined the College of Foreign Affairs, a diplomatic career being the most prestigious of all the civil service careers available to a young nobleman.[10] He took the oath to the emperor on June 15, 1817.[11] In May 1820, after three years in Saint Petersburg— years in which Pushkin earned recognition as a poet but did not advance in rank—he was transferred to Ekaterinoslav to serve under Ivan Inzov, the head of a chancellery that supervised foreign colonists. At the same time, Inzov was made the acting governor-general of Novorossiia and vice regent (*namestnik*) of Bessarabia, and Pushkin moved with his chancellery to Kishinev, where he served until the summer of 1823. He then transferred to Odessa, to serve under M. S. Vorontsov, who replaced Inzov as governor-general and *namestnik*. In June 1824, amid worsening relations with Vorontsov and after a series of missteps (such as his refusing to fulfill Vorontsov's order to inspect damage inflicted by locusts in Kherson guberniya and sending by imperial post a letter in which he discussed his atheism—as was discovered when it was opened by the police), Pushkin handed in his resignation, citing his poor health. The petition was readily granted, and Pushkin was retired without the customary promotion to the next rank, which clearly indicated imperial displeasure with his service and behavior. He was ordered to reside on his father's estate in Mikhailovskoe under police surveillance.

Two generally accepted opinions dominate interpretations of Pushkin's early service career: that between 1817 and 1824 Pushkin was not very serious about his service duties, and that he was exiled to the south as a punishment for writing anti-government poetry. Both opinions need to be reexamined. The position that Pushkin held upon graduation was supernumerary (his salary of seven hundred rubles a year came from the state treasury, not the College) and thus perhaps could be considered a sinecure that required little work. Contemporary memoirs and later biographers seem to agree that Pushkin took advantage of this situation.[12] If he did, his behavior was exceptional: many of his classmates were appointed to similar positions, and, judging by their careers, they did not neglect their duties.[13] However, evidence exists that Pushkin was not as completely idle as the cited sources suggest. His position required regular presence at the office and fulfillment of certain duties, such as being on call to receive diplomatic mail, and there are no indications that he neglected them.[14] Furthermore, in his unpublished notebook, Vladimir Sollogub, one of Pushkin's acquaintances in the 1830s, records a story Pushkin told him, in which he mentions being on call: "Pushkin recounted that, when he served at the Ministry of Foreign Affairs, he once was on duty together with one very old clerk."[15] Pushkin also worked as a translator; this is how he is referred to in a letter written by the head of the College, Count Ioann Kapodistria, at the time of Pushkin's transfer to Ekaterinoslav: "Yesterday the Emperor ordered the College to give Mr. Pushkin, translator, 1,000 rubles for travel expenses."[16] In Kishinev Pushkin continued to translate for Inzov's office: in his letter to Kapodistria of April 28, 1821, Inzov reports that he has given the poet the task of "translating Moldavian laws written in French into Russian." Likewise, he writes to P. M. Volkonsky on December 1, 1821: "Mr. Pushkin, who is attached to my office, is well-behaved. I occupy him with correspondence in French and with translations from Russian to French, because, given his lack of experience, I cannot trust him with other paperwork."[17] There is evidence that Pushkin's supervisors were reasonably content with his performance.[18]

The scarcity of documents concerning Pushkin's early service, both in Saint Petersburg and in the south, makes it difficult to decide how involved in his service Pushkin actually was. While all the formal aspects of his early career are documented, the only extant evidence of the particular service duties Pushkin performed is the cited documents.[19] Perhaps he did not take advantage of the career opportunities he was given—unlike some of his classmates or A. S. Griboedov, who was appointed to the College at the same time but with a lower rank (provincial secretary, twelfth class), yet by the time of his death in 1829 had attained the rank of state councilor (fifth class).[20]

However, the very absence of a paper trail may be suspicious. At the time of his service in Petersburg and Kishinev, Pushkin belonged to a circle of people, many of them in diplomatic service themselves, who, according to Mariia Maiofis's reconstruction of their activities, participated in Count Kapodistria's Russian modernization project, which proposed major reforms including the introduction of a constitution and the abolition of serfdom.[21] Initially supported by the tsar, Kapodistria's plans failed to take hold and eventually lost the tsar's support. In 1822 his disagreements with Alexander over internal and foreign policies resulted in his leaving his post at the College and going abroad, never to return to Russia. He officially resigned the post in 1827. Maiofis points out the conspicuous absence from the appropriate archives of many documents concerning Kapodistria and his circle; she suggests that documents related to Kapodistria's project were actively destroyed throughout the 1820s.[22] It is not inconceivable that Pushkin's service documents were among them.

Pushkin formally served under Kapodistria from the moment he took the oath until the latter left Russia. Furthermore, Kapodistria's young associates were the poet's close friends and benefactors; all of them, including Kapodistria, were members of Arzamas, a literary association founded by S. S. Uvarov, the infamous minister of public education under Nicholas I, but at the time an ambitious statesman of liberal persuasion. Among the members of Arzamas were several diplomats (D. N. Bludov, D. V. Dashkov) as well as poets (P. A. Viazemsky, V. A. Zhukovsky, K. N. Batiushkov). Kapodistria was elected an honorary member in March 1816. Pushkin joined on April 7, 1818, at the last official meeting of the association.[23] As Maiofis argues, the members of

Arzamas, striving to make Russia a truly European nation, considered "demonstrating the great success of Russian literature and enlightenment" instrumental to this task.[24] Their encouragement of Pushkin's literary talent should be seen in this context. Furthermore, it was no coincidence that the poetry that supposedly inflamed the tsar's anger against Pushkin was in line with Kapodistria's and his associates' modernization plans—and was, arguably, not far removed from the tsar's own ideas at the time.

Pushkin thus could have been sent away for reasons other than political. In January 1820 he learned about the rumor circulating in Saint Petersburg that he had been flogged by the police. Pushkin was devastated to the point of contemplating suicide, and, as he wrote in an unsent letter to Alexander I on September 1825, decided to behave so defiantly and provocatively that the government would be forced to exile him to Siberia. Widely circulating his unpublished and thus uncensored poems was part of his strategy, which apparently indeed led to his removal from the capital.[25] This removal was supposed to be temporary and was represented as a service reassignment: not only was Pushkin given 1,000 rubles for travel expenses (a surprisingly large sum), but he also served as a courier, bringing Inzov his letter of appointment as acting governor-general and vice regent. Also, the lengthy trip to the Caucasus and Crimea that Pushkin undertook right after his arrival in Ekaterinoslav was likely sanctioned in advance.[26]

To be sure, Alexander was not amused by Pushkin's provocative behavior, and several older friends had to intercede on his behalf, Kapodistria among them.[27] It was in fact Kapodistria who arranged with the tsar the details of Pushkin's departure for the south, as is evident from the rough draft of his letter to Inzov, approved by Alexander.[28] The letter gives a mostly positive characterization of Pushkin, citing his "unusual talent" and intellect (but also his absence of moral fortitude) and expressing the conviction that it was possible "to make out of him an excellent servant of the state or, at least, a first-rate writer." It also seems to imply that Kapodistria expected to take Pushkin under his protection upon his return to Saint Petersburg: "Mr. Pushkin, it seems, wants to choose a diplomatic career and to begin it in [my] department. There is nothing I wish more than to give him a position close to me, but he will receive this favor only through you, when you tell me that he deserves it."[29] It is significant in this context that Pushkin's duties under Inzov were connected with Kapodistria's pet project: providing laws for the newly acquired province.

Pushkin apparently began to view his temporary reassignment as an exile in the spring of 1821, a year after his departure from Petersburg: it was only then that he began to model his authorial image not on Byron but on Ovid, and Alexander became a "sly Augustus" in his eyes.[30] However, it appears that Pushkin's status did not change unequivocally until after Kapodistria's fall. At that time, Inzov was also dismissed as vice regent, and Vorontsov appointed in his stead.[31] Pushkin's friends (especially A. I. Turgenev and Zhukovsky) had a high opinion of Vorontsov and urged Pushkin to transfer to his office in Odessa, which he did.[32] This was a fatal mistake: the two did not get along. Furthermore, while Kapodistria had valued Pushkin's poetic gift, Vorontsov did not. He wrote to P. D. Kiselev on March 6, 1824: "I am not a great admirer of his gift: one cannot be a true poet without constantly working on expanding one's knowledge, and his is not sufficient."[33] In response to Vorontsov's exacting treatment of him, Pushkin flaunted his lack of ability as a bureaucrat and refused to fulfill his duties. The poet's insubordination in the locust affair, his caustic epigrams directed at the *namestnik* (whose wife he was reportedly courting), and, finally, the letter about atheism that the police read led to his dismissal from service.

Whether Pushkin was a participant in Kapodistria's modernization project; a happy-go-lucky, good-for-nothing playboy; or (as he wrote at the height of his conflict with Vorontsov in an unsent letter to one of his supervisors) a poet who had chosen "a different destiny" and therefore "for seven years had not engaged in service, had not written a single paper, and had not had any dealings with a single one of his superiors"; or even all three combined, one fact is certain: he was not promoted during his years of service and remained in the rank of collegiate secretary throughout his forced retirement.[34] It is also clear that eventually he began to worry about this. On April 16, 1830, soon after his engagement to Nataliia Goncharova, Pushkin wrote to A. Kh. Benkendorf expressing his discontent with his service status: "I was dismissed from service in 1824, and this stain still remains. Having finished the Lyceum in 1817 with the rank of the tenth class, I never received the two ranks that were mine by right, because my superiors passed me over when it was time to recommend me [for promotion], and I didn't find it necessary to remind [them] about myself."[35] Concerned primarily with removing the stigma of his forced retirement to mollify his future in-laws, Pushkin did not ask to return to service at that time, citing his literary activities as his main occupation and source of income. However, a little more than a year later, in July 1831, he repeated his complaints in another letter to Benkendorf: "My present rank (the very same with which I graduated from the Lyceum) unfortunately impedes me in my service career. I was listed [*schitalsia*] at the College of Foreign Affairs from 1817 to 1824. For time in grade [*za vyslugu let*], I should have been promoted twice, that is, to the ranks of titular [councilor] and collegiate assessor, but my former supervisors kept forgetting to nominate me. I don't know whether I can still receive what I was entitled to."[36] In this letter, Pushkin offers his services to the tsar, as both a journalist and a historiographer:

> If my lord emperor wishes to use my quill, I will strive to fulfill his will with exactitude and zeal, and I am ready to serve him to the best of my abilities. In Russia periodical editions don't represent different political parties (which we don't have), and the government doesn't need to have its own official journal. Nonetheless, general opinion needs to be guided. I would happily undertake editing a *political and literary journal*, that is, the kind of journal that would publish political and foreign news. I would unite gifted writers around it and thus would draw closer to the government useful people who now still shy away from it, thinking it to be hostile to enlightenment.
>
> Permission to do historical research in our state archives and libraries would more suit my occupation and inclinations. I don't dare or wish, after the late [*nezabvennyi*] Karamzin, to take upon myself the title of historiographer, but I can in time fulfill my long-held desire to write a history of Peter the Great and his successors up to Peter III.[37]

From the way Pushkin phrases his offer of services, it seems that his desire to work in the archives was stronger than his wish to edit a journal (although he actually had plans to publish such a journal and made attempts to receive permission to do so). In any case, on November 14, 1831, he was reinstated at the College in the rank of collegiate secretary, and on December 6 was promoted to the rank of titular councilor (ninth class).[38] Pushkin's new service position brought him a yearly income of 5,000 rubles (a sum much larger than what a titular councilor normally received) and access to the imperial archives. On December 31, 1833, Pushkin was granted the title of *kammerjunker*, and his official service designation became "titular councilor with the title of *kammerjunker*." He never advanced any further.[39]

As mentioned earlier, Pushkin's return to service is usually explained by his desire to have access to the imperial archives. However, from his letter to Benkendorf it is evident that he was also ready to serve the emperor as a journalist. The desire to serve the government that Pushkin expresses here needs to be taken seriously; not long before he wrote to Benkendorf offering his services, he jotted down a program for a periodical, concluding with the following two points: "I offer my journal to the government, as an instrument of its influence on the general opinion. Officialism [*ofitsial'nost'*]."[40] The program is similar to one the members of Arzamas had developed in the late 1810s. It is therefore noteworthy that when Pushkin wrote this program and the letter to Benkendorf he was in touch with two former Arzamasians, Filipp Vigel and Uvarov.[41] Indeed, in July 1831, Vigel wrote to Pushkin expressing his and Uvarov's support for his new project. In his letter, Vigel informs Pushkin that not only does Uvarov know about his plan for a journal, but he "approves of it, is enthusiastic about it," and is ready to talk about it with Benkendorf (whose endorsement would be needed to start a new publication).[42] In her book, Maiofis offers a thorough discussion of the reasons for Uvarov's alleged enthusiastic reaction: she convincingly argues that, at the time Arzamas was active, Arzamasians saw themselves not as private persons getting together to dine on goose, have a good time, and poke fun at their literary opponents but as high-minded patriots aspiring to advise the tsar on matters of internal and foreign affairs at a time when, they believed, radical changes in these areas were imminent. Maiofis also contends that this spirit was rekindled at the beginning of Nicholas's reign, and that the three former Arzamasians—Uvarov, Vigel, and Pushkin—could have been united by it.[43] Despite Uvarov's supposed enthusiasm, Pushkin's project failed, but the poet's relatively good and collaborative relations with Uvarov continued, though gradually deteriorating, until December 1835, when Pushkin wrote a poem viciously mocking Uvarov, "On the Recovery of Lucullus," after which, as is well known, their relations swiftly went downhill, ending in mutual vitriolic hatred.

Pushkin the *Kammerjunker*

In 1831 Uvarov was on the verge of becoming one of the most powerful statesmen in the Nicholaevan empire: in 1832 he would be appointed deputy minister, and in 1833, minister of public education. The same year he would come up with his famous (or infamous) triad, Orthodoxy,

Autocracy, and Nationality, which would become the ideological basis of Nicholas's reign. Uvarov's support would thus have been a serious help not only for Pushkin's plan to launch a pro-government periodical but also for his service career. In his letter to Pushkin, Vigel assures him that Uvarov will support him in all possible ways, including making him an honorary member of his Academy of Sciences, facilitating his election to the Russian Academy, and helping him receive the court title of *kammerherr*.[44] Uvarov did facilitate Pushkin's election to the Russian Academy on January 7, 1833, but his appointment as *kammerherr* never took place.[45]

Instead, on December 31, 1833, Pushkin was made a *kammerjunker*. His diary and letters testify that he found the title insulting. Many contemporaries testified that Pushkin also expressed his indignation publicly, pulling no punches. For example, his brother, Lev Pushkin, reported the following to Iakov Polonsky, a poet and his good acquaintance: "My brother [. . .] first learned about his *kammerjunker*'s title at a ball in the house of Count Aleksei Fedorovich Orlov. It infuriated [*vzbesilo*] him to such a degree that friends had to take him to the Count's study and there calm him down in every possible way. I cannot comfortably repeat here everything that the enraged poet, foaming at the mouth, said about his appointment."[46] Pushkin's close friend P. V. Nashchokin told a very similar story to Petr Bartenev (who, as is well known, interviewed many of Pushkin's contemporaries to collect information about the poet): "His friends, Viel'gorsky and Zhukovsky, had to throw cold water on the newly minted *kammerjunker*, so agitated was he by this appointment! If not for them, he would have gone to the palace, beside himself, flaring up, his face burning, and said rude things to the tsar himself."[47]

The extent of Pushkin's public protestation is questioned by his friend S. A. Sobolevsky, who attached a comment to Bartenev's record of Nashchokin's comments about Pushkin's rage: "Nonsense. Pushkin was too well-mannered [for this]."[48] Bartenev seems to agree: "Soon (as can be seen from his letter to Nashchokin) [Pushkin] realized that the tsar didn't want to offend him and calmed down."[49] Indeed, in the letter mentioned by Bartenev, written in March 1834, Pushkin notes: "Certainly, having made me a *kammerjunker*, the tsar was thinking of my rank and not of my age—surely, he didn't want to pique me."[50]

A few words on the history of the *kammerjunker* title can help clarify the matter. Beginning in 1809, *kammerjunker*, hitherto a rank of the ninth class in court service (that is, formally the same as titular councilor in civil service), ceased to be a rank and became an honorary title (*zvanie*). From then on, every *kammerjunker* had to be in the military or civil service. At first, there was no consistent correspondence between this title and rank, but in 1836, about three years after Pushkin was made a *kammerjunker*, a correspondence was established, and the title could be granted only to persons of the ninth to the fourth class. For *kammerherrs* the corresponding ranks were fifth to third class.[51] Pushkin's fellow *kammerjunkers* (161 persons) included people from the fourteenth (one person) to the fifth (two persons) classes. Forty-two *kammerjunkers* in this group had the rank of titular councilor, and twenty-one, collegiate assessor (eighth class).[52] From Nicholas's point of view, the title of *kammerjunker* corresponded to Pushkin's service rank.[53]

With respect to Pushkin's age as well, Nicholas seems to be not entirely off the mark. According to S. A. Reiser, who succeeded in finding dates of birth for 86 percent of Pushkin's fellow *kammerjunkers*, thirteen were born between 1791 and 1799; and twenty-three, between 1801 and 1812. Of these younger *kammerjunkers*, only nine were born after 1805— that is, were significantly younger than Pushkin.[54] At the same time, at age thirty-four, Pushkin was not the oldest in the group: some of his fellow *kammerjunkers* were over forty. Pushkin may have been upset because the majority became *kammerjunkers* at a younger age: according to Reiser's calculations, one usually "became a *kammerjunker* between the ages of 16 and 39," most receiving the title between twenty and twenty-five.[55]

Pushkin the *Kammerherr*

The extent to which Pushkin really came to terms with the *kammerjunker* title can be called into question, however: his mood remained noticeably depressed throughout the summer of 1834, and on June 25 he attempted to resign from service, asking only that the tsar not suspend his archival privileges. The resignation was accepted, archival privileges revoked, and Pushkin was able to remain in service and thus retain his access to state archives only thanks to Zhukovsky's active intercession.[56]

In addition to Pushkin's unhappiness about the title's low status, he could have been upset by the rumors that it was granted to him so that his beautiful wife could be invited to court balls. The question of whether Nicholas's alleged improper interest in Nataliia Nikolaevna Pushkina was indeed the impulse behind his granting Pushkin the title is beyond the scope of this chapter. True or not, contemporary speculations on this matter undoubtedly distressed Pushkin; no wonder he referred to them repeatedly in his correspondence and his diary. Furthermore, he apparently also vented his frustration in the 1834 fairy tale *The Golden Cockerel*: the sexual undertones of the entire *kammerjunker* episode, including speculations about Nataliia Nikolaevna and the tsar, seem to have been translated into sexual motifs in the tale.[57]

However, the rumors concerning Pushkin himself are far more important; they perhaps allow the reconstruction of contemporary opinion about Pushkin's receiving the title of *kammerjunker*. How did they see the incident and his reaction to it? Was it viewed as it is now by the majority of scholars and educated Russians, namely, that the title was unexpected, unwanted, insulting, and was accepted only because it was impossible to decline a favor from the tsar? Or was their view perhaps different? Did Pushkin's contemporaries sympathize with his situation? If his enemies did not, did his friends? Granted, such a reconstruction can only be speculative, but it is worth attempting, if only to complicate the currently accepted image of Pushkin's stoically suffering an insult he could not avenge. Perhaps looking at the situation through a different lens will provide a picture somewhat closer to the actual situation.

Many contemporaries registered Pushkin's discomfort, perhaps indignation and even wrath, in reaction to receiving the title, and this is what the existing cultural memory has preserved. What is not often recalled is that for many around Pushkin, including those who liked and even loved him, his situation was comical, and Pushkin knew it. On January 7, 1834, he wrote in his diary: "The other day Grand Duke [Michael] congratulated me in the theater: 'Thank you very much, your highness,' [I replied]; 'Until now everyone was laughing at me, you are the first to congratulate me.'"[58]

Indeed, they were laughing. Several days after Pushkin's encounter with the grand duke, on January 20 (that is, less than a month after the title was officially conferred), Sofiia Karamzina, the historian's daughter, writing to Ivan Dmitriev, described Pushkin's feelings rather flippantly: "Pushkin was deeply afraid [*krepko boialsia*] of bad jokes on account of his unexpected *kammerjunker* status, but now he has calmed down, attends balls, and enjoys the solemn beauty of his wife" (Karamzina goes on to joke about Nataliia Nikolaevna's jealousy of Pushkin's attentions to other women).[59] However, it is likely that Pushkin calmed down (if he actually did) not because there were no jokes, but because he could do little to prevent them. Petr Viazemsky's son Pavel, who knew Pushkin quite well, writes in his memoirs: "Friends didn't spare Pushkin's pride [*samoliubie*] on account of his belated *kammerjunker* title. I remember Sobolevsky's poem: 'Pushkin kammeriunker, / Razzolochennyi kak kliunker'" (Pushkin the *kammerjunker*, / gilded like a golden coin). Pavel Viazemsky continues: "It was Sobolevsky who invented the name *kliunker* for a golden coin, using it as proof that there is a word that rhymes with *kammerjunker*."[60] The joker, one of the poet's closest friends, is referring here to the *kammerjunker* uniform, which featured rich golden decorations. He bends over backwards to ridicule his friend, inventing a new meaning for a word of German derivation, which, according to Dahl's dictionary, actually meant a train of carts carrying gold.

Petr Viazemsky (who is considered one of Pushkin's closest friends, even though—especially toward the end of Pushkin's life—it is possible to question the genuineness of his friendship) made similar jokes. On May 28, 1834, he wrote to Pushkin, forwarding to him Ivan Miatlev's invitation for dinner: "Come without fail. It will be really fun. You have to be there at 4 o'clock, that is, today. In addition, Miatlev is

> Любезный родственник, поэт и камер-гер.
> А ты ему родня, поэт и камер-юнкер:
> Мы выпьем у него шампанского на клункер,
> И будут нам стихи, на м<ате>рный манер.[61]

[A dear relative, a poet, and *kammerherr*. / And you are his relative, a poet, and *kammerjunker*. / At his place we will drink champagne worth a *klunker* / And [Miatlev—known for his burlesque poetry] will read his obscene poetry to us.]

Viazemsky is, of course, quoting Vasily Pushkin's 1812 poem "To P. N. Priklonsky," which begins with the line "Dear relative, poet and *kammerherr*"—a line that entered the parlance of the Pushkin circle and was used by Pushkin in his own poem addressed to Viazemsky on the occasion of his receiving the title of *kammerherr* on August 5, 1831, which begins "Dear Viazemsky, poet and *kammerherr*." In his invitation, Viazemsky jokingly presents himself, Miatlev, and Pushkin as members of the same family by pointing out that all three of them have court titles. Given the fact that both Viazemsky and Miatlev were *kammerherrs*, whereas Pushkin was only a *kammerjunker*, it is doubtful that Pushkin was entirely amused by Viazemsky's joke.

An additional insult in this joke comes from the sexual associations of the word *kammerherr* itself. Not only does the German *herr* sound like a vulgar Russian synonym for penis, but a detail of the *kammerherr*'s uniform, a golden key that was worn on the lower back, invited homosexual connotations: "In the Arzamasian parlance [it] was interpreted as 'the key to one's bottom' (*kliuch k zadu*), implying the way the distinction was allegedly often earned."[62] The title of *kammerjunker*, or junior *kammerherr*, by definition must have been even less respectable.

In this context, the allegations that Pushkin actively sought out the title of *kammerjunker* had to be even more upsetting for him than the needling but friendly jokes. Such allegations seem to have been rather widespread. Iakov Polonsky wrote down his own reminiscences about the episode: "Some of his enemies spread rumors and even published that Pushkin attained this title by using intrigue and flattery." He then goes on to quote Lev Pushkin's refutation of these rumors.[63] Pushkin's good friend N. M. Smirnov records similar allegations in his 1842 memoir: "Moreover, in relation to this case a vile lampoon appeared, in which they talked about the change in Pushkin's feelings, alleged that he had become a fawner, a petty person [*malodushnyi*], and he, who valued his fame, was afraid that this opinion would be accepted by the public and would deprive him of his popularity [*narodnosti*]."[64] Likewise, Nashchokin reported to Bartenev: "Many accused [Pushkin] of seeking out the *kammerjunker* title."[65] In his memoirs, V. I. Safonovich, a casual acquaintance of Pushkin, gives us a taste of what people outside Pushkin's inner circle said and thought: "Pushkin was a kind of enigmatic, two-faced [*dvulichnoe*] creature. He was eager to be accepted among the aristocracy [*kidalsia v znat'*]—but [at the same time,] wanted to be popular; he would appear in a salon—but would behave grossly [*griazno*]; [he] would seek the good graces of people with influence and of the upper echelons—but had nothing genial [*gratsioznogo*] in his manner and behaved haughtily. He was both a conservative and a revolutionary. He accepted the title of *kammerjunker* with pleasure, but would mill [*vertelsia*] around people who didn't particularly like the court."[66]

To add insult to injury, many among Pushkin's contemporaries believed that he was upset not because he had been granted an unwanted court title, but because, in his view, this title was not high enough; they believed that had he received the title of *kammerherr* he would have accepted it gladly. In his earlier (1834) description of Pushkin's reaction to receiving the title, Smirnov explains his displeasure precisely in this way: "He claimed that it would be strange if he put on a court uniform—he, the former critic of the court; *mais le fin mot de la chose* [but the final word on the matter] [was] that he was annoyed that he had not been made a *kammerherr*. The Emperor didn't figure this out [*ne dogadalsia*], and he was given the golden uniform [of *kammerjunker*], so that he, and especially his beautiful wife, could be invited to court."[67] Likewise, Petr Viazemsky wrote to Grand Prince Michael soon after the poet's death, on February 14, 1837: "I have to admit: Pushkin didn't like his *kammerjunker* uniform. What he didn't like in it was not the court service, but the uniform of a *kammerjunker*. Despite my friendship with him, I will not hide that he was conceited and vain. The *kammerherr*'s key was a distinction that he would have appreciated; but it seemed to him improper that at his age, at the height of his career he was made *kammerjunker* in the manner of youths and society debutants. This is the entire truth about his prejudice against the uniform. It came not out of opposition, not out of liberalism, but out of vainglory and personal touchiness."[68] Accurate or not (and regardless of what one thinks about Viazemsky's true feelings toward Pushkin), this is strong testimony, especially from a person who had witnessed his friend's death two weeks before.

The rumors about Pushkin's alleged desire for a higher title were apparently quite prevalent. Pushkinist Leonid Grossman writes in his 1934 article: "Such opinions spread widely in Petersburg 'high society,' giving rise to ironic remarks, epigrams, lampoons [*paskvili*], and caricatures."[69] Significantly, Smirnov mentions a "vile lampoon" (*merzkii paskvil'*) in his 1842 memoir. Grossman does not give any concrete references to epigrams and lampoons in his article, but analyzes in detail a caricatured portrait of Pushkin that depicts him holding the chamberlain's key in his hand and pressing it to his lips (see figure 1). The meaning of the caricature is clear: Pushkin's kissing the key represents his alleged passionate desire to become a *kammerherr*. It also implies the sexual overtones of this desire, which suggests that the *kammerherr* jokes spread well beyond Pushkin's immediate circle. Grossman does not discuss the possible provenance of the caricature, but dates this amateur drawing to somewhere between 1834 and 1836, 1834 being the most probable date.

We have no evidence that Pushkin was aware of the gossip that he desired the *kammerherr*'s key, but he certainly knew the rumor that he actively sought out the title of *kammerjunker*. According to Nashchokin (as recorded by Bartenev), Pushkin repudiated this rumor in the following way: "When [Pushkin] told Nashchokin about this [rumor], he argued that he could not have sought it out, because three years earlier

Figure 1. Alexander Pushkin with a *kammerherr*'s key (reproduced in *Literaturnoe nasledstvo* 16–18 [1934]: 983)

Benkendorf himself had offered him the title of *kammerherr*, but he rejected it, noting, 'You want me to be reproached like Voltaire'" (who was reproached for accepting a position at the court of Friedrich the Great).[70]

It is hard to tell what exactly Pushkin had in mind when he mentioned Benkendorf's offer. One possible basis for Pushkin's assertion can perhaps be found in his correspondence with Elizaveta Khitrovo, Mikhail Kutuzov's daughter and a high society lady with considerable influence, who happened to have tender feelings for Pushkin. In her letter to the poet, written in May 1830, shortly before his marriage to Nataliia Goncharova, Khitrovo first forgives him his impending marriage and then proposes to help him relaunch his career, citing the tsar's benevolent attitude toward him and promising, in order to help, to "tear herself into forty-six thousand pieces for him."[71] Responding to her, Pushkin says, "Thanks, but no thanks," expressing an aversion to civil service and court titles: "It is very kind on your part, madam, to take an interest in my situation in relation to the master [that is, Nicholas]. But what sort of a position, in your opinion, can I take at his side? I don't see a single proper one. I abhor paperwork. [. . .] To be a *kammerjunker* doesn't befit my age; besides, what would I do at court? Neither my income nor my occupation allows me this."[72] It is interesting to consider the French term for the court title that Pushkin rejects in this letter: *gentilhomme de la chambre*. The French system of the Officers of the Crown was of course quite different from the Russian Table of Ranks, and the French term not only did not directly correspond to anything in the Russian Table of Ranks but also seems to have been used by Russians rather loosely, as it could be applied both to *kammerherrs* and *kammerjunkers*. For example, A. B. Kurakin (who became a *kammerjunker* in 1771) is called "Gentilhomme de la Chambre de sa majesté imperial de toutes les Russies" in the title of his letter published in 1775 by François Henri Turpin as an introduction to Turpin's tragedy *Cyrus*. Presumably, this is how Kurakin the *kammerjunker* signed his letter. S. G. Domashnev, who received the title of *kammerjunker* in 1773 and that of *kammerherr* in 1778, signed his *Discours sur l'importance de l'histoire*, delivered in 1776 at the Academy of Sciences in Petersburg (of which he was appointed director in 1775) and published in 1778, "M. de Domaschneff, gentilhomme de la Chambre de l'imperatrice." Because this was published the same year he received his title of *kammerherr*, it is difficult to decide which title is actually meant. Finally, in the rough draft of a letter in French written in March 1794 from Petersburg to an unknown person (perhaps

S. R. Vorontsov), F. V. Rostopchin, updating his correspondent on rumors about upcoming diplomatic appointments, informs him that Baron Gustav Ernest (Gustav Ottonovich) Stackelberg is said to be slated for an appointment to Copenhagen and had been made a *gentilhomme de la chambre*. Since G. E. Stackelberg was made *kammerjunker* in 1789 and *kammerherr* in 1794, it is far more likely that Rostopchin has in mind the latter appointment and thus uses *gentilhomme de la chambre* for *kammerherr*.[73] In short, Russians used *gentilhomme de la chambre* to indicate both *kammerherr* and *kammerjunker*, but Pushkin's assertion in his letter to Khitrovo that the title of *gentilhomme de la chambre* doesn't befit his age suggests that he was rejecting the idea of the title of *kammerjunker*, not *kammerherr*.

It is not known whether Khitrovo followed up on her offer despite Pushkin's refusal or, if she did, whether any rumors were generated by her actions. It is equally impossible to determine whether the title of *kammerherr* was actually offered to Pushkin at that point. If it was, and Pushkin declined (which is highly doubtful, since, even coming from Benkendorf, it would have had to be authorized by Nicholas, and imperial appointments could not be refused), an added irony of his reference to Voltaire would have been the fact that the French philosophe carried both titles: *gentilhomme de la chambre du Roy* in France and *kammerherr* at Friedrich's court.

It is also possible that Nashchokin's story echoes a different set of events, partly described in Filipp Vigel's 1831 letter quoted earlier in this chapter, in which Vigel asserts that in addition to supporting Pushkin's plans for a new journal, Uvarov is ready, even eager, to promote Pushkin's social standing in any way possible. Most importantly, Vigel suggests that Uvarov may help him obtain the title of *kammerherr*: "As a poet, you don't have to serve, but why shouldn't you become a courtier? If a laurel wreath decorates the brow of a son of Apollo, why couldn't the *kammerherr*'s key decorate the behind of a scion of an ancient noble family?"[74] Given the fact that both Vigel and Uvarov were known homosexuals, Vigel's proposition had to have sounded at least somewhat provocative.

It is impossible to say what in Vigel's letter originates with Uvarov and what he included on his own initiative. In October 1831 Uvarov translated into French (or rather transposed) Pushkin's "To the Slanderers of Russia" ("Klevetnikam Rossii"; he sent it to Pushkin on October 8).[75] In January 1833 he facilitated Pushkin's election to the Russian Academy. Of course, Pushkin's appointment as *kammerherr* never took place, but whether Uvarov undertook any steps in this direction is impossible to determine. In any case, Pushkin's alleged assertion that he was offered and refused the title may have originated in this episode (as he asserted to Nashchokin in 1834, this offer was made "three years ago"; the chronology thus matches). One thing is still certain: it could not have been an official appointment or even a real offer; if it were, Pushkin would not have been in a position to refuse it. Eventually, Pushkin petitioned to be reinstated at the College of Foreign Affairs, was allowed to return to service, and was promoted to the rank of titular councilor. He was made *kammerjunker*, not *kammerherr*—most likely because, according to Reiser's article analyzing the ranks and ages of Pushkin's fellow *kammerjunkers*, as a titular councilor, "according to the rules and traditions, Pushkin could not lay claim to the title of *kammerherr*."[76]

Pushkin the Servitor: The View of His Contemporaries

Such is the tentative (and, at times, blurry) history of Pushkin's service. It is tentative not only because relevant documentation is lacking but also because existing biases interfere. It is tempting to see Pushkin in a heroic light, as a person who consistently opposed what currently is often regarded as an oppressive government. At times Pushkin obliged, but at least twice in his life (at the turn of the 1810s and in the early 1830s) he may have seriously striven to cooperate with this government. If he did, both times he did so while he was employed in state service. What was an accepted behavior in Pushkin's time may seem improper in the present day, and this sense of impropriety makes it more difficult to see Pushkin's service career as it was. In addition, a modern biased sense of justice may make one resent Pushkin's apparent lack of service success.

To illustrate this bias, it is worth pointing out that Russian cultural memory has preserved a legend, popular among amateur historians, that toward the very end of his life—or even after his death—Pushkin was granted the title of *kammerherr*.[77] This legend is based mostly on wishful thinking but also on the fact that in the documents of the military court investigation held after Pushkin's fatal duel, he is consistently called *"kammerherr."*[78] All the investigators, as well as his dueling adversary Georges-Charles de Heeckeren d'Anthès and Pushkin's second, Konstantin Danzas, use this title. The only person who calls Pushkin *kammerjunker* is Petr Viazemsky.[79] Finally, an inquiry about Pushkin's title was made to the Court Chancellery; and after the response came back stating that it was *kammerjunker*, all parties used the correct title.[80] The story of the post-mortem promotion reflects not facts but Pushkin's unshakably high status in Russian cultural memory.

Pushkin's contemporaries looked at his service career through a different lens, in some respects more distortive than ours, but in others, perhaps, more accurate. Most importantly, they did not regard Pushkin's service career and rank as something irrelevant. Two examples illustrate this point. One is Uvarov's alleged indignation over V. F. Odoevsky's obituary for Pushkin, in which Odoevsky famously called him "the sun of our poetry." The obituary was published by A. A. Kraevsky in *Literary Supplements* to the *Russian Invalid* (*Literaturnye pribavleniia k Russkomu invalidu*) that he edited at the time. The next day Kraevsky was summoned to the Ministry of Public Education and dressed down by an official:

> I have to pass on to you [. . .] that the minister (Sergei Semenovich Uvarov) is very, very cross with you. Why this publication about Pushkin? Why this black frame around the news of the death of a person of low rank, without any real position in the state service? Well, that would still be not too bad! But what kind of expressions did you use?! "Sun of poetry!!" For pity's sake, why such an honor? "Pushkin died half-way through his great career!" What kind of career? Sergei Semenovich has rightly pointed out: was Pushkin a military leader, a commander, a minister, a statesman? Finally, he died at almost forty. To write little verses [*stishki*] doesn't mean, as Sergei Semenovich has put it, to have a great career! The Minister has authorized me to admonish you and to remind you that, as a clerk at the Ministry of Public Education, you in particular should refrain from such publications.[81]

Granted, by the time of Pushkin's death, Uvarov had developed so passionate a hatred for the poet that it by itself can explain his rage over what he perceived as an overwrought obituary. But Uvarov was not alone in considering Pushkin's achievements as a writer insufficient to offset his low service rank. Nashchokin's wife recounts a high-ranking military officer's reaction to the news of Pushkin's widow's impending marriage to P. P. Lanskoi: "After Nataliia Nikolaevna's engagement,

General Vrangel, the commander of the Moscow artillery, dropped by. I asked him: 'Have you heard the news?'—'What news?' he asked. 'Pushkina is going to marry.'—'Whom?'—'General Lanskoi.'—'Good for her! At least he is a general, not some Pushkin or other, a man without a name and status.'"[82]

Significantly, it was not only high-ranking officials who paid attention to Pushkin's lack of service success: even contemporaries who knew his worth as a writer noticed his low service rank. In his "Poetic Journey through the Wide World," the second chapter in his *Fantastic Travels of Baron Brambeus (Fantasticheskie puteshestviia Barona Brambeusa,* 1833), Osip Senkovsky tells the story of a collegiate secretary who has remained in this rank for five years and is desperate for promotion. The first-person narrator complains: "I felt that I was created for higher ranks and higher sensations, but some magical, invisible force fettered my existence to the tenth class with a heavy chain; it seemed to me that I would never get out of it [*iz nego ne vylezu*], that when all of humanity was promoted to the rank of titular councilor, I alone on the entire globe would remain a collegiate secretary."[83] Angry and frustrated, he becomes "an awful free-thinker," stops "going to the office," and begins "going to [his] supervisor's wife instead in order to turn" his supervisor's attention to himself.[84]

The narrator's situation is complicated by the fact that in his soul he is not a bureaucrat but a poet: "My soul could not fit the narrow confines of the tenth class anymore; [. . .] I was born a poet, a romantic, and my soul required strong sensations."[85] The narrator reads new romantic literature, dreams of horrifying adventures and awful misfortunes that would make his life more exciting, and, since "all great poets gamble," he gambles. Fleeing the wrath of two collegiate registrars who lost fifty thousand rubles to him, the narrator moves to Moscow, then goes to Ukraine, Novorossia, and, finally, to Odessa. Eventually he ends up in Constantinople, where he experiences a passionate love, a series of humiliating frustrations, and a near-mortal illness. As a result, he loses his romantic disposition and becomes a scholar. (Many twists of the plot not directly useful for the task at hand are omitted here.)

At first glance, the story of a collegiate secretary with the soul of a poet waiting for years to become a titular councilor looks too generic to be a reference to Pushkin. No doubt there were many collegiate secretaries who did not get promoted; some of them were likely to become freethinkers, many considered themselves poets, and some of them gambled; yet others had love affairs with the wives of their superiors; some of them could have ended up serving in Odessa; and some perhaps were thinking of running off to Greece. However, taken together, these traits begin to coalesce into a grotesque portrait of someone resembling Pushkin: a freethinking collegiate secretary, a poet and a gambler, traveling to the south of Russia and ending up in Odessa where he had (or was rumored to have had) a love affair with the wife of his superior. Pushkin's Greek sympathies were well known, and, according to his letter to his brother Lev, he considered running off to Constantinople.[86] The romantic narrative poems written by Pushkin during his stay in the south add another relevant connection. Finally, it was shortly before Senkovsky wrote his "Poetic Journey" that Pushkin was promoted to the rank of titular councilor. His longish stint as a collegiate secretary could have attracted attention at that point.

Even more important, of course, is the fact that the story contains references to Pushkin's works. It begins with two lines of dots with a question mark at the end. This is a feature of the romantic fragment in general, but it is also a feature of Pushkin's *Eugene Onegin*, with its omitted stanzas replaced by dots. More references to *Eugene Onegin* follow. Arriving in Moscow, Senkovsky's narrator characterizes it thus: "No, it is boring in Moscow. What can I see there? The ruins of ancient boyar pride, over which bridegroom-profiteers [*zhenikhi-spekulianty*] languidly find their way in rented carriages. Piles made up of the debris of estates freed from mortgage obligations, upon which brides sit, dressed in fine clothes [*razodetye v pukh*], twiddling their thumbs and counting the stars on the chests of those who come from Petersburg!"[87] Compare chapter 7 of *Eugene Onegin*, in which Tatiana is taken to Moscow, to "the marriage market," and is chosen by the "haughty general" from Petersburg to be his wife. Also compare Pushkin's portrayal of Moscow as a ruined seat of ancient boyars in his essay "A Journey from Moscow to Petersburg." Written in 1833–35 and not published in Pushkin's lifetime, it contains his views on the status of the Russian nobility as they took shape in the late 1820s and the early 1830s. It is not improbable that Pushkin shared his views with his fellow literati, and they could have been known to Senkovsky.

Another reference to *Eugene Onegin* (or, rather, to "Fragments from Onegin's Journey" ["Otryvki iz puteshestviia Onegina"]) is the scene of the narrator's arrival in Odessa: his carriage gets stuck in the middle of a huge mud puddle, in which his coachman promptly drowns and which prevents the narrator from leaving the carriage until morning, when he is removed from it by locals. Compare "Fragments from Onegin's Journey":

> В Одессе пыльной, я сказал.
> Я б мог сказать: в Одессе грязной –
> И тут бы, право, не солгал.
> В году недель пять-шесть Одесса,
> По воле бурного Зевеса,
> Потоплена, запружена,
> В густой грязи погружена.
> Все домы на аршин загрязнут,
> Лишь на ходулях пешеход
> По улице дерзает вброд;
> Кареты, люди тонут, вязнут.[88]

[I said, "In dusty Odessa." I could have said, "In muddy Odessa," and, honestly, I wouldn't have lied. Five or six weeks a year, at the pleasure of stormy Zeus, Odessa is flooded, inundated, submerged in thick mud. All the houses are sunk in two feet of mud, and only on stilts do pedestrians dare to walk down the street. Carriages and people drown, get stuck.]

Finally, Senkovsky's narrator directly refers to *Eugene Onegin*: "If I return to Petersburg at some point in time, I will compose a novel in verse, that is, a *poema*, in which I will paint in mud the grandiose picture of my wanderings and my sensations."[89] It is rather obvious that in his "Poetic Journey" Senkovsky is mocking Pushkin's service career and marks his mockery with references to Pushkin's life and, especially, works.

It is noteworthy that "Poetic Journey" was written at a time when the relations between Senkovsky and Pushkin were quite friendly—as they remained, with only a few small glitches, for the rest of Pushkin's life. In his letter to Pushkin written in the winter of 1834, Senkovsky praised "The Queen of Spades" as a new word in Russian prose.[90] Pushkin published many of his works, including "The Queen of Spades," in Senkovsky's *Library for Reading* (*Biblioteka dlia chteniia*). Only after Pushkin decided to publish his own periodical, *The Contemporary*, did Senkovsky's attitude seem to worsen, and in 1836 the *Library for Reading* published several pieces that mocked Pushkin's ostensibly diminishing writerly reputation and his alleged ineptitude as a journalist.[91] If a change in Senkovsky's attitude did indeed occur, it did not last, particularly after *The Contemporary* published a refutation of Gogol's attack on Senkovsky in his article "On the Movement of Journalistic Literature in 1834 and 1835."[92]

Nonetheless, Senkovsky's occasional use of the pseudonym A. Belkin (which combines the last name of the supposed author of Pushkin's *Tales of the Late Ivan Petrovich Belkin* with Pushkin's own first initial) has been interpreted as his criticism of Pushkin's prose. Three tales published in the *Library for Reading* are signed "A. Belkin": "A Tale Lost to the World" ("Poteriannaia dlia sveta povest'," 1835), "A Turkish Gypsy" ("Turetskaia tsyganka," 1835), and "Dzhulio" (1836; signed "T.M.F.V.—A. Belkin").[93] Of these three, "A Turkish Gypsy" has recently been shown to be a translation by E. F. Korsh of "The Gipsy of Sardis" by Philip Slingsby (a pseudonym of Nathaniel Parker Willis), and the only gesture toward Pushkin that can be found in the tale is the chosen pseudonym.[94] "A Tale Lost to the World" can perhaps be linked to Pushkin and read as Senkovsky's criticism of Pushkin's apparent refusal to work in the genre of the high-society tale (*svetskaia povest'*) advocated by Senkovsky. Indeed, instead of high-society characters, the tale features a group of low-ranking insignificant civil servants going on a picnic. The following passage can be connected to Pushkin's discussion of ranks in "The Station Master": "Galaktion Andreich [. . .] sang on this occasion a long Little Russian [*malorossiiskuiu*] aria [. . .] about the disadvantages of high ranks. Luka Lukich was the first to point out: 'Here, for example, Iakov Petrovich: he has attained the rank of the seventh class and willy-nilly has to take the first place in an omnibus. Why wouldn't he climb to the roof [where the rest of the group was riding]!'— This followed by comments about the independence and sweet proximity to nature of ranks of the fourteenth, twelfth, and tenth classes, partly even the ninth."[95] This description of a bunch of low-ranking clerks is a likely reference to Pushkin: not only are these clerks not able to attain a rank higher than that of the tenth or ninth classes (that is, the two ranks held by Pushkin), but they obviously do not even want to rise any higher (recall Pushkin's claim in "The Station Master" that low rank bestows narrative ability). The fact that one of the group tells a story that nobody can remember could be another jab at Pushkin's *Tales*, echoing Faddei Bulgarin's criticism of *The Tales of Belkin*: "While you read, everything seems to be nice, smooth, and fluid; when you finish, everything is forgotten."[96]

If this reading is correct, Senkovsky seems to continue using the rank system to mark his references to Pushkin, but even in a polemical context these references remained mild and by and large harmless.[97] They likely were the product of Senkovsky's general propensity for playfulness rather than actual malice and enmity toward Pushkin.[98] Nonetheless, Senkovsky's mocking of Pushkin's low rank confirms the general awareness of Pushkin's lack of service success.

Another case is Gogol, and more specifically, his "Notes of a Madman." The question of Pushkin's and Gogol's relationship remains contentious in both Russian and Western scholarship. Gogol's attitude toward Pushkin was far more complex and ambiguous than the fervent admiration Gogol claimed to feel.[99] Furthermore, Gogol could deliver his disagreements with Pushkin in the form of praise, as is evident in his 1832 article "A Few Words about Pushkin" ("Neskol'ko slov o Pushkine"), included in his 1835 collection *Arabesques* (*Arabeski*). The article is usually read as Gogol's praise of Pushkin as the first and only Russian national poet. However, as Edyta Bojanowska demonstrates, this praise can hardly be accepted at face value.[100]

The ambiguity of Gogol's attitude toward Pushkin also manifests itself in his story "Notes of a Madman" ("Zapiski sumasshedshego"), included in *Arabesques* under the title "Scraps from the Notes of a Madman" ("Klochki iz zapisok sumasshedshego"). In fact, in "Notes of a Madman," Gogol mentions Pushkin directly. Poprishchin copies a poem by Nikolai Nikolev and comments: "Pushkin's work, no doubt [*Dolzhno byt', Pushkina sochinenie*]."[101] Poprishchin's comment is usually interpreted as a sign of his ignorance and bad literary taste, but it is possible to see in it Gogol's mockery—very mild, but still mockery—of Pushkin's poetry and especially of his reputation as a poet. In this connection it is essential to note that in his article "A Few Words about Pushkin," Gogol discusses the widespread problem of literary works falsely attributed to Pushkin. While talking about the rapid spread of Pushkin's fame, he notes that Pushkin's name by itself guarantees a work's success and is used for this purpose by "idle scribblers [*dosuzhimi marateliami*]." Gogol affixes a footnote to this allegation, in which he says the following: "A multitude of the most ludicrous poems were disseminated under Pushkin's name. This is the usual fate of a talented man who enjoys great renown. At first it seems funny, but then it becomes aggravating, when one ceases to be young [*vykhodish' iz molodosti*] and sees that this nonsense doesn't stop. In this way they began to attribute to Pushkin "Medicine for Cholera," "The First Night," and the like."[102] The question arises, who is the butt of Gogol's joke here: the ignorant readers, the sly usurpers of Pushkin's name—or Pushkin himself, whose reputation somehow allowed the most absurd works, whether literary or not, to be attributed to him? One may suspect that the vexation shown here by Gogol is not quite sincere: as with Poprishchin's comment, Gogol's footnote leaves in doubt both the quality of Pushkin's real works and the actual worth of his literary fame.

Further, a somewhat critical (or, at least, ironic) attitude toward Pushkin manifests itself in "Notes of a Madman," not only in Poprishchin's mistaken remark about the authorship of Nikolev's poem but also in Gogol's play with the relative worth of the rank of titular councilor and the title of *kammerjunker*. It seems likely that the joke is at least partly aimed at Pushkin, mocking his rank and, especially, his well-known vexation over receiving the title of *kammerjunker*.

"Notes of a Madman" was written in the late summer–early autumn of 1834, that is, about six to eight months after Pushkin received his supposedly insulting title. The event therefore had to be fresh in Gogol's memory. An additional argument in support of the supposition that "Notes of a Madman" relates to Pushkin is provided by Gogol's manuscript of the story, as described by N. S. Tikhonravov: "In Gogol's notebook [. . .] 'Notes of a Madman' is on pages 208 through 220. There is no title. Instead of that, there is written 'O P.,' that is 'o Pushkine' [about Pushkin]."[103] Tikhonravov surmises that this is an indication that Gogol wrote his article "A Few Words about Pushkin" earlier than "Notes of a Madman"—which is, of course, true, but does not mean that Gogol didn't use "O P." as a temporary substitute title to indicate the story's theme. "A Few Words about Pushkin" is found earlier in the same notebook, beginning on page 136, where the article is also titled "O P."[104] It is quite logical that the two works about Pushkin included in *Arabesques* have the same temporary title, indicating their similar subject matter.[105]

It is likely that the Pushkin connection explains Gogol's choice of Poprishchin's rank (titular councilor) and his rival Teplov's title (*kammerjunker*). Gogol's story culminates in a conflict between Poprishchin and Teplov over Sophie's hand—a conflict entirely imagined by the former. Poprishchin loses this imaginary competition, and the loss plunges him irreversibly into madness. He explains his defeat by the insurmountable vertical rift in status between a titular councilor and a *kammerjunker*. In his opinion, the status of a *kammerjunker* is equal to that of a general. Having found out about Sophie's engagement, he complains: "Always either a *kammerjunker* or a general. Everything that is best in this world, everything falls either to *kammerjunkers* or to generals. The moment you find a poor little treasure [*bednoe bogatstvo*] for yourself, you think you can reach it with your hand [*dumaesh' dostat' ego rukoiu*]—but a *kammer-junker* or a general filches it from you [*sryvaet u tebia*]."[106] Poprishchin is, of course, mistaken: according to Reiser's analysis, Teplov's rank could not have differed very much from Poprishchin's (ninth class), whereas generals belonged to the first four classes. Curiously, Poprishchin's mistake is a reversal of Pushkin's assessment of the title of *kammerjunker*: whereas Titular Councilor Poprishchin considers the *kammerjunker*'s title much higher than his own, Titular Councilor Pushkin considers it much lower. Their behavior, nonetheless, is similar; Pushkin's contemporaries described his reaction to receiving the *kammerjunker*'s title as that of a person who had lost his mind: "beside himself, flaring up, his face burning," "foaming at the mouth." According to Nashchokin, a treatment similar to what Poprishchin gets in the insane asylum—cold water poured on his head—was applied to Pushkin by his friends to calm down the poet, who had lost his temper. It is not impossible that Gogol had heard these stories about Pushkin's rage and his friends' actions prior to his work on "Notes of a Madman."

Poprishchin's insistent claims that only noblemen can write well and therefore he, as a true nobleman, is an exceptionally good writer, whereas non-nobles, especially tradesmen (or bourgeois, *meshchane*) can never be good writers, also signal Pushkin's implicit presence in the story. These claims are likely to refer to Pushkin's poem "My Gene-alogy" (1830), especially to the repeated phrase "I am a tradesman/bourgeois [*Ia meshchanin*]." They may also allude to debates about the so-called literary aristocracy in general, which are reflected in "My Genealogy."[107]

Gogol held an ambivalent position in these debates: while he attempted to adopt the modes of behavior accepted in Pushkin's circles and even "joined in the polemics of Pushkin's associates against such rivals as Sękowski and Bulgarin," both his precarious societal position and his literary innovations placed him outside the behavioral and literary conventions shared by Pushkin and his friends.[108] Furthermore, Gogol's article "A Few Words about Pushkin" contains Gogol's concrete, albeit tacit, disagreements with Pushkin as an esthete and literary aristo-crat. Gogol rejects what he considers to be Pushkin's stance as a "poet's poet" as well as his "elitist esthetics," "refined hermeticism," and "dis-junction from the current Russian reality."[109] The concluding lines of

Gogol's article in particular portray Pushkin's position in literature as elitist and unacceptable to Gogol himself: "The more a poet becomes a poet, the more he depicts feelings that are familiar to poets alone—the more visibly the crowd that surrounds him diminishes, and in the end it becomes so small that [the poet] can count his true admirers on his own fingers."[110]

The so-called literary aristocrats' view of literature and the writer's role was not only unacceptable for Gogol aesthetically but may also have piqued him personally. In particular, "My Genealogy" could have been directly offensive to Gogol, specifically with its assertion that the clearly autobiographical lyrical persona's ancestors "did not jump over to the princes from the Ukrainians [*v kniaz'ia ne prygal iz khokhlov*]." This line, directed at Aleksandr Bezborodko, who had a breathtaking career under Catherine the Great, could have offended Gogol with its use of the word *khokhol*, a pejorative name for Ukrainians.[111] Gogol may have felt the offense even more keenly, however, because the person derided was the founder of Gogol's alma mater, the Nezhin Gymnasium. In this connection, it is noteworthy that the theme of rapid social ascent, "jumping" from "tradesmen/bourgeois" or "even peasants" to grandees and sometimes even sovereigns is so prominent in "Notes of a Madman."[112]

As a newcomer and upstart in the literary arena, Gogol needed help and support from writers with status and reputation, especially literary aristocrats. At the same time, his incomplete acceptance by the circle of his benefactors, his provincialism, and his marginal position among the members of the high society to which his benefactors belonged complicated his relations with them. He felt awkward among them, and resented his dependence upon people whose views he did not always share, and whose jokes and comments may have hurt his feelings both as an author and as a social outsider.

One of the ways Gogol used to smooth out the awkwardness of his relations with his friends of higher rank was the exaggeration of his closeness to this social circle in general and to Pushkin in particular. As many scholars point out, Gogol used this method especially vigorously after Pushkin's death, when the late poet could not refute his assertions. It is at this time that Gogol speaks especially frequently about Pushkin's passing along to him the plots of *The Inspector General* and *Dead Souls*.[113] Gogol's other way of dealing with the problem is less obvious and requires a close reading of his works. It involved including in his works implicit disagreements with the views of his "sworn friend" or even stealthy mockery of him. This sly strategy worked particularly well while Pushkin was alive, since Gogol could be reasonably sure his benefactor was smart enough not to acknowledge that he recognized himself in Gogol's portrayals. He would never "shriek out of stupid shock: that's me!"[114]

In his "Poetic Journey through the Wide World," Senkovsky ties his narrator to Pushkin by repeatedly referring to his works, and yet scholars have so thoroughly repressed the memory of Pushkin's service career that they fail to connect the dots and see the great poet in the laughable collegiate secretary striving to become a titular councilor. Granted, Senkovsky's works are not widely read, and his references to Pushkin could simply have been overlooked, but Gogol's story is a universally acknowledged classic and therefore provides an even better illustration of how inattention to Pushkin's service career blinds scholars to what seems to be a rather obvious reference to it. The taboo that persists in regard to the topic of Pushkin the servitor prevents not only an adequate reconstruction of Pushkin's life but also an adequate reading of some of the best-known masterpieces of Russian literature.

The Anxiety of Rank in Pushkin's Prose Fiction

Pushkin turned to prose fiction late in his creative life: in 1827, when he began working on *The Blackamoor of Peter the Great*, a historical novel about his black ancestor Ibrahim Gannibal. It is noteworthy that of about thirty contemplated works Pushkin completed only four: *The Tales of Belkin*, "The Queen of Spades," "Kirdzhali," and *The Captain's Daughter*.[115] The rest of Pushkin's attempts at prose fiction remained in various states of incompletion, ranging from several relatively polished chapters (*The Blackamoor*, *Dubrovsky*, and *Egyptian Nights*), to fragments that begin in medias res and end as abruptly ("The Guests Were Arriving at the Dacha," "In the Corner of a Small Square," and "We Were Spending the Evening at the Dacha"), to notes of several lines or paragraphs.

Paul Debreczeny, in his study of Pushkin's prose fiction, explains the large number of abandoned projects by Pushkin's inexperience as a prose writer and his search for an effective narrative voice.[116] In contrast, Monika Greenleaf argues that Pushkin's tendency to abandon his prose projects can be accounted for by his general bent toward fragmentariness.[117] She develops Iury Tynianov's idea that there are no firm boundaries between Pushkin's "sketched programs and his finished prose" and that sometimes his "rough drafts became in themselves finished products." Tynianov points to "Kirdzhali" and *A Journey to Arzrum* as examples of published work in which "the boundary between a program and a [finished] work" is not fully established.[118] *The Blackamoor of Peter the Great* is yet another example of a work that Pushkin never finished but parts of which he nonetheless published.[119]

Scholarship has also begun to plumb the connection between Pushkin's "life text" and his literary texts, which frequently reveals different forms of anxiety surfacing as a theme in his poetry and prose.[120] Reading Pushkin's "life text" and his literary texts together, Catharine T. Nepomnyashchy suggests that Pushkin's anxieties could have played a role in his abandoning some of his prose pieces. She argues that Pushkin's uneasiness about his mixed racial origin, intensified by his plans to marry, could have made it impossible for him to continue the story of his African protagonist in *The Blackamoor of Peter the Great*. Nepomnyashchy also suggests that Pushkin's disquiet about the increasing commercialization of literature and the corresponding rise of prose fiction could also be a strong factor in his not finishing *The Blackamoor* and, later, *Egyptian Nights*. It is significant that both sets of anxieties were linked to Pushkin's uneasiness about selling things that should not be sold: people (Gannibal, allegedly bought at the slave market in Istanbul), love (Cleopatra's selling her nights in one of the poems Pushkin planned to insert in *Egyptian Nights*), or the fruits of artistic creation (the Italian *improvisatore*'s selling the poetry he composes on demand for his audience).[121]

Thus the same autobiographical impulses that spurred Pushkin's creativity—in particular, personal concerns—also at times gave him writer's block. This section will probe another set of anxieties, this one about rank and social status, which forms a theme in Pushkin's prose fiction. Pushkin's uneasiness about his social status in general, and his service rank in particular, and the way it makes itself evident in his poetry has been thoroughly studied.[122] Its manifestations in his prose fiction, however, have been largely neglected. At the same time, close examination of Pushkin's prose shows that the issue of rank and status not only is present in many of his prose works but also frequently constitutes the core of the narrative. Furthermore, it often has clear personal significance. The rest of this section examines some of Pushkin's anxieties over rank and social status as they reveal themselves in his prose fiction.

In the first of *The Tales of Belkin*, "The Shot," Pushkin's discomfort with his social standing is revealed rather directly. In this story of an interrupted duel, Silvio's dueling opponent, Count B***, is portrayed as a representative of the "new aristocracy," a powerful and wealthy group within the nobility that had risen to prominence in the eighteenth century, in many cases thanks to their personal ties to monarchs. Silvio calls him "a young man from a rich and distinguished family [*znatnoi familii*]" and "a brilliant child of fortune [*blistatel'nyi schastlivets*]." He then again stresses the count's social prominence and wealth: "Picture [. . .] an exalted [*gromkoe*] name, and money, more that he could count, in an inexhaustible supply."[123] The young man's title suggests the recent origin of both his exalted name and wealth (the first Russian count was Boris Sheremetev, who received the title in 1706, as a reward for putting down a revolt in Astrakhan).

It is not clear whether the protagonist is a middling nobleman or a foreigner: Silvio, the narrator informs us, is not his real name. If he were the former, his social standing would put him on par with Pushkin, whose family was neither prominent nor rich. To compensate for his family's lack of present prominence, Pushkin laid claim to an old and respectable bloodline and asserted his ancestors' historical significance. He attributed the Pushkins' current marginality to their ancestors' allegedly independent behavior at several historical turning points in the seventeenth and eighteenth centuries, when they had to take sides in the struggle for the throne and made noble choices that allegedly caused their marginalization.[124] Mark Altshuller, however, has demonstrated the fictional character of Pushkin's accounts about his ancestors' historical prominence and their political independence.[125]

It is thus likely that Silvio's conflict with Count B*** is as much over a difference in social standing as it is over their rivalry in reckless behavior (as Silvio seems to claim). This assumption is supported by Silvio's conduct as a duelist: it mimics that of many middling Russian noblemen, including Pushkin himself, who resorted to unconventional dueling behavior (*breterstvo*, from the French *bretteur*, a reckless and relentless duelist) to force socially superior opponents to acknowledge their equal status.[126] Silvio resents Count B***'s nonchalant conduct at the dueling site, rightly seeing it as dismissive and insulting. He wants the count to take him seriously, and to achieve this he violates the rules of proper dueling (as *bretteurs* often did) by interrupting the duel and getting the count to agree to withstand his shot at any time in the future Silvio finds convenient.

However, despite Pushkin's similarity to Silvio with respect to social standing and dueling behavior, it seems that he was not completely certain whose side to take in the conflict he described, Silvio's or the count's, which signals his ambivalence regarding his own position vis-à-vis the two groups of nobility. It is telling that Pushkin distributes features of his own real-life behavior between Silvio and Count B***. Not only does he ascribe to Silvio *bretteur* behavior characteristic of himself, especially in his youth, but he also makes him join Alexander Ypsilanti's uprising against the Turks (in which, the narrator reports, Silvio is killed)—an action Pushkin himself contemplated in the early 1820s. At the same time, the count's conduct at the dueling site (eating cherries under the barrel of a gun) echoes Pushkin's nonchalance during his 1822 duel with the officer Zubov. Unlike Count B***, however, Pushkin withstood Zubov's shot and subsequently refused either to return fire or to reconcile—a harsher insult than the one initially inflicted on Count B*** by Silvio, who does not refuse to shoot at the count, but delays his shot indefinitely: while this action is against the rules, it is not insulting in and of itself.

It is noteworthy that Pushkin initially ended the story at that point: the manuscript of the first version ends with the claim that "the ending has been lost." In this version, the count, like Zubov, would have been left in a position that was considered dishonorable: he would have shot at his opponent, but would never himself have endured the danger of being shot at. Two days later Pushkin added chapter 2, the account of Silvio's revenge, which turns out to be far more insulting than the original refusal to continue the duel.[127] He arrives at the estate of the newly wedded count and demands his turn at a shot. The count, whose nonchalance is now all but gone, complies, and Silvio is about to shoot at him, but is reluctant to do so because the count is unarmed. He convinces the count to begin the duel from scratch. The count again wins the right to shoot first, and does so. He misses and hits a painting on the wall instead. Silvio now prepares to shoot, even as the count's bride arrives at the scene and begs him to spare her husband. Satisfied with the sight of the count's distress, Silvio leaves, but not before demonstrating his superior marksmanship by sending a bullet into the hole left by the count's bullet. The count is thus made aware that he remains alive only thanks to Silvio's magnanimity—if magnanimity it is. The count is fully aware of the dishonor inflicted on him by Silvio: he has shot at his opponent twice, and his opponent has never returned fire. The count's situation is thus even worse than that of Pushkin's opponent Zubov.

"The Shot" was written in September 1830 at Boldino, where Pushkin went to take possession of the nearby village of Kistenevka, allotted to him by his father on the occasion of his impending marriage. His situation thus resembled that of Count B*** as depicted in chapter 2 of the story. The fact that Pushkin was quarantined in Boldino because of a cholera epidemic and was in danger of dying emphasizes the similarity. Identifying with the newly married Count B***, who was facing death because of his youthful imprudence, Pushkin may have been rethinking his own former dueling behavior. The story reworks the denouement of the Zubov episode, thereby presenting a different perspective on Pushkin's mistreatment of the officer; the mature Pushkin, about to be married, is perhaps not as enthusiastic about Silvio's and, by extension, his own youthful cruelty.

Pushkin's insulting conduct with Zubov was typical for the Kishinev period of his life. His years in Kishinev (a location that was clearly on his mind when he wrote chapter 1 of "The Shot") were particularly difficult for him socially. Lotman writes: "A collegiate secretary and a versifier [*stikhotvorets*] in a world where everything was defined by rank, a person without means amidst people well provided for and spending money freely, a twenty-year-old youth amidst seasoned military officers or grand Moldavian boyars, Pushkin was a person whose dignity was constantly being assaulted."[128] One line of defense was Pushkin's perpetual readiness to duel. It is well known that his mentor in dueling affairs in Kishinev was Lieutenant Colonel I. P. Liprandy, a famous *bretteur* and Pushkin's acknowledged original both for the character of Silvio and for the story's narrator, Lieutenant Colonel I. L. P.

Not only does Liprandy split into two characters in "The Shot," but one of them, the narrator, undergoes a strange metamorphosis in the course of the story: while in chapter 1 he is independent and dignified in his interactions with Silvio, in chapter 2 he inexplicably assumes an obsequious tone with Count B***. The narrator himself explains it with reference to his current poverty: "Having grown unaccustomed to luxury in my poor corner [. . .] I now felt timid" (72; 8:1:71). While this might explain a momentary awkwardness, it cannot justify the narrator's servile tone throughout his brief conversation with the count, in which he addresses him by title (Your Excellency, *Vashe siiatel'stvo*) nine times. Moreover, he twice uses the title not as an address but as a substitute for the pronoun "you" ("I bet Your Excellency could not hit"; 73; 8:1:72). Such usage powerfully signals the speaker's implied lower status.

The narrator's behavior is particularly conspicuous because there is no reason for him to feel so inferior. Granted, at the time of his visit to Count B***'s estate, Lieutenant Colonel I. L. P. is retired and living in his ancestral "poor little village" (71; 8:1:70). Nonetheless, his status as a gentleman, his respectable military rank (seventh class), and his education (in the past, Silvio liked to talk to him "about different subjects" [68; 8:1:67]) make him the count's equal in everything but title and wealth. Furthermore, the narrator seems to be the only true exponent of the code of honor in the story: it is against his reaction that the behavior of the two duelists is measured. This gives him an enormous moral advantage over the count, who twice shoots at Silvio and does not endure a single shot himself.

Every first-person narrator is simultaneously the author's creation and, in spite of any sophisticated reader attempts to resist this identification, his alter ego, and I. L. P.'s behavior with the count echoes Pushkin's own insecurities, both those of the Kishinev period and especially those of the time he wrote the story. About to be married and facing a cholera epidemic, he would have identified with Count B***. At the same time, living in Boldino, near his ancestral "poor little village" of Kistenevka, Pushkin, like the story's narrator, could not have failed to perceive the vast distance between himself and the count; unlike the count, he had no title, no luxurious estate, no rich bride, and a paltry independent income. Furthermore, unlike I. L. P., he had no respectable service rank, and, as his April 1830 letter to Benkendorf quoted earlier in this chapter indicates, this did bother him as he was preparing to marry Nataliia Goncharova. The lack of a stable income was also a cause for concern for Pushkin the bridegroom: the letters he wrote to friends when leaving for Boldino convey his worry that his royalties would not cover the cost of his wedding and impending household expenses. It could be that Pushkin attempted to purge himself symbolically of these worries by making his look-alike narrator in "The Shot" fawn before the count. At the same time, he also makes the count humble himself before the narrator by revealing the conclusion of his duel with Silvio. The exorcism worked: as is well known, Pushkin's involuntary sojourn at Boldino made the autumn of 1830 one of the most productive, and thus lucrative, periods of his life.[129]

The theme of service and rank returns in "The Stationmaster," another of *The Tales of Belkin*. The entire story, of course, is about differences in social status: its main character, the humble stationmaster Samson Vyrin, loses his beautiful daughter Dunia to Minsky, a dashing young aristocrat and cavalry captain (seventh class). Convinced that Minsky will abandon his socially inferior lover, Vyrin travels to Saint Petersburg to save her but is thrown out both from Minsky's quarters and from the apartment he keeps for Dunia. Years later Dunia shows up in her native village dressed as a grand dame and with three children in tow, only to learn that her father has drunk himself to death.

This inverted version of both the prodigal son and the fallen woman stories begins with a lengthy discussion of the system of ranks in Russia. The first paragraph portrays the sorry lot of stationmasters, whose rank of collegiate registrar (fourteenth class) barely protects them from physical abuse at the hands of irate high-ranking travelers demanding horses. It also outlines the complicated rank system that governs the dispensation of horses at post stations.

The third paragraph of the story describes the narrator's past youthful resentment of the rank system, which governs not only the dispensation of horses at post stations but also the distribution of food at governors' dinner tables. By the time he tells the story, however, the narrator's rank has risen (the fictitious editor A. P. informs us that Belkin heard "The Stationmaster" from Titular Councilor A. G. N.), and his resentment has apparently dissipated: "Nowadays both the one and the other seem to me to be in the order of things." He now seems to find wisdom in the rank system—or does he? He concludes wryly: "Indeed what would happen to us if the rule convenient to all, 'Let rank yield to rank,' were to be replaced by some other, such as 'Let mind yield to mind'? What arguments would arise! And whom would the butler serve first?" (94; 8:1:98). Such a "defense" of the rank system actually mocks it as an absurdity bound to create awkward situations not only for the young A. G. N. but also, by extension, for the low-ranking Pushkin.

The first paragraph of the story ends the discussion of the sad lot of stationmasters, harassed because of their low service rank, rather unexpectedly, with a statement on the low-ranking stationmasters' narrative talents. They are declared better narrators than high-ranking officials: "For my part, I must confess that I would rather listen to them than to some official of the sixth class traveling on government business."[130] In the third paragraph the narrator, seriously or not, hails the rank system that governs social interactions in Imperial Russia. He then abruptly returns to his story, leaving the reader to wonder how his apparent approval of the hierarchy of rank reflects on his own ability as a narrator and, most importantly, on his previous statement that the hierarchy of narrative talent runs contrary to that of rank.

As a matter of fact, in Pushkin's prose of the 1830s, none of the first-person narrators are socially prominent. The narrator of "The Shot" is seized with a sudden social inferiority complex. The narrator of "The

Stationmaster," for all his apparent service success, remains a modest titular councilor. The rank of the alleged author of *The Tales of Belkin* is not identified, but it is unlikely that this dull-minded fellow could have made a decent career in his seven years in an undistinguished infantry regiment. The narrator of the unfinished "A History of the Village of Goriukhino" ("Istoriia sela Goriukhina," 1830), Belkin's double (initially, Pushkin planned to make the story another of Belkin's creations), began his service as a cadet (*iunker*) and, it seems, was able to rise only to the first commissioned officer's rank, that of warrant officer (*praporshchik*, fourteenth class). Even Petr Grinev, the narrator of Pushkin's last work of prose fiction, *The Captain's Daughter* (*Kapitanskaia dochka*, 1836), who, like Pushkin, is of a "good old family," is unable to rise above the very same rank of warrant officer (Debreczeny translates *praporshchik* as ensign). In *Pushkin and Romantic Fashion*, Greenleaf suggests: "The poet in prose was one step away from the mad clerk, the next figure into which modern society would project its own sense of disorientation and self-pity."[131] This implies that Pushkin's narrators of prose fiction are one step away from Gogol's pathetic characters Aksenty Poprishchin and Akaky Bashmachkin, titular councilors scribbling away in mad inspiration.

As, of course, is the future Titular Councilor Alexander Pushkin. In a fit of self-mockery, he gets the narrator of "A History of the Village of Goriukhino" in trouble with higher-ranking officers for his love of writing and writers. Still a cadet, he spends a week in Saint Petersburg on official duty and, sitting in a café, spots "B., the author" (123; 8:1:130). He chases after him to pay his respects, but, to his utter chagrin, he bumps into one higher-ranking officer after another, and every one of them stops him and demands that he stand at attention. B. disappears, and the poor cadet catches up with some solicitor instead. Chasing after B.—that is, Faddei Bulgarin, a financially successful prose writer and, in the 1830s, Pushkin's bitter enemy—and being stopped at every step by one's superiors could serve as a comic representation of Pushkin's own struggle for both respectable social status and financial success as a writer.

The unfinished novel *Dubrovsky* (1833) returns to a theme highly important for Pushkin and prominent in "The Shot," that of the heterogeneity within the noble class. The novel's events are set in motion by a conflict between a wealthy and powerful upstart (Troekurov) and a middling nobleman (Andrei Dubrovsky). Pushkin begins by establishing the two characters' essential equality as noblemen: "Of the same age, born of the same social class, and educated the same way, they were to some extent similar in character and disposition" (146; 8:1:162). This is how middling nobility and Pushkin himself would have wanted to see relations within the noble class. However, just as this way of thinking did not work in real life, it does not work in the novel: Troekurov accepts Dubrovsky as his equal only up to a certain point. As soon as he feels Dubrovsky has slighted him, he forgets their old friendship and begins to behave like an all-powerful and ruthless new aristocrat: he takes away Dubrovsky's village, Kistenevka (which, tellingly, is named after the village allotted to Pushkin himself in 1830).

Although Troekurov is introduced as a person "of distinguished birth" (*znatnyi rod*; 145; 8:1:161), Pushkin indicates that his prominence is of recent origin. The ruling read during the court procedure that deprives Dubrovsky of his estate suggests that Troekurov's father was of humble station: he began his career in the rank of provincial secretary (thirteenth class at the time) and eventually rose to that of collegiate assessor (eighth class).[132] Not only were provincial officials at the bottom of the state service hierarchy, but it is not even certain that Troekurov's father was a hereditary nobleman, for while the court ruling refers to the "noble birth" of every noble person mentioned, it says no such thing about the elder Troekurov. True, he did rise to the rank that would have secured him a place in the hereditary noble class, and his son rose even higher, to the rank of general *en chef*—that is, full general (second class). Yet, for all his service success, Troekurov is an upstart and behaves like one. He is boorish and enjoys flattery. Most conspicuously, he lacks the sense of honor expected from a gentleman: he agrees to take his friend's estate by means of chicanery.

In contrast, Dubrovsky is portrayed as a man of honor. A retired lieutenant of the guards (ninth class), he is independent and dignified despite his modest financial situation. He knows how to respond to an offense to his honor. In his reply to Troekurov's insulting demands, he writes: "I do not intend to tolerate jests from your serfs, nor will I tolerate them from you, for I am not a buffoon but a nobleman of ancient lineage [*starinnyi dvorianin*]" (148; 8:1:164). The last clause of his retort echoes the response of the nineteen-year-old Pushkin to a certain Major Denisevich, who declined Pushkin's challenge to a duel because of the challenger's youth and low service rank. To this, Pushkin responded: "I am a Russian nobleman [*Ia russkii dvorianin*]." Denisevich was forced to apologize.[133] The connection is made stronger by Dubrovsky's concluding his letter with a formula that may indicate his readiness to duel: "I remain your humble servant [*Za sim ostaius' pokornym ko uslugam*]"

(148; 8:1:164). Pushkin thus "lends" Andrei Dubrovsky not only the name of his estate but also his own behavior as a gentleman as well as his own understanding of what the relations between noblemen—regardless of how much money they have—are supposed to be. Andrei Dubrovsky's sad lot suggests that in the 1830s Pushkin may have been more pessimistic about establishing equality within the noble class than he was in the late 1810s.

Pushkin and the Marketplace

Money, of course, was one important factor creating inequality within the noble class: Troekurov is rich, and Dubrovsky poor. By the 1830s, money had also become a particularly thorny issue within the community of writers: it divided them into two groups, commercially successful professionals and writers who either did not want to or could not achieve financial success and support themselves by their literary labors. Unlike in the eighteenth century, the competition now was not between high-minded Western-educated nobles and writers catering to the poorly educated masses but within the former group. Writers who had maintained friendly relations in the 1820s now often became bitter enemies over this issue.

Pushkin's position on publishing for money and achieving commercial success was complex and changed over time.[134] In his younger years, when he fashioned himself as a society man and dandy, the specter of the patronage system inherited from the eighteenth century particularly worried him, and he was on the alert for any attempts to treat him like a client looking for patronage. He wrote to Viazemsky as late as June 7, 1824: "None of us would want *the magnanimous patronage of an enlightened grandee*. This fell into decay [*obvetshalo*] with Lomonosov. Our present-day literature is and has to be nobly independent."[135] In the 1830s, without abandoning the dandy persona altogether, Pushkin came to respect the professionalism of some of his eighteenth-century predecessors. He began to acknowledge Sumarokov's devotion to writing; Trediakovsky, the butt of Pushkin's jokes in the 1820s, also receives high praise in the "Journey from Moscow to Petersburg," as well as in Pushkin's other writings in the 1830s.[136] Pushkin thus made his peace with professionalism that did not involve competition in the book market.

The 1830s, however, presented Pushkin with exactly this problem: how did one become a financially successful writer in the rapidly growing book market? That is, how should one go about becoming a professional in terms of commercial success? Faddei Bulgarin was quite successful financially at that time—and not as a journalist as he was in the 1820s but as a prose writer. Did Pushkin want to follow in Bulgarin's footsteps? If he did, how far was he prepared to go to earn a hefty income by writing? Which artistic principles was he prepared to sacrifice? Pushkin confronts these questions most directly in *Egyptian Nights* (1835), another unfinished prose piece. At the center of this piece is a new (and disturbing) view of professionalism and the commercialization of literature.

As a young man, Pushkin seemed to have easily resolved for himself the conflict between artistic freedom and taking money for his published art: he kept a conceptual separation between the spheres of creativity and commerce. The formula he uses in his March 8, 1824, letter to Viazemsky, "I write for myself and publish for money," summarizes his position well.[137] The same year Pushkin wrote a poem, "Conversation of a Bookseller with a Poet," that develops a similar idea. The bookseller suggests to the initially reluctant poet: "Inspiration cannot be sold, / But a manuscript can." The poet readily agrees and concludes the conversation with the following statement, characteristically rendered in prose: "You're absolutely right. Here's my manuscript. Let's make a contract."[138] This position allowed Pushkin to earn decent money without compromising his artistic independence. Furthermore, in the late 1820s his rising popularity as a poet ensured his substantial commercial success.[139]

Pushkin still appears to be subscribing to this formula in the 1830s, when he writes in his April 1834 letter to M. P. Pogodin: "I write a lot to myself [*pro sebia*], and publish out of necessity [*ponevole*] and solely for money."[140] He further explains his attitude toward money in a July 1834 letter to his wife: "I don't like money much, but I respect it as the only decent means to be independent [*ia den'gi malo liubliu—no uvazhaiu v nikh edinstvennyi sposob blagopristoinoi nezavisimosti*]."[141] But how well did Pushkin's formula from the 1820s work in the 1830s, when not only had Pushkin's reputation as a poetic genius begun to fade but the market for literature had also changed dramatically due to the emergence of entertainment literature, in particular the novel? The very tone Pushkin uses to formulate his attitude toward publishing for money has changed noticeably: he now sounds bitter. Entertainment literature by definition caters to a mass readership, requiring the writer to adapt to its tastes. However, this was not something Pushkin was prepared to do.[142] This is evident in his letter to Pogodin, where the statement about writing "to himself" and publishing for money is followed by the angry explanation: "Who cares [okhota] to appear before a public that doesn't understand you, in order that four fools [duraka] may curse you in their journals for six months all but obscenely [tol'ko chto ne pomaternu]. There was a time when literature was a noble, aristocratic career [poprishche]. Now it is a flea market [vshivyi rynok]. So be it."[143] The word "aristocratic" likely refers to the "literary aristocracy" controversy (1828–31) and the fact that, in the eyes of the "foolish" critics, the "aristocratic party" to which Pushkin belonged lost to the group of literati that included Bulgarin. In this respect it is crucial to note that the first half of Pushkin's letter to Pogodin speaks indignantly of Bulgarin: Pushkin refuses Pogodin's invitation to read his poetry at a meeting of the Society of Lovers of Russian Literature, arguing that to have been elected to the Society together with Bulgarin was the equivalent of a slap in the face. Said election had taken place in 1829, that is, five years before the letter was written, but Pushkin's indignation comes through as fresh and hot as if the election had happened just the day before.

Pushkin's new thinking shapes his concept of the professional writer in *Egyptian Nights*. One of the two main characters in the novella, Charsky, is a society man and poet who conceals his gift, calling inspiration rubbish (*drian'*), and hides from everyone when it overcomes him. He does this because, as a nobleman, he cannot accept the idea of writing for profit. Charsky cannot resolve the "conflict between social position, literary commerce, and inspiration."[144] In contrast, Charsky's foil in the story, the Italian *improvisatore*, is a thorough professional. To be sure, the *improvisatore* represents the commercialization of literature in its crudest form: he sells the fruits of his inspiration directly to consumers, as if from a market stall. And yet, it is to him that Pushkin planned to lend his own poetry in this unfinished work. But is Pushkin comfortable with this identification? Is Charsky not his true alter ego?[145]

This question does not have a clear-cut answer. On the one hand, Charsky, a high-society man, resembles Pushkin in many respects; on the other, Pushkin seems to distance himself from him. The story explains that he is a poet, but not what kind of poet. His poetry is not included in the text of *Egyptian Nights*, and Pushkin did not plan to include it, in contrast to that of the Italian. Furthermore, it seems that Charsky does not publish his poems at all, even anonymously as his eighteenth-century predecessors sometimes did. In this, Charsky differs from Pushkin, who published his first poem when he was fourteen years old, signing it with a very transparent pen name (*Aleksandr N. k. sh. p.*), and never stopped publishing. To be sure, Pushkin did not publish everything he wrote, circulating some poems in manuscript and suppressing others altogether. But in general he was a publishing author throughout his life—even after his relations both with critics and readers began to sour in the late 1820s.[146] Furthermore, Charsky is rich, free of family obligations, and thus does not need to publish for money. Pushkin, in contrast, was short of money all his life, and particularly in the 1830s, when his growing family, life in the capital, gambling, and inability to economize forced him to amass enormous debts. Not simply publishing, but publishing for money was something he not only wanted to but had to do.

In *Egyptian Nights* the situation is further complicated by the fact that, repulsive as he is, the improviser clearly possesses a poetic gift. In fact, he is a genius, and his inspiration is of divine origin; as in Pushkin's poems "Prophet" ("Prorok," 1826) and "The Poet" ("Poet," 1827), when inspiration comes to him, he changes into a different, loftier person: "But the improviser already sensed the divine presence. . . . He signaled to the musicians to play. . . . His face grew alarmingly pale; he trembled as if in fever; his eyes sparkled with wondrous fire; he smoothed his black hair with his hand, wiped the beads of sweat off his high forehead with a handkerchief . . . and suddenly stepped forward, folding his arms across his chest. . . . The music stopped. . . . The improvisation began" (258; 8:1:274). Charsky acknowledges the Italian's genius after he hears his first improvisation: "The Italian grew silent. . . . Charsky sat without a word, astonished and moved" (255; 8:1:269). His subsequent praise of the Italian's talent is very similar to Pushkin's reaction to Adam Mickiewicz's improvisation, which he heard during the Polish poet's stay in Russia. According to Antoni Edward Odyniec, Pushkin exclaimed: "Quel genie! quel feu sacre! que suis-je aupres de lui?"[147] However, even though the Italian is a genius, like Mickiewicz and Pushkin himself, are the goods he offers truly salable at the market, flea or otherwise? Are there buyers for the poetic production of a genius? In other words, would the improviser be able to make a profit without Charsky's helping him at every turn, effectively serving as his patron? Is he, after all, a practical model for Pushkin to follow? The unfinished novella leaves these questions unanswered.

If the improviser is a questionable model for Pushkin, then so is Charsky, and not only because he is a rich dilettante free not to publish for money but also because his status vis-à-vis the state is different from

Pushkin's. It is said of Charsky that state service "placed no great burden on him" (249; 8:1:263). In contrast, it certainly burdened Pushkin in the 1830s, curtailing his independence. He writes to his wife in September 1835, regretting that he cannot abandon the service: "The tsar doesn't allow me to become [*zapisat'sia*] either a landowner or a journalist."[148] Apparently, Pushkin refers here to his attempt, in the summer of 1834, to hand in his resignation in order to move his family to the countryside, where he hoped to be able both to live within his means and to produce literary works according to his taste and publish or not publish them at will.

Having to sell one's literary production at the flea market together with Bulgarin and his ilk makes Pushkin's earlier comfortable duality of creativity and commerce unworkable; in order to sell successfully at the flea market, one needs to have something the customer wants to buy, and Pushkin believed that he could not provide such goods: as he writes to his wife in the letter quoted above, "To write books for money, as God is my witness, I cannot."[149] At the same time, what his genius could provide was not profitably salable anymore.

It seems that around the time he wrote *Egyptian Nights*, Pushkin found himself in a real bind: his attempt to retire from service and move away from Saint Petersburg failed, wiping out his last chance to be a professional yet nobly independent author. As the unfinished *Egyptian Nights* demonstrates, he could not afford (and, likely, did not want) to follow Charsky's example of writing exclusively "to himself"; even though he stopped publishing his poetry in 1836, he still published *The Captain's Daughter* and continued to put out his journal *The Contemporary*. At the same time, having tried on the *improvisatore*'s role, he realized that the marketplace was problematic for him as well, both because selling his literary works at a flea market was not for him and because there might be no buyers for the works of a genius. It is impossible to tell what kind of modus vivendi Pushkin would have worked out had he lived, but in his lifetime he was not able to come up with a new formula that would reconcile creative freedom, professionalism, and the marketplace to his satisfaction.

3

The Hierarchy of Ranks
according to Gogol

When readers of Russian literature want to learn about state service and the value of particular ranks in Imperial Russia, especially civil ones, they often see the works of Nikolai Gogol as their best source of information. Indeed, who else among Russian writers paid so much attention to state servitors? Beginning with "Notes of a Madman" and ending with *Selected Passages from Correspondence with Friends* (*Vybrannye mesta iz perepiski s druz'iami*, 1847), Gogol's works are overpopulated with all kinds of bureaucrats, from the lowest to the highest ranking. Could there be a better way to learn about the Table of Ranks, gaining knowledge and having fun at the same time?

While the readers of the Petersburg Tales, *The Inspector General*, and *Dead Souls* will most definitely have fun, they should be very cautious about relying on Gogol's works for historically accurate information on the rank system. All the terms are right, all the titles are correct—but do they mean what they are supposed to mean? A close reading of Gogol's fiction shows that very often they do not. Gogol shamelessly replaces the hierarchy of ranks created by Peter the Great with his own. It seems to be just as orderly as Peter's, but it is not. It seems to re-create the historical reality, but it does not. One cannot rely on it to learn what the Table of Ranks and service hierarchy in Imperial Russia were really like—Gogol the writer is anything but reliable.

Gogol's documentation of his own life (in letters and elsewhere) is equally unreliable. It is therefore exceptionally difficult to compose a credible biography of Gogol: his notorious secretiveness coupled with his inclination to invent "facts" about his life oftentimes make this task an exercise in guesswork.[1] Writing about Gogol's service career is no exception. It is particularly difficult, not only because of missing information and inconsistencies between documents but also because, at times, Gogol appears to have "edited" the history of his service, adding and subtracting as he saw fit. Nonetheless, a credible reconstruction of Gogol's service career is possible on the basis of available published documents (see next section). Although Gogol's correspondence, in particular his letters to his mother, provides valuable information, it is treated with caution in the second section of this chapter, since it not only often presents contradictory views on Gogol's planned and actual service career but also distorts reality. The final section of this chapter reexamines some of the literary works in which Gogol depicts state service and the system of ranks. It focuses on his descriptions of the civil service (of which Gogol had some personal experience), referring to the military service (which Gogol never experienced) only occasionally.

Gogol's Service Career: An Attempt at a Reconstruction

Having graduated in 1828 from the Nezhin (Nizhyn) Lyceum of Higher Arts, Gogol received the right to enter the service at the lowest rank, fourteenth class (notably, Pushkin graduated from his more prestigious educational institution with the rank of collegiate secretary, tenth class). Like Pushkin, Gogol was not among the best students in his grade and thus lost the opportunity to graduate with the right to the rank of the twelfth class. Unlike Pushkin, Gogol did not have a high-status service position waiting for him upon graduation, and to get one, he had to rely on his own initiative and the meager connections his family had in Saint Petersburg. After his arrival in the capital in December 1828, it took the young provincial nearly a year to find a position. As his letters to his mother indicate, it was a difficult experience for him that resulted in some strange behavior (such as his notorious unexpected trip abroad in August–September 1829) as well as in less than truthful reports to his mother about his life in Saint Petersburg and his search for a service position.

As with many other episodes in Gogol's life, the picture of the beginning of his service career is murky: it is not even clear what his first place of service was. According to the archival documents published by V. V. Gippius in 1936, his first place of employment was the Department of State Economy and Public Buildings in the Ministry of Internal

Affairs.[2] However, according to F. V. Bulgarin's memoir—published in 1854 in response to the first biography of Gogol by P. A. Kulish—in late 1829 or early 1830, the desperate Gogol arrived at Bulgarin's, introduced himself, presented the journalist with a flattering poem, and asked him for help in finding a position. Bulgarin allegedly obliged, securing Gogol a position in the Chancellery of the Third Section through its director, M. Ia. Fon-Fok. Bulgarin continues: "I don't remember how long Gogol served in this chancellery, to which he came only to collect his pay; but I know that [eventually] a friend of Gogol's brought his letter of resignation [*pros'ba ob otstavke*] to the chancellery and collected his [service] documents. And Gogol himself disappeared nobody knew where!"[3] Abram Reitblat, in his analysis of this episode of Gogol's service career, suggests that Bulgarin's claim is at least partially correct: "It seems to us quite plausible that in the second half of 1829 Gogol visited Bulgarin, asked him for help, was recommended to the Chancellery of the Third Section, and wrote a petition to be accepted for service there. However, having been accepted, Gogol apparently didn't serve and soon withdrew his documents."[4] Granted, what Reitblat offers is a conjecture. It is nonetheless worthwhile to keep in mind that in his letters Gogol several times mentions a position (or positions) ostensibly available to him but never accepted.

Gogol's stint in the Department of State Economy and Public Buildings is better documented, even though many details remain vague. He was appointed to the Department on November 15, 1829, on a trial basis (*na ispytanie*). It is not known to what sort of a position Gogol was appointed, but apparently it did not suit him, because on February 25, 1830, he petitioned the director of the Department for the return of his service documents on the grounds that he was not planning to remain in the Department.[5] During his time in the Department, Gogol was not sworn in, and therefore the rank of collegiate registrar was not conferred on him: his petition was signed "Student Nikolai Gogol-Ianovsky."[6] It is noteworthy that his service record, compiled sometime after he left his last service position—that of adjunct professor at Saint Petersburg University—does not mention his time in the Department of State Economy and Public Buildings at all.[7]

It is likely that Gogol decided to abandon the Department of State Economy and Public Buildings to accept a better position with a higher salary (600 rubles as opposed to 360 rubles a year) in the Department of Domains at the Ministry of the Imperial Court.[8] It has not been positively determined who helped him secure this position: some name A. A. Troshchinsky, a nephew of Gogol's old family friend and patron D. P. Troshchinsky.[9] I. G. Iampol'sky, who published a set of Gogol's service documents concerning his second service position, believed that it could have been V. I. Panaev, a minor writer and, at the time, a section chief at the Department of Domains.[10] In any case, on March 27, 1830, Gogol petitioned to be appointed to a position under Panaev, was offered the position of scribe (*pisets*), and began his service on April 10, 1830. On June 3 of the same year, Gogol was sworn in and confirmed in the rank of collegiate registrar. On July 22 he was promoted to the position of deputy desk chief (*pomoshchnik stolonachal'nika*), and his yearly pay was increased to 750 rubles.[11] Despite the promotion, he remained in the Department for less than a year, submitting his letter of resignation in February 1831. His petition was granted on March 9.[12] Gogol left without collecting his papers, which he finally requested in January 1832.[13]

Gogol left the Department of Domains to begin a more prestigious and, he hoped, more promising and exciting career. By that time, the young writer had made acquaintances with established literati—V. A. Zhukovsky and P. A. Pletnev among others. As N. A. Belozerskaia writes in her introduction to the publication of several important documents pertaining to Gogol's service as an educator, "In 1831, [Gogol] procured an [introductory] letter to Zhukovsky, who entrusted him [*sdal ego na ruki*] to Pletnev."[14] Pletnev, in addition to his activities as critic, journalist, and publisher, was a prominent educator and served at the time as inspector of classes at the Patriotic Institute, a school for the daughters of fallen officers, one of the charities under the auspices of Dowager Empress Maria Fedorovna. On Pletnev's recommendation, on February 9, 1831, Gogol was appointed to the Institute as a teacher of history with a yearly salary of 400 rubles. He began service on March 10, the day after his resignation from the Department of Domains was accepted.[15] As he wrote to his mother on April 16, 1831, he hoped also to teach at several other schools, but his plans were not realized, and he ended up supplementing his salary with private lessons.[16]

The chronology of Gogol's life published in volume 10 of his *Complete Works* indicates that his initial appointment was as a junior teacher (*mladshii uchitel'*) of history.[17] Even though the compiler of the chronology, G. S. Vinogradov, refers to the service record published by I. A. Linnichenko, in fact the record does not mention Gogol's appointment as a junior teacher. According to this record, Gogol was appointed as a senior teacher (*starshii uchitel'*) on April 1, 1831, at the rank of titular councilor. To quote the record: "By the Highest vouchsafement [*s Vyso-chaishego soizvoleniia*] of Her Imperial Majesty [Gogol] was appointed to the Patriotic Institute as Senior Teacher of history, being, according to the decree of April 1, 1831, in the rank of Titular Councilor from the day of assuming the current position on March 10, 1831."[18] Gogol thus was rapidly promoted from the fourteenth class to the ninth. However, in her official correspondence with the court the head of the Institute, Louisa Wistinghausen (Vistingauzen), consistently presents Gogol's rank as that of the fourteenth class; the documents issued by the court do the same.[19] This can possibly be explained by the fact that the term "titular" meant something like "nominal." According to the Table of Ranks, this rank was given to professors at the Academy and other teachers, including, apparently, those at the Patriotic Institute.[20] Presumably, the rank was linked to the position and thus could be retracted when the person left it. However, this did not affect clerks who gained this rank through the civil service.

At first, Gogol was very enthusiastic about his teaching obligations, and it seemed that his career path had finally been established. Beginning in 1832, his salary was increased to 1,200 rubles, his egregious three-month lateness in returning from a leave of absence in the summer of 1832 was essentially forgiven, and, against all the rules, two of his sisters were accepted as students at the Institute gratis. Furthermore, on March 9, 1834, together with some of his colleagues, Gogol was nominated for an award and received a diamond ring from the empress.[21] Finally, when, in the summer of 1834, Gogol applied for a position as adjunct professor in the Department of General History at Saint Petersburg University, his application was successful.[22] The appointment took place on July 24, 1834, and for a while Gogol continued teaching at both the Institute and the University. The position of university adjunct professor afforded Gogol the rank of collegiate assessor, eighth class.[23]

Gradually, however, Gogol became bored and disillusioned with his duties at the Patriotic Institute. Nonetheless, he remained there until the summer of 1835, when again failing to return promptly from a leave of absence, he was dismissed and replaced.[24] As is well known, despite his initial enthusiasm, Gogol's university career was also not successful, and on December 31, 1835, he was dismissed, ostensibly on the occasion of the restructuring of the university.[25] After this last attempt at a service career, Gogol never served again.

Gogol's Service Career:
Self-Presentation

It is instructive to compare the information on Gogol's service gleaned from official documents with what he wrote to his correspondents, especially to his mother, M. I. Gogol, about his attitude toward service and his search for a position, as well as his impressions of civil service in general and his own service experiences in particular. The picture that emerges is rather inconsistent. Not only are there factual disparities in Gogol's reports on the subject of service, but they also display striking variations in style: many times in his correspondence of 1827–35, Gogol would unexpectedly switch from astonishingly ostentatious descriptions of his future service achievements to no less astonishingly scornful and dismissive comments on what can be gained through service—and back.

If one can trust Gogol's letters, as a young man he gave serious thought to his future service career. At that time, it seems that he saw it above all as selfless service to the fatherland. On October 3, 1827, while still a student in the Nezhin Lyceum, he wrote to his relative Petr Kosiarovsky about his supposedly well-thought-out plans for a career in law:

Even far back, almost from the age of meager understanding [*pochti neponimaniia*], I burned with an inextinguishable zeal to make my life necessary for the good of the state [*nuzhnoiu dlia blaga gosudarstva*]; I had a burning, boiling desire to be of use, if only in the slightest [*prinesti khotia maleishuiu pol'zu*]. Anxious thoughts that I would not be able to [*ne budu moch'*], that they would bar my way [*pregradiat mne dorogu*], that they would not give me the opportunity to be of the slightest use to [the state], would cast me into a deep despondency. Cold sweat would break out [*proskakival*] on my face when I thought that, perhaps, I was destined to perish in the dust, not having distinguished [*ne oznachiv*] my name with a single beautiful deed—[destined] to be in the world and not leave a mark of my existence—this [thought] was terrible to me. I examined in my mind all stations [*sostoianiia*], all positions [*dolzhnosti*] in the state and settled on one. On law [*iustitsii*]. I saw that in this field [*zdes'*] there will be the most labor, that only in this field can I be a benefactor [*blago-deianie (sic)*], only in this field will I truly be useful to humanity. Injustice, the greatest misfortune in the world, ripped at my

heart more than anything else. I swore not to waste a single
minute of my short life without doing good [*ne sdelav blaga*].
(10:111–12)

The awkwardly highfalutin style undermines (perhaps unwittingly)
the veracity of Gogol's outpouring. As a result, it remains unclear
whether, as he claims, he indeed "for two years continuously studied
the laws of other nations, as well as natural [law], the basis for all other
kinds, and am now studying ours [*otechestvennye*]" (10:112).[26] Nonetheless, it is noteworthy that Gogol found it necessary to make such claims
and to position himself not only as a future ardent servant of the state but
also as a benefactor of humanity. Furthermore, he considered himself
well prepared for both roles.

Almost immediately upon Gogol's arrival in Saint Petersburg, his
enthusiasm for service seems to fade. His first letter from the capital to
M. I. Gogol, written on January 3, 1829, already reflects his apparently
changing mood: "I am seized by misery [*khandra*] or something like
that, and for almost a week I have been sitting on my hands [*sizhu
podzhavshi ruki*] doing nothing. Could it be because of failures that have
made me totally indifferent [*obravnodushili*] to everything?" (10:136). It
is not clear what failures he is referring to, since at that point he has
been in the capital for only about a week. However, as Gogol becomes
better acquainted with the Saint Petersburg bureaucracy, his outlook
appears to turn even more pessimistic. He writes to his mother on April
30, 1829, sharing his unfavorable view of the capital and its inhabitants:
"The silence there is remarkable, no spirit sparkles in the people, everyone [around] is a servitor or an official [*sluzhashchie da dolzhnostnye*],
everyone talks about their departments and ministries [*kollegiiakh*],
everything is oppressed, everything is steeped in the idle, petty toil in
which their life is uselessly wasted" (10:139).[27]

Gogol's letter of May 22, 1829, reflects his growing frustration and
anxiety in a somewhat peculiar way: it offers M. I. Gogol two elaborate
lies. The first is of a personal nature: it is a complaint about Gogol's
ruined plans for a trip abroad. He claims that a friend, whom he does
not name, invited him to go along and promised to pay all his expenses.
However, the trip did not take place due to the friend's sudden death:
"My hopes (that is, a small portion of them) weren't realized; it's a good
thing I didn't give myself over to them [*ne vdavalsia uveritel'no im*]; it's a
good thing that I have enough of a reserve of doubt about everything
that may happen. Here is the essence [of what happened]: my modest

talents were acknowledged, and I had an excellent chance to go to foreign lands. This trip, usually associated with great expense, would cost me nothing, everything would have been paid for, and my smallest needs during the trip would have been satisfied. But imagine my misfortune. [. . .] My magnanimous friend, who was to provide all this, suddenly died, and his intentions and my expectations went down the drain [*lopnuli*]" (10:143). Gogol concludes the story with an expression of his deep sorrow about the loss of the only true friend he supposedly ever had. The commentary to this letter in Gogol's *Complete Works* refutes the veracity of this story: "In the entire corpus of biographical literature about Gogol there is not a single fact confirming that Gogol had a 'friend' who was ready to offer him an opportunity 'to go to foreign lands.' A. S. Danilevsky [Gogol's classmate in the Nezhin Lyceum], who lived with him in Petersburg [at that time], denied the existence of such a friend" (10:420). The commentators agree with Gogol's biographer, V. I. Shenrok, who suggests that Gogol was trying to prepare his mother for news about the trip abroad that he was about to undertake on his own.[28]

In the next paragraph, Gogol informs his mother about a service position that looks more than suitable for a young man without any experience. Gogol, however, finds it beneath him:

> So I am to remain in Petersburg now. I am being offered a position with a salary of 1,000 rubles a year. But should I sell my health and precious time for a sum [*tsenu*] that would barely cover my room and board for the year? And [sell it] in order to do nonsense. How can this be acceptable? [*Na chto eto pokhozhe?*] To have no more than two free hours a day, and the rest of the time not to be able to step away from the desk and to [have to] copy old gibberish and nonsense produced by Messrs. Desk Chiefs [*gospod stolonachal'nikov*]. [. . .] So I am standing in thought and on my life path [*sic*], awaiting the resolution of some of my expectations. It is possible that soon [*na dniakh*] there will become available a position a bit more lucrative and noble, but I have to admit that if there too I will have to waste so much time on silly tasks, then—I am not taking it [*to ia—sluga pokornyi*]. (10:143–44)

Not only was 1,000 rubles a year decent pay for a starting position (Gogol himself would later accept much less), but there is no evidence that Gogol was even offered such a position at that time, let alone expecting to be offered a better one. Together with the lie about the generous friend who died, both claims about available service positions look like pure inventions, the purpose of which remains speculative. Was Gogol indeed laying the groundwork for a trip abroad unsanctioned by his mother? Was he preparing his mother for his request for money in the following paragraph of the same letter? Was he hoping to convince his mother that the state service was not his calling? Significantly, in the same letter, after reminding M. I. Gogol about his requests to her for reports on Ukrainian customs, Gogol hints at his literary activities and the hopes he was placing in them: "I have planned my time in such a way that even leisure itself [*samoe otdokhnovenie*], if not now, then very soon will bring me substantial profit [*sushchestvennuiu pol'zu*]" (10:144).

In late July, Gogol reports to his mother that he has become convinced that a service career would be a betrayal of his true calling. He reproaches himself for even thinking about sacrificing his divine gift to it: "And I have dared to cast away this divine destiny and to crawl on my belly [*presmykat'sia*] in this capital among those servitors, who spend their lives so fruitlessly! One thing is to crawl in a place where every minute of life isn't wasted, where every minute [brings] a rich supply of experience and knowledge. But to pass your life where [*izzhit' tam vek, gde*] there is absolutely nothing ahead of you, where all the years spent in inconsequential activities will resound in your soul as a painful reproach— this is mortifying [*ubivstvenno (sic)*]!" (10:146). Even a successful service career now seems unacceptable to Gogol: "What kind of happiness is it to serve until you get some kind of state councilor rank at the age of 50, to receive a salary that is barely sufficient to support yourself properly, and to be powerless to bring the least little bit [*na kopeiku*] of good to humanity?" (10:146). It is astonishing how easily this young man of no means and few prospects scorns the rank of state councilor (fifth class), a rank as unattainable to him at the time as it would later be to his unsuccessful servitors Poprishchin and Bashmachkin portrayed in "Notes of a Madman" and "The Overcoat," respectively.

Having forgotten the passionate desire to get to Petersburg as soon as possible expressed so frequently in his letters from Nezhin to his friends, Gogol now claims that he agreed to move to the capital only to oblige his mother: "If a nobleman really needs to serve, he ought better to serve in his own province. But no, he has to drag himself [*nado potaskat'sia*] to Petersburg, where not only will he not get anything, but will haul [*peretaskaiut*] a lot of money from home and spend it here in great quantity. Despite all this I had decided [*reshilsia*], to please you, to serve here no matter what it took, but God didn't wish it [*no bogu ne bylo etogo ugodno*]" (10:146–47). Gogol concludes the letter with an announcement of his impending trip abroad, citing as reasons for his departure not only his disappointment in the very idea of service but also a purely imaginary unrequited love for a high-society woman. He declares that he will finance his trip with the money his mother had sent him to pay interest to the Custody Board (*Opekunskii Sovet*). In compensation, he offers to transfer all rights to his estate to his mother.[29]

The trip did not improve Gogol's mood: in addition to despondency over his failure to secure a service position (or gain fame as a writer) in Saint Petersburg, he also evidently began to feel guilty about disappointing his mother. Several days after his departure, on August 1, 1829, he writes to her from Lubeck, asking for forgiveness, explaining the trip as motivated by his poor health, and claiming that a position is awaiting him in Petersburg (which he could have and wanted to accept, "but some silly human preconceptions and prejudices" stopped him; 10:152). In about two weeks, on August 13, he writes to her again, promising to return soon and to continue looking for a service position. He once more claims that a position is awaiting him in Petersburg: "At least now I will have enough energy [*v silakh*] to take a position that has been offered me in Petersburg" (10:155). Reitblat suggests that both times Gogol may have been hinting at the position procured for him by Bulgarin.[30] While the dates do not agree (in his memoir, Bulgarin claims that Gogol petitioned him for a position in late 1829 or early 1830, and Gogol writes about August 1829 as the time when the position was available), Reitblat's supposition is not entirely impossible. However, it is more likely to be the same imaginary position Gogol mentions in his letter of May 30.

Upon his return to Saint Petersburg, Gogol seems to have resumed his positive attitude toward service (perhaps for his mother's sake). He writes to her on October 27, 1829, with faith and even enthusiasm: "Soon I hope to receive a position [*opredelit'sia na sluzhbu*]. Then, with renewed energy, I will take up the work and will devote all my life to it" (10:160). This time Gogol's efforts proved successful: from November 15, 1829, to February 25, 1830, he did serve in the Department of State Economy and Public Buildings. However, as he presents it in his correspondence with his mother, it was not a happy time for him. On February 2, 1830, he writes: "Once again I'm going to the office every day, and—with difficulty, much difficulty—getting by [*perebivaius'*]"

(10:166). Since the rest of the passage describes his impoverished lifestyle, it seems that by "getting by" Gogol is referring to his financial
situation rather than the stress caused by going to the office regularly.

Soon after resigning from the Department of State Economy and
Public Buildings, Gogol applied for the position in the Department of
Domains; and on April 10, he began his service there. Even though the
new position was financially superior to the old one, Gogol's letter to
his mother of April 2 is hesitant and self-contradictory in its assessment
of his situation:

> After endless searching, I finally managed to find a position,
> quite unenviable, however. [. . .] And I have to admit that I am
> in a terrible state of bewilderment [*v uzhasnom nedoumenii*]; I
> don't know where to begin, to what to apply myself [*k chemu
> obratit'sia*], what to do. Often it occurs to me to abandon every-
> thing and leave Petersburg. But, at the same time, suddenly all
> the advantages of service present themselves to me and [the ad-
> vantages] of everything that I would have to forfeit in departing
> from here. Comparing my position with the positions occupied
> by others, I immediately see that the position that I occupy is not
> the worst, that many people, even a great many [*mnogie, ves'ma
> dazhe mnogie*] would want to have it, that I need only to redouble
> my patience and I can hope to be promoted. (10:168–69)

Unexpectedly, Gogol concludes his relatively optimistic evaluation of
his service prospects with a complaint about his poor financial circumstances in comparison to those "many" who are envious about his service position: "But those many receive enough from home to support
themselves, and I have to live exclusively on my salary" (10:169). This
complaint is followed by several pages of detailed description of his
disastrous financial situation. To make it look even more disastrous,
Gogol cites a reduced number for his yearly salary—500 rubles instead
of 600—and includes lists of receipts and expenditures for December
1829 and January 1830 that demonstrate that he is consistently in the red.

Gogol's account of his service in his next letter to his mother, written
on June 3, 1830, is also mixed. He begins with praising his immediate
superiors, V. I. Panaev ("a very good man, whom I truly respect in my
heart") and his desk chief, D. I. Ermolaev ("admittedly, a pretty nice
[*nedurnoi*] man and not without education [*vospitaniia*]"; 10:176). Then,
however, he points out that making a good career at present is much

more difficult than in earlier epochs, such as the reigns of Catherine and Paul. First he remarks that bribe-taking is not as prevalent and easy now as it was in the eighteenth century: "Now bribe-taking by messrs. servitors [*gospod sluzhashchikh*] there [referring to the offices, the Senate among them, listed in his previous sentence] is quite restricted; even if some [bribe-taking] happens, [the bribes] are too insignificant and can barely serve as a small aid in supporting their meager [*skudnoe*] existence" (10:177). Then Gogol reminds his mother that another source of income, estates granted by the monarch for good service, are also not available under Nicholas: "In the olden times, a man who had served several years with good faith and fidelity [*veroiu i pravdoiu*] would be given whole estates, with a thousand peasant souls and more. Now, as you know yourself, they don't give [you] anything like that" (10:177). Gogol's conclusion, nonetheless, seems oddly optimistic. It is also marked by excessively lofty expressions: "So, you will ask, are there now no advantages to serving? On the contrary, they exist, especially for a man who has an intellect [*um*] that knows how to make use of this situation, who sets himself a goal; having reached it [*stavshi na kotoruiu*], he can act freely [*v sostoianii dat' obshirnyi prostor svoim deistviiam*], become indispensable to the huge immensity of the state [*ogromnoi masse gosudarstvennoi*]. This intellect [*um*] has to have an iron will and patience, until he reaches his destiny" (10:177). Gogol goes on for a while in the same vein, concluding that without these exceptional qualities, all a servitor would gain after thirty-five years of service is his pension. Gogol does not want to end up like that: "To serve having no other goal besides this is not a great good [*nebol'shoe blago*]" (10:178). His goal is of a higher nature: "I am even now of the opinion that a man needs only to wish in order to get what he wishes, if what he wishes is possible. To be sure, what is necessary [*podrazumevaetsia*] here is patience and firmness" (10:178). It looks as if Gogol is aiming high in his service career, but the strange stipulation "if what he wishes is possible" undermines his apparent resolve to reach a higher goal. And indeed, the goal he states further on in the letter is much more modest and within the reach of an average servitor: "In a year, and maybe even sooner, I hope to receive a permanent position [*shtatnoe mesto*]" (10:178). His career record, however, indicates that this actually happened much sooner, a month and a half after he wrote the cited letter. Gogol proudly reports in a letter of September 1: "My service is going very well; my superiors are all excellent people. I have served for only four months, but already received a permanent position—which many don't receive even after five years of service, and some don't receive even after ten years" (10:182).

Gogol continues to send optimistic reports to his mother ("Everything is going well with me," 10:184)—up until the spring of 1831, when he informs her that he has left the Department of Domains to assume new duties at the Patriotic Institute. In a letter of April 16, he writes that he is ill with hemorrhoids, and doctors have advised him to avoid sitting for extended periods of time. "I am very glad this has happened: because of it [I could] leave this inconsequential [*nichtozhnuiu*] job— inconsequential, I think, for me, because some other person would be God knows how happy to take the position that I have left. But my path is different, my road is straighter, and there is more energy in my soul to march forward with sure steps" (10:194). He then tells his mother about his new appointment as a teacher of history at the Patriotic Institute. Curiously, it seems he wanted to inform her that his appointment came with the rank of titular councilor, but for some reason thought better of it: he begins to write *Chiny idut* ("ranks are coming"), but then crosses the words out (10:194).

For a while Gogol writes to his mother only about the advantages of his new position—mostly, about being able to enroll his sisters in an excellent school. Later, he updates her on their progress. He does not inform her about his attempts to receive the professorship in Kiev, only hinting at some service prospects in a letter of July 10, 1834. It is not clear when he informed her about his appointment as an adjunct professor at Saint Petersburg University. The first time he mentions it is in a letter of August 1, 1834. He writes about this appointment as if his mother already knows about it: "You complain that I report nothing about my service and so on. What can I tell you: you yourself know where I am. I have, however, discarded an extra burden and given up other activities.[31] Now I am just a professor in our [*zdeshnem*] university and don't have any other position, because I have neither the desire to take it, nor the time" (10:333). Gogol's claim that he is "just a professor" is not accurate, since he was dismissed from the Patriotic Institute only in June 1835, which means that at the time the letter was written he still held two positions. Furthermore, he does not inform his mother of the true nature of his professorship, letting her believe that his position was that of a full professor (*ordinarnyi professor*), not an adjunct (*ad"iunkt* or *extraordinarnyi professor*).

The last time Gogol discusses service and ranks with his mother is in the letter of November 6, 1834. He writes, with some sarcasm directed at M. I. Gogol's supposed obsession with rank: "You would like to know in what field I am a professor in our [*zdeshnem*] university. I teach [*chitaiu*] the history of the Middle Ages. You haven't yet lost your passion [*ne okhladeli ot strasti*] for ranks and think that I should receive a higher rank. Not at all, I am still what I used to be, that is, a collegiate assessor and nothing more" (10:343). He proceeds in the same dismissive and, at the same time, somewhat bitter tone: "If there were any kind of advantage for me in [having a higher] rank, I wouldn't, of course, neglect to use it. I am not so dumb as to let it slip. But my circumstances and my situation are such. [. . .] But I cannot explain it to you. We cannot understand each other and would just waste paper [trying to reach an understanding]. Let us drop [the topic of] ranks. I love you, [love you] as a singular and exemplary mother—what more do you need? You, surely, love me too to such a degree that you would refrain from reminding me of this topic and in your next letter, surely, will not say a word about it" (10:343). What do Gogol's remarks indicate, however? Is he simply annoyed by his mother's meddling? What is the nature of the circumstances that he mentions but refuses to explain? Is he trying to conceal from his mother that he is not a full professor with the corresponding rank of court councilor (seventh class)? Is he himself upset by his lack of service success? Is he disappointed with his teaching at the university, and did this disappointment color his response to his mother? His letter to M. P. Pogodin, written about a month later, on December 14, 1834, suggests as much: "Do you know what it means not to find sympathy [*sochuvstviia*], not to meet with any response? I teach [*chitaiu*] alone, absolutely alone in this [*zdeshnem*] university. Nobody listens to me, in no one have I seen even once that vivid truth has stricken him [*ni na odnom ni razu ne vstretil ia, chtoby porazila ego iarkaia istina*]. And because of this I now absolutely abandon any artistic polish and all the more [abandon] the desire to awaken my sleepy audience. [. . .] If only one student creature [*studencheskoe sushchestvo*] would understand me. They all are as bleak as Petersburg" (10:344). Here again, it is unclear whether the professor lost inspiration because of the sleepy audience or the audience grew sleepy because of the uninspiring professor. Gogol's dismissal from the university suggests the latter. Remarkably, Gogol apparently did not inform his mother of his dismissal.

One may argue that Gogol's predilection for lying to his mother and his reluctance to share the details of his life with her resulted from a normal (if at times not entirely healthy) filial desire to protect his privacy.[32] And yet, Gogol was hardly less secretive and untruthful with other people in his life. P. V. Annenkov, in his memoir about Gogol, explains Gogol's inclination to invent some things and conceal others by his playfulness and love of mystery. In "Gogol in Rome in the Summer of 1841" (1857), Annenkov reports the following episode: "Gogol, by his nature, tried to influence the crowd by his external behavior [*vneshnim svoim sushchestvovaniem*]. He loved to present himself in a certain mysterious perspective and to conceal from [the crowd] some details that could particularly affect it. For example, after publishing his *Evenings*, passing through Moscow—where, by the way, he was received with great respect by the local literati—he arranged things at the city gate in such a way as to sign himself in and get into the *Moscow News* not as a collegiate registrar, which he was, but as a collegiate assessor. 'This is necessary [. . .],' he told his friend who accompanied him."[33] The story is, however, of doubtful veracity, since in 1832, when Gogol indeed twice passed through Moscow on the way from Petersburg to Ukraine and back, he already had the rank of titular councilor, and therefore would not have been able, as Annenkov explained it to M. M. Stasiulevich, who questioned the story, to "erase" (*podchistit'*) "the term 'registrar' in his travel voucher and replace it with a different one: 'assessor.'"[34] Or did his travel documents list him as having the rank of the fourteenth class, that is, of collegiate registrar (as the head of the Patriotic Institute and the court documents refer to him)? In this case, perhaps Gogol did erase the hateful "registrar" and replace it with the more respectable "assessor." However, in his compilation *Gogol in Life* (1933), V. V. Veresaev attaches the following note to the excerpts from Annenkov's memoir and his correspondence with Stasiulevich: "In every issue of the *Moscow News* at that time they would publish 'News about Those Persons of the [Highest] Eight Ranks Who Came to This Capital and Those Who Left It,' beginning with full generals and actual privy councilors and ending with majors and collegiate assessors. We have inspected the newspaper for the entire year of 1832 and didn't find there the name of Gogol or Ianovsky. Let us point out as a fun fact [*kur'ez*] that in one issue 'Collegiate Assessor Kovalev' is registered as coming in." Veresaev helpfully adds for those not in the know: "This was the name of the main character of Gogol's tale 'The Nose.'"[35]

The entire episode, beginning with Annenkov's most probably fictional report and ending with Veresaev's finding in the paper the namesake of Gogol's character, illustrates how very challenging it can be to establish the facts of Gogol's life, largely due to the way Gogol presented himself to others. Did Annenkov invent the story or did he simply uncritically accept someone else's report? The latter is more probable, and in this case, could it be Gogol himself who was the original reporter? It is likely he was. But what can be made of the appearance of Collegiate Assessor Kovalev's name in the paper? In this instance, Gogol could not be responsible, but could Gogol perhaps have seen it in the paper during his two visits to Moscow in 1832 and later used it in his tale? This is particularly probable if Gogol indeed was the author of the fictional story about his assuming the rank of collegiate assessor. These and many other questions are likely destined to remain without definite answers, and they do affect our perception of Gogol's biography, including his service career, making us doubt and question the available facts, particularly as presented by Gogol himself.

What is quite certain, however, is that Gogol's experience in the state service was not extensive. If the time during which he taught is excluded (and teaching is markedly different in nature from serving as a clerk), Gogol's cumulative time in state offices was no more than a year and a half long—even if the days on which Gogol simply did not go in to the office are not subtracted.[36] Thus his understanding of this sphere of Russian life was not as thorough as is often believed. His presentation of the world of Russian bureaucracy in his fiction is therefore as much an invention, a simulacrum, as his presentation of Ukrainian villages and towns (about which he learned much from his mother's letters and invented even more) or Russian provincial space (which, as S. A. Vengerov pointed out in his 1913 article "Gogol Absolutely Didn't Know Real Russian Life," Gogol observed mostly from the inside of his carriage during his infrequent travels across Russia).[37]

This is not to say that Gogol was totally unfamiliar with the hierarchy of ranks and the general configuration of the state service of his day; every nobleman, however inexperienced, had to know about the system of ranks and the structure of the Russian bureaucracy. Even before entering the state service, the young Gogol was certainly aware that his father had retired in the rank of collegiate assessor and that his mother remained for the duration of her life a collegiate assessor's widow (*kollezhskaia assessorsha*, just as Korobochka is a *kollezhskaia sekretarsha*, which tells us that her late husband retired in the rank of collegiate secretary; see 6:50). The Table of Ranks was the hierarchy into which Gogol was born and in which he was expected to function. Outside this system a nobleman was a nobody—very much like the young Gogol himself, who continued to retain the status of "student" up to the moment he was confirmed in the rank that was due to him thanks to his education. His status as a student did not depend on his actually being in school or on his age, but solely on the fact that he had not yet earned a place in the hierarchy of ranks.

Even though Gogol was certainly familiar with the Russian bureaucracy of his time, in his fiction he displays a curious inconsistency in his treatment of service and ranks, and this inconsistency is similar to what can be observed in his letters. The value of a given rank is often fluid in Gogol's fictional world—now higher than the Table of Ranks would indicate, now lower. Gogol's fictional servitors themselves also often misunderstand or misrepresent the ranks they hold, sometimes exaggerating their significance and sometimes underestimating it. Why did Gogol play with the system of ranks like this? Can it perhaps be explained by his relatively short experience as a servitor? Or was it rather a reflection of his own fluctuating views on the service, now as the highest duty, now as the lowest chore? Or perhaps his free play with the Table of Ranks had artistic value for him? If it did, what was the nature of this value? The following section addresses some of these questions.

The Table of Ranks in Gogol's Fiction

Service and ranks first appear in Gogol's fiction in one of his Dikanka stories, "Ivan Fedorovich Shponka and His Auntie" ("Ivan Fedorovich Shpon'ka i ego tetushka," 1832). In this story, a painful boyhood punishment for taking a bribe (in the form of a *blin*) leads the title character to choose the military over the civil service: "Right away [the teacher] flogged Ivan Fedorovich on his hands very painfully. And rightly so: the hands were guilty of taking [the *blin*], not some other part of his body. [. . .] Perhaps this very incident was the reason why he never had the slightest desire to enter the civil service, having concluded from his experience [*vidia na opyte*] that it is not always possible to hide the evidence [*khoronit' kontsy*]" (1:285–86). Recall, in this context, Gogol's letter to his mother of June 3, 1830, in which he explains to her the difficulty of bribe-taking under Nicholas.

Shponka's military service is presented as exceedingly successful: he began it in the rank of warrant officer (*praporshchik*, fourteenth class) and "in a short time, eleven years after receiving the rank of warrant officer, he was promoted to the rank of second lieutenant" (*podporuchik*, thirteenth class; 1:286). The narrator of the story points out that such a high rank did not make Shponka unduly proud: "Some other person in his place, having received such a rank, would have been puffed up, but pride was entirely unknown to him, and having become a second lieutenant, he remained the same Ivan Fedorovich as he once was in the rank of warrant officer" (1:286). Ivan's auntie agrees with the narrator's high appraisal of the second lieutenant's rank: she calls it "not insignificant" (*nemalovazhnyi*) in her letter encouraging Shponka to retire (1:286). Upon retirement, Shponka, as a servitor in good standing, is promoted to the rank of lieutenant (*poruchik*, twelfth class), which later his auntie calls "significant," arguing that all he needs now is a wife and children: "You already have a good rank. It's time to think about children. You certainly [*nepremenno*] need a wife" (1:306).

The value of rank is obviously (and comically) exaggerated here. Is it done to emphasize the low expectations of service success prevalent in Shponka's milieu? Or is the point to indicate Shponka's lack of ambition and diminished masculinity, which make the very idea of having a wife terrifying to him? It is noteworthy that Afanasy Ivanovich of "Old-World Landowners" ("Starosvetskie pomeshchiki," 1835; included in Gogol's second collection of stories, *Mirgorod*) retired as a second major, eighth class. His status as a married man and his claim to Pul'kheria Ivanovna that he is ready to rejoin the military in case of war, jocular though it is, call attention to his masculinity as compared with Shponka's conspicuous lack thereof, and perhaps explain Afanasy's superior rank.

This is the extent of Gogol's engagement with the subject of state service in his first two collections of stories. Beginning in the mid-1830s, however, rank becomes a virtually indispensable element in Gogol's prose and drama. At times, he presents it as an absolutely essential component of any piece of literature, something that the reader expects and demands. At least twice his narrators claim that without naming a character's rank one cannot write a credible story. In "The Overcoat," the story's narrator comments in parentheses on this ostensibly obligatory feature of Russian prose: "As for his rank (since in Russia [*u nas*] one has first of all to declare the rank [of a character]), he [Akaky Bashmachkin] was what is called an eternal titular councilor" (3:141). In *Dead Souls*, the narrator not only stresses the necessity of declaring each character's rank but also claims that the value of this rank is of the uttermost importance for the reader, who needs to assess his own rank vis-à-vis that of a character:

> But the author has serious scruples [*ves'ma sovestitsia*] about occupying his readers for so long with people of low class,

knowing from experience how reluctant they are to become
acquainted with low estates. Such is the Russian: [he has] a strong
passion for associating with those who are at least one rank
above him; and a nodding acquaintance with a count or a prince
is better for him than any kind of close friendship. The author
is even afraid for his hero, who is only a collegiate councilor.
Court councilors, perhaps, will make his acquaintance, but as
for those who are close to the rank of general, these people, God
knows, will perhaps even cast one of those contemptuous
glances that are so proudly cast by a person at everything that
creeps under his feet; or, even worse, perhaps, will pass by
[*proidut*] with an inattention pernicious for the author. But however lamentable [*priskorbno*] the former and the latter might be,
we need, nonetheless, to return to our hero. (6:20–21)

Collegiate councilor is, of course, a respectable rank (sixth class), as is,
for that matter, court councilor (seventh class). Both lose only in comparison with the first four classes (the slot for fifth class in the military had
been empty since the late eighteenth century), those of major-general,
lieutenant-general, general, and general–field marshal. What is remarkable here, however, is the clear sense of hierarchy, so rarely present
in such an unshakable form in Gogol's works. The hierarchy is always
there, of course, but Gogol tends to destabilize it by various means,
from tossing several different ranks into the same category and then
reshuffling them, to making the dead titular councilor Akaky ignore
the hierarchy altogether and snatch overcoats from every bureaucrat he
meets, "disregarding rank and title [*ne razbiraia china i zvaniia*]" (3:169).[38]

Ranks figure prominently in four of Gogol's "Petersburg Tales":
"Nevsky Prospect" ("Nevskii prospekt," 1834), "The Nose" ("Nos,"
1833), "The Overcoat" ("Shinel,'" 1842), and "Notes of a Madman"
("Zapiski sumasshedchego," 1834).[39] In "Nevsky Prospect," in particular, the entire hierarchy of ranks periodically floods the eponymous
street, and this hierarchy is not stable, as the Table of Ranks would have
it: instead, it changes and shifts depending on the time of the day. This
story is also somewhat lopsided, repeatedly mentioning some ranks
and ignoring others.

The first group of bureaucrats, showing up on Nevsky Prospect early
in the afternoon, consists of those whose life is not strictly regimented
by their service; around 2:00 p.m., the crowd of retired servitors "is
joined by those to whom an enviable fate has allotted the blessed title of

officials on special assignments [*chinovnikov po osobennym porucheniiam*]. They are joined by those who serve in the College of Foreign Affairs and are distinguished by the nobility of their employment [*zaniatii*] and habits" (3:12). By the nature of their occupation, members of the first group stand somewhat outside the service hierarchy, usually being subordinated to one particular high-ranking official. The second group is distinguished by the type of their service, which was considered the most prestigious of all the varieties of civil service. The narrator cannot conceal his ostensible envy for their comparative freedom from service obligations and their advantageous position in the service hierarchy, exclaiming with an exaggerated rapture: "My God, what kind of beautiful positions and types of service there are! How they elevate and delight one's soul! Alas, I don't serve and am deprived of the pleasure of experiencing [*videt'*] refined treatment at the hands of my superiors" (3:12).

Later in the afternoon, Nevsky Prospect is filled with several other groups of civil servants returning home from their offices:

> At three o'clock there is a new change. Suddenly, spring comes to Nevsky Prospect: clerks in green uniforms cover it all.[40] The hungry titular, court, and other kinds of councilors try to speed up with all their might and main. The young collegiate registrars, gubernial and collegiate secretaries still hasten to use their time to stroll along Nevsky Prospect with deportment showing that they have by no means spent six hours in an office [*prisutstvie*]. But the old collegiate secretaries, titular and court councilors walk fast, looking down: they don't care [*im ne do togo*] to look at passers-by; they haven't detached themselves yet from their preoccupations [*zaboty*]; in their heads there is a jumble [*eralash*] and an entire archive of cases begun and not yet finished. For a long time, instead of a shop sign, they see a box with papers or the round face of the head of the chancellery. (3:14)

Notably, all clerks walk fast, but for different, although not always clearly defined, reasons. At the same time, they are distinguished not by their ranks but by their level of hunger, as well as by age and, presumably, experience. The narrator does not indicate why councilors, regardless of their rank, are in general hungrier than registrars and secretaries or why older collegiate secretaries are more preoccupied with service than their younger counterparts. The result is the formation of three different types of hierarchies—one of hungry clerks; another of evidently less hungry clerks who, moreover, like to promenade along Nevsky Prospect to parade themselves as free of any service concerns; and the third, of clerks fixated on their service duties. The existence of these three groups undermines the vertical and rigid hierarchy of the Table of Ranks, presenting it as unstable and fluid.

In the evening yet another crowd of clerks appears on Nevsky Prospect, arranged according to yet another principle: "Young gubernial registrars, and gubernial and collegiate secretaries walk back and forth along [the prospect] for a very long time. But old collegiate registrars and titular and court councilors for the most part stay at home—either because they are married or because their live-in German cooks cook very well. You will [also] meet here those respectable old men who at two o'clock strolled along Nevsky Prospect with such gravitas and amazing nobility. [Now] you will see them running just as the young collegiate registrars do, in order to look under the hat of a lady they see from afar" (3:15). The main differentiation in this description is, curiously, by presence and absence, and here again a difference not in rank is stressed but in age or marital status (the cooks obviously play the same role as the wives). Then, however, the age hierarchy collapses, and old high-ranking bureaucrats are seen running after prostitutes as fast as young collegiate registrars do. Once again, the clearly structured Table of Ranks is rendered as shifting and even reversed.

The narrative technique Gogol used to portray the world of service in "Nevsky Prospect" makes it difficult for the reader to see the incongruities that this portrayal contains. While Gogol creates specific classifications of servitors, he either makes it tricky to distinguish between different classes (as is the case with the clerks who are all hurrying, but for different reasons) or simply breaks the differences down (as with the clerks who chase after prostitutes). His narrative defies logic, which prevents the reader from seeing the actual absurdity of his classifications.

Furthermore, Gogol's picture of the world of state service is not only distorted but also incomplete. For example, not one of the described groups includes collegiate assessors. Why this omission? Is Gogol protecting from derision his father's rank or his own? Or is he saving this rank for his next story, "The Nose"? In addition, the world of "Nevsky Prospect" is overwhelmingly a world of civil servitors. One of the very few characters with military rank in "Nevsky Prospect" is Lieutenant Pirogov. It is curious that the story's narrator presents Pirogov not so much as an individual but as a representative of a group. Even though, unlike the civil servants appearing on Nevsky Prospect, he has a name, he nonetheless lacks individuality almost to the same degree that they do: "But before we tell who Lieutenant Pirogov was, it would do no harm [*ne meshaet*] to tell something about the society to which Pirogov belonged. There are officers who comprise some kind of a middle class of society [*kakoi-to srednii klass obshchestva*] in Saint Petersburg. At a soiree, at a dinner at the home of a state councilor or an actual state councilor who has gained [*vysluzhil*] this rank by working hard for forty years, you will always find one of them" (3:34). Having described their attractiveness to the pale and bland daughters of said councilors, as well as their literary preferences (Bulgarin, Pushkin, and Grech), the narrator concludes with the following passage, presenting Pirogov as someone very much content with his place in the service hierarchy: "He was very fond of his rank, which he had received not long ago, and even though sometimes, lying on a sofa, he would say, 'Ooh, ooh! Vanity, all is vanity! What does it matter that I am a lieutenant?' still he was secretly very flattered by his new rank [*dostoinstvo*]. In conversation, he would often try to hint at it; and once, when some scribe coming his way looked discourteous to him, he immediately stopped him and in a few sharp words let him know that the man standing before him was a lieutenant, not some other kind of an officer" (3:36). If the exclamation "Vanity, all is vanity" quotes the book of Ecclesiastes, the phrase "What does it matter that I am a lieutenant?" echoes the complaint of Aksenty Poprishchin of "Notes of a Madman" in his diary: "Why am I a titular councilor and what for [*s kakoi stati*] am I a titular councilor?" (3:206). Pirogov, however, reverses the meaning of Poprishchin's complaint, turning it into a hidden boast. The irony of this reversal is that it is not quite clear what Pirogov is boasting about: the rank of lieutenant was not particularly impressive (recall the mockery with which Gogol's narrator presents Shponka's satisfaction at receiving it upon his retirement). It is actually less impressive than titular councilor: lieutenants belonged to the twelfth class (unless the lieutenant in question served in the guards), whereas titular councilors belonged to the ninth, and therefore, even if the fact that the value of the military ranks was higher is taken into account, a titular councilor still outranked a lieutenant. Nonetheless, Pirogov is proud of his rank and is liked by the daughters of higher-ranking officials, whereas Poprishchin undervalues his rank and fails to attract the daughter of his superior. It is also noteworthy that, regardless of their status as servitors, by the end of their respective stories both Pirogov and Poprishchin are physically abused, and Pirogov easily survives the dishonor, while Poprishchin is ruined. This contrast further complicates the seemingly stable and logical hierarchy of ranks.

If collegiate assessors are absent from "Nevsky Prospect," it is, of course, Collegiate Assessor Kovalev who is the central character in "The Nose." Even though Kovalev is a so-called Caucasian collegiate assessor (which means that he was promoted to this rank speedily and without the required examination, in order to entice him and others like him to serve in the Caucasus during Russia's conquest of the region), he, like Pirogov, is very proud of his rank: "He had been in this rank for only two years and therefore couldn't forget about it even for a minute" (3:53). Furthermore, Kovalev cleverly uses the fact that both the rank of collegiate assessor and that of major were of the eighth class, disregarding, to his advantage, the greater value of the latter rank: "And to give himself more nobility and weight, he never called himself a collegiate assessor, but always a major" (3:53). The narrator promises to follow suit ("Therefore we too will from now on call this collegiate assessor a major," 3:53), but in fact he often wavers and uses Kovalev's civil rank.

The rank of collegiate assessor is also special because in Gogol's time it afforded its bearer hereditary nobility (whereas the next-lower rank, that of titular councilor, afforded only "personal" nobility, which the bearer could not pass on to his children). Gogol's narrator does not inform us of Kovalev's lineage, and therefore it remains unknown whether he was born a noble or earned nobility through his rank. If the latter is the case, his desire to marry (however vaguely indicated) can be explained by, among other things, his wish to establish a new noble line.

Kovalev's conflict in the story is, of course, with his runaway nose, which somehow turns into a person—and, moreover, into a person of a higher rank. In Kovalev's estimation, the Nose is a state councilor (fifth class): "He was wearing a uniform embroidered with gold, with a large stand-up collar; he wore chamois pantaloons, and had a sword at his side. The hat with plumes allowed one to conclude that he had the rank [schitalsia v range] of state councilor" (3:55). Kovalev's "reading" of the Nose's uniform, however, seems to be seriously off: the uniform of state councilors did not include plumes on the hat; plumes could signal either a high military rank (that of admiral or adjutant-general in the imperial suite) or a court title.[41] The Nose is obviously not in the Navy or other military service, and thus the plumes should signal his connection with the court.[42] The Nose's declaration that he is a scholar or an educator (po uchenoi chasti, 3:56), however, undermines this assumption and leaves the reader as confused as Kovalev.

The Nose then does his own reading of Kovalev's uniform. His point is that their types of service are different, which precludes the possibility of their having any connection: "I am on my own. In addition, we cannot have any kind of close relations. Judging by the buttons on your uniform, you must be serving either in the Senate or, at least, in the Ministry of Justice [*po iustitsii*]. And I am in science/education" (3:55). The buttons of the Senate and the Ministry of Justice uniforms were indeed similar,[43] but while the story does not tell in what department Kovalev served during his time in the Caucasus, it could not have been in either the Senate or the Ministry of Justice, since both were located in Saint Petersburg. The Nose's "reading" of Kovalev's uniform is thus also off. Whereas for a modern reader Kovalev's and the Nose's mistakes are imperceptible, they must have been very clear to contemporary readers and undoubtedly added to the general sense of confusion and unreality reigning in the story.

In any case, the Nose's resplendent uniform intimidates Kovalev: "'How can I approach him?' Kovalev thought. 'Everything—his uniform, his hat—indicates that he is a state councilor. Devil knows how to do it!'" (3:55). The difference of three classes may be intimidating; however, not only is the higher-ranking bureaucrat Kovalev's own nose, but Kovalev does not seem to be a person easily intimidated by rank: he is acquainted with the widow of a state councilor and is courting her daughter. Moreover, he has arrived in Saint Petersburg in search of a position as a vice-governor, executor, or even governor (3:54, 3:56). All of these positions required a higher rank than collegiate assessor: an executor in a "good" department (such as the First Department in the Senate) could easily be a collegiate councilor (sixth class), the position of vice-governor as a rule required the rank of state councilor, and a governor was normally expected to have the rank of actual state councilor (fourth class). Kovalev's view of the value of various ranks is inconsistent: he exaggerates the importance of his own rank but is intimidated by his own nose, when he realizes that it/he outranks him.

The value of ranks in the fictional world of Gogol's Petersburg tales is thus unstable. "Nevsky Prospect" presents at least three shifting hierarchies. In "The Nose," Kovalev is not quite sure of the value of ranks, including his own: he both exaggerates and understates its importance. However, the most intriguing distortion of the value of ranks is found in Gogol's portrayals of two titular councilors, Aksenty Poprishchin in "Notes of a Madman" and, especially, Akaky Bashmachkin in "The Overcoat."

The inherent ambiguity of the rank of titular councilor is important here. First, the original meaning of the word "titular," that is, "nominal," undermined its authenticity, particularly initially, in the eighteenth century, but perhaps for even longer. Second, in Gogol's time, it was a rank that afforded a civil servant "personal" nobility, which in a way also lacked authenticity, because it could not be passed down to the bearer's children. Finally, and most importantly, Alexander's decree of 1809, "On the rules of promotion in ranks in civil service and on examinations in knowledge [*v naukakh*] for promotion to collegiate assessor and state councilor," stated: "From the time of the publication of this decree, nobody will be promoted to the rank of collegiate assessor even if [this person] has served the required number of years as a titular councilor, unless in addition to excellent recommendations from his superiors he presents a certificate from one of the imperial universities [certifying] that he has studied in it with success the disciplines that are useful for the civil service or, by undergoing an examination, earns recognition of his knowledge."[44] The decree had implications primarily for servitors who entered the service without much formal education and made their way up the service ladder by personal effort; the cultural elite was not affected by it.

Gogol's two titular councilors, Poprishchin and Bashmachkin, most probably felt the sting of the decree: there are no indications that either attended the university. It is unknown whether they attempted to pass the examination, but most probably they did not. It is likely for these reasons that they were both destined to remain "perpetual titular councilors" (3:141). But, at the same time, it is important to remember that the rank of titular councilor was of a respectable ninth class. It also bestowed personal nobility, which was probably irrelevant for Poprishchin, who repeatedly asserts in his diary that he is a hereditary nobleman, but probably significant for Bashmachkin, whose father was a titular councilor himself and thus, if not a nobleman by birth, unable to pass noble status down to his son.

Whether because of the ambiguity of his rank or for some other reason, Poprishchin's status as a servitor is presented in the story in a noticeably equivocal way. On the one hand, he is portrayed as a lowly feeble-minded clerk whose service obligations seem to consist exclusively of sharpening quills for the head of his department; apparently, he is incapable of doing anything more complicated. On the other hand, not only does he have a relatively high rank but his position in the department is quite considerable; he is a desk chief (3:209), which means that several clerks are working under him.[45] Desk chiefs were normally supposed to have the rank of court councilor, not titular councilor. It is not clear why Gogol chose a lower rank for his desk chief in "Notes." Could it be because Poprishchin serves in a department of special importance? He himself points this out in the very first entry of his diary: "True, our service is noble, everything is so clean—you won't see anything like it in a gubernial office: the desks are of mahogany, and all superiors use the formal 'you' [*na vy*]" (3:194). The description recalls the characterization of the Ministry of Foreign Affairs in "Nevsky Prospect." Perhaps the importance of the department could elevate the value of the ranks of clerks serving in it. This can explain that the young Gogol was made a deputy desk chief in the Department of Domains at the Ministry of the Imperial Court when he was in the rank of collegiate registrar (the lowest, fourteenth class).

Another possible explanation is that Poprishchin is exceptionally good in his position as desk chief, compensating for his lack of formal education with practical knowledge and experience. Many contemporaries reacted to the 1809 decree with criticism, pointing out that civil servants did not necessarily need to be versed in the disciplines taught at the universities or certified by examinations and could rely on what they had learned through performing their service duties. One such opponent of the decree was Nikolai Karamzin, who wrote in his 1811 "Note on Ancient and New Russia" ("Zapiska o drevnei i novoi Rossii"): "Until now in the most enlightened states they have required from bureaucrats only the knowledge for their office: from an engineer, [they require] the science of engineering, from a judge, a knowledge of the law, and so on. In our country [*u nas*], however, the chair of the Civil Chamber is obliged to know Homer and Theocritus; a secretary in the Senate, the properties of oxygen and all gases; a vice governor, Pythagorean figures; the supervisor in a madhouse, Roman law. Otherwise they will die collegiate or titular councilors. Neither forty years of state service nor important achievements free them from the obligation to learn things that are entirely alien and useless to us."[46] The position of desk chief obviously required service experience and a knowledge of procedures beyond the sharpening of quills and, as Gogol himself points out in his letter to M. I. Gogol, "some education" (or refinement, *vospitanie*; 10:176), especially in the "noble" type of department where Poprishchin serves. It is impossible to tell for sure whether Poprishchin was ever a good bureaucrat: when he appears on the pages of the story, his mental state has already begun to deteriorate. Already in the first entry of his diary Poprishchin writes that the head of his division is not happy with his performance: "He has been telling me for quite a while: 'Why, dear fellow, do you always have such a jumble in your head? Sometimes you dart around like a scalded cat [*kak ugorelyi*], at times you confuse a case in such a manner that Satan himself cannot untangle it'" (3:193). The syntax suggests that this is a relatively new development: "He has been telling me for quite a while" presupposes that before that Poprishchin's performance was at least adequate and perhaps superior, since he was entrusted with the position of desk chief despite his inadequate rank.

As for *vospitanie*, the narrator repeatedly indicates that Poprishchin is not terribly sophisticated; he thinks he is, believing that reading poetry (however bad) and attending the theater (where he prefers to watch vulgar vaudevilles) qualifies him as a cultured nobleman, but it does not.[47] In addition to his lack of polish, it seems that Poprishchin's age creates a problem for him as a successful servitor: he is forty-two years old and still a titular councilor. But he himself initially does not think that his age is impeding his career or, by extension, his success in love. In his diatribe against the head of his division (who, incidentally, is a court councilor, seventh class), Poprishchin declares: "So what, I also can get a higher rank [*mogu dosluzhit'sia*]. I'm still forty-two years old; that's the time when real service is just beginning. Wait, my friend! We will also become a colonel [sixth class] or, God willing, perhaps something even better" (3:198).

Obviously, at this point Poprishchin sees his rank of titular councilor as a good stepping-stone to a fulfilling career. Perhaps he still thinks he can pass the required examination: he certainly believes himself to be an exceptionally good writer. However, when confronted with failure in love, Poprishchin becomes utterly disappointed in his rank, blaming it for his inability to win Sophie's hand and, at the same time, questioning the fairness of his having such a rank: "Why am I a titular councilor and what for am I a titular councilor? [. . .] I would like to know why I am a titular councilor. Why specifically a titular councilor?" (3:206). The readers are left with the same question: what was Gogol's reason for making his character a titular councilor, a rank that seems simultaneously too high and too low for him? But before answering this question, it is useful first to consider Gogol's other titular councilor, Akaky Akakievich Bashmachkin.

If in "Notes of a Madman" the possibility exists that before his mental illness Poprishchin was worthy of the rank of titular councilor (even if not of the hand of Sophie), in "The Overcoat," the problem is that Akaky's service abilities are so obviously deficient that his having this rank is simply not plausible. The narrator calls him a "perpetual titular councilor," which could mean that, at the beginning of his service career, he, like Poprishchin, was promoted on some grounds, but then, due to his lack of education and inability to pass the required examination, his career stalled, and he remained in the same rank forever. But what could the grounds for Akaky's initial promotion have been? It is obvious that his first position was that of a scribe, a copyist, which means that his rank most likely was the lowest one, fourteenth class (compare this with Gogol's first service position as a scribe, which he held with the rank of collegiate registrar). When the reader first meets him, he is still a copyist, since, as the narrator tells us, he is unable to perform any duty except for mechanically copying documents. It looks as if Akaky's incapacity would have precluded any promotion, even for time in service.

The narrator, however, almost makes us believe that Akaky began his career in the rank of titular councilor or was even born to this rank. Calling him "a perpetual titular councilor," he says that, even as a newborn, Akaky already knew what his rank would be: "The child was baptized, and during this [rite] he cried and made a face, as if he foresaw that he would be a titular councilor" (3:142). The narrator presents having the rank of titular councilor as a misfortune, as a sign of a total failure in one's service career, which in Akaky's case is obviously wrong: for a clerk of his low abilities, it is an unprecedented and unbelievable success.

In Poprishchin's case, it is possible to surmise that, as a young man, he had enough ability to climb the ladder of ranks, reaching the rank of titular councilor and even the position of desk chief. He apparently remains a perpetual titular councilor because of his lack of education and, later, mental disease. It is much more difficult to explain Gogol's giving the lowly scribe Akaky Bashmachkin the relatively high rank of titular councilor instead of the more fitting rank of collegiate registrar. Was he simply following a literary tradition, as he himself makes the reader believe by saying that Akaky was "a perpetual titular councilor, who, as is well known, has been laughed at and joked about to their hearts' content by various writers" (3:141)? Explaining Gogol's reference to "various writers" laughing and joking about perpetual titular councilors, Viktor Vinogradov notes that this is a reference to Bulgarin's 1835 *Memoirs of Titular Councilor Chukhin, or, A Simple Story of an Ordinary Life*. Vinogradov points out that in the early draft this ironical reference obviously targeted Bulgarin alone, but in the final version Gogol generalized it, implying the existence of a sizable group of writers taunting titular councilors.[48] However, who are these writers? Even Bulgarin's Chukhin is not a "perpetual titular councilor": the memoir ends with his promotion to this rank, after which he retires to live on his estate in Livonia. However, he is thinking about returning to service in order to receive the next rank, that of collegiate assessor, and the hereditary nobility that came with it.[49] So are the "various writers" mocking titular councilors nothing but Gogol's invention, just like Rudy Panko and other narrators in the Dikanka stories and *Mirgorod*? Was Gogol actually not following the tradition of laughing at titular councilors but creating it?

If this is so, by presenting two characters in this rank who, for different reasons, cannot inspire much respect on the part of the reader, Gogol succeeded in creating a powerful image of the titular councilor as a good-for-nothing failure of a servitor. He also succeeded in bequeathing it to later generations of writers: the image kept reappearing throughout the nineteenth century. Dostoevsky solidified this image in the characters of Makar Devushkin of *Poor Folk* and Iakov Goliadkin of *The Double*, and continued to use the rank, sometimes carrying on the tradition (Marmeladov of *Crime and Punishment*) and sometimes playing with it (Fedor Karamazov of *The Brothers Karamazov*). The tradition of presenting titular councilors as perpetual failures culminated in the 1860s in a poem by P. I. Veinberg, the first stanza of which reads like an abridged "Notes of a Madman":

> Он был титулярный советник,
> Она—генеральская дочь;
> Он робко в любви объяснился,
> Она прогнала его прочь.[50]

[He was a titular councilor, / She was a general's daughter; / He timidly declared his love, / She chased him away]

A. S. Dargomyzhsky set the poem to music, assuring its popularity and its survival into the twenty-first century.[51] Thanks to the initial effort by Gogol to muddle the significance of the rank of titular councilor and the later images of lowly clerks of this rank by his successors, as well as the present lack of a clear understanding of the rank system, both Poprishchin and Bashmachkin remain paragons of catastrophic ineffectuality, and their rank has become a byword for an abortive service career. Reactions to their lack of success may vary from pity to contempt, but the idea of failure is firmly attached to their names and entrenched in our consciousness. The portrait of a titular councilor created by Gogol is thus a simulacrum that has successfully replaced what historical sources suggest about this rank.

The Inspector General is another example of Gogol's clever distortion of the factual picture. Significantly, a lack of stability in the value of ranks is the most pronounced feature of this comedy. In his imagination, the protagonist Ivan Khlestakov effortlessly rises from his position of scribe ("You, perhaps, think that I only copy," 4:48) with a likely corresponding rank of collegiate registrar, first to the rank of collegiate assessor (4:48), then to the position of director of a department (with the corresponding rank of general), and, finally, almost to the rank of field marshal (first class). Frightened by this idea, Khlestakov cannot even finish saying "field marshal": "Tomorrow I will be made a field marsh . . ." (4:50). It is particularly important, however, that the bureaucrats of the provincial town Khlestakov visits also lose their sense of the proper hierarchy of ranks and help him create the confusion. The mayor of the town in particular is infected by Khlestakov's fantasies: it is he who by the end of the play actually believes that he can leave behind his relatively low rank of collegiate assessor (to which his service position normally corresponded) and become a general.

It is crucial that in *After the Performance (Teatral'nyi raz"ezd*, 1836)— in which Gogol reacts to the failure of the comedy's first staging— the spectators of the play, discussing it as they leave the theater, focus on the question of whether the representation of bureaucrats is plausible or not. Spectators who are bureaucrats are particularly concerned with this question, and their opinions vary. The following dialogue is characteristic:

> *Voice of a gentleman of positive quality* [*pooshchritel'nogo svoistva*]: "He must be a rogue [*bestiia*], a rascal of an author, [he] has learned everything, knows everything."
>
> *Voice of an angry bureaucrat, who, however, is obviously experienced*: "What does he know? The hell he knows. And he lies, lies: everything he has written, everything is a lie [*vraki*]. And bribes are taken in a totally different way, for that matter. . . ."
>
> *Voice of another bureaucrat from the crowd*: "Well, you say: it's funny, it's funny! Do you know why it's funny? Because they [the characters] all are [real] personalities [*lichnosti*]. Everybody he has represented is his own grandma or auntie. That's why this is funny!" (5:163)

It seems that by introducing conflicting opinions about the play, Gogol invites the reader to consider the veracity of his representation of the world of bureaucracy and perhaps to doubt it. The invitation is certainly seductive, particularly given the phantasmagorical way Gogol portrays his bureaucrats: the accuracy of his portrayal is illusory, but somehow it has the potential to replace reality.

As Gogol's correspondence demonstrates, his attitude toward state service was ambiguous from beginning to end: at times he presented it as the highest of callings, as the noble way to serve the state and even humankind, whereas on other occasions he presented it as a senseless and torturous waste of time. Something similar can be seen in Gogol's fiction. His presentation of the world of state service is rarely accurate. The value of ranks fluctuates whimsically, and the hierarchy of ranks is usually distorted. One may argue that Gogol's incoherent portrayal of the world of service reflected the fact that there was more than one hierarchy that affected the status of a servitor in Russia: different types of service had different reputations; the level of a servitor's education affected his standing, as did his position within the noble estate and the prestige, economic status, and connections of his family. But the Table of Ranks still mattered, and the value of one's rank was keenly felt (as Gogol himself mockingly acknowledges in the passage on ranks in *Dead Souls*). The rules for promotion still existed and were well known both to Gogol and his readers. Although today's readers may have trouble perceiving the incongruities in his portrayals of the world of service, his contemporaries likely did not.

And yet, for all the discrepancies and distortions in Gogol's representation of the world of Russian state service, it is strangely convincing. Gogol's discursive strategies discourage readers from questioning what he presents as its reality. Gogol's copy of reality has become, to use Jean Baudrillard's term, *hyperreal*, actually preventing the reader from distinguishing what is incorrect or deceptive in the picture. To a large degree, the way people now think of the world of state service is determined by Gogol's portrayal of it in his fiction. Furthermore, even knowing its inaccuracy does not prevent us from thoroughly enjoying it.

4

Poets in the Military

Denis Davydov, Aleksandr Polezhaev, and Mikhail Lermontov

Many Russian writers of noble status began their service in the military (Sumarokov, Derzhavin, Murav'ev, Karamzin, Dmitriev, to name just a few), but a relatively small number of them stayed in the military for the duration of their time in service. They left for various reasons, but one of the most powerful incentives was the desire to rise in rank: transferring to the civil service allowed one to gain at least one class in the Table of Ranks (two if the transfer was from one of the guards regiments). The more comfortable and less regulated life of a civil servant was certainly also appealing for many. The reasons some nobles stayed in the military differed as well: for some the military service was their true calling, whereas others were compelled to stay by circumstances or even forced to join the military as a punishment. The three poets, Denis Davydov, Aleksandr Polezhaev, and Mikhail Lermontov, whose cases are discussed in this chapter, present all three of these situations. The chapter ascertains whether military service affected the poets' self-perception differently than did civil service. It also examines the military theme in their poetry.

Denis Davydov (1784–1839) was the most enthusiastic and successful soldier of the three: he participated in eight wars, including the 1806–7 campaign against Napoleon, in which Napoleon defeated the so-called Fourth Coalition; the Russo-Swedish War of 1808–9; and the 1812 Patriotic War, during which Davydov came up with a plan to organize guerrillas, performing raids on the French Army rear areas. Davydov described his experience in the *Essay on a Theory of Guerilla Warfare* (*Opyt teorii partizanskogo deistviia*, 1821) and the *Diary of Guerilla Operations of 1812* (*Dnevnik partizanskikh deistvii 1812 goda*, 1814–38). He also wrote several other pieces on military history, but most importantly he was a well-known and strikingly original poet. On friendly terms with many prominent poets of his time, he left his distinct mark on early nineteenth-century poetry, including Pushkin's. Most significantly, Davydov's careers as a poet and a soldier were closely intertwined.

Davydov's military career, although quite successful (he rose to the rank of lieutenant-general, third class), was never entirely smooth. His family, a respectable one with a strong tradition of military service, was persecuted during the reign of Paul, and therefore Davydov was at first unable to enlist in the prestigious Cavalier Guards Regiment. In September 1801, after Paul was assassinated, Davydov did enter the regiment, though initially his small stature posed an obstacle (cavalier guards were supposed to be over six feet, whereas Davydov reportedly was barely over five). Still, he eventually enlisted and began service in the rank of *estandart-iunker*, which was just below the first officer's rank of cornet (at the time, twelfth class in the cavalier guards), to which he was promoted in September 1802. He was promoted again, in November 1803, to the rank of lieutenant (ninth class in the cavalier guards).

At that time, Davydov already wrote poetry. According to his 1828 autobiography, his first attempts at writing date to his adolescence, when he read some of his friends' poems published in Karamzin's almanac *Aonids* and decided to follow suit.[1] He acknowledges that his first experiments were weak and derivative. Nonetheless, Davydov persevered, and eventually made a name for himself. His three politically charged satirical fables earned him both renown as a poet and an unfavorable reputation with Alexander I that negatively influenced his military career.

In September 1804 Davydov was transferred to the Belorussian Hussar Regiment in the rank of captain of horse (*rotmistr*, ninth class). A transfer from a prestigious guards regiment stationed in the capital to a regular provincial cavalry regiment was normally used as punishment. The manner in which Davydov described the transfer in his 1828 autobiography (written in the third person) implies that it was not a positive development, even though he attempts to make light of it: "In 1804 the fate that governs people, or the people who direct her blows, forced our prankster [*povesa*] to transfer to the Belorussian Hussar Regiment, which was then stationed in Kiev guberniya, near Zvenigorodka. The

young captain of horse [*rotmistr*] twiddled his moustache, tilted his
shako toward one ear, *drew himself up tight, tautened himself* [*zatianulsia,
natianulsia*—both words are in italics in the original, implying that they
are terms], and began to dance the mazurka till he dropped [*i pustilsia
pliasat' mazurku do upadu*]."[2] Davydov does not explain the reason for
his transfer, but it was apparently caused by three satirical fables, written
in 1803 and 1804, that could be read as critical of the government and
the tsar himself. In the first of them, "The Head and the Feet" ("Golova
i nogi"), the criticism is general and does not necessarily describe a
specifically Russian situation. In this poem, the feet warn the head that
they "have the right to trip / And can at some time, having tripped,—
how can we avoid this?— / Smash Your Majesty against a rock."[3] In
another fable, "A True Story, or a Fable, Call It What You Will" ("Byl' ili
basnia, kak kto khochet nazovi"; also known as "The River and the
Mirror," "Reka i zerkalo"), Siberia is mentioned as a place of political
exile, which, of course, directly points to Russia. In this poem, a despot
is about to execute a nobleman for his honest criticism of his policies.
The nobleman explains to the despot, however, that, having broken the
mirror that truthfully shows his image, the despot will still see his ugly
reflection in every river but will not be able to destroy all of them. The
despot takes the nobleman's point and commutes his death sentence to
Siberian exile. The fable ends with a caustic quatrain that plays on the
two meanings of the word "fable" (*basnia*):

Монарха речь сия так сильно убедила,
Что он велел ему и жизнь и волю дать . . .
Постойте, виноват!—велел в Сибирь сослать,
А то бы эта быль на басню походила.[4]

[The monarch was so convinced by these words that he ordered
to give him back both his life and his freedom. . . . Wait, I'm
sorry! He ordered him exiled to Siberia—otherwise this truthful
tale would resemble a fable/falsehood.]

These two poems were offensive enough to warrant Davydov's transfer,
but the 1804 piece "The She-Eagle, the Ruff, and the Grouse" ("Orlitsa,
turukhtan i teterev")—which very transparently refers to Catherine the
Great, Paul, and Alexander I, respectively—was even more provocative.[5]
It praises Catherine the she-eagle; portrays Paul the ruff as a cruel
despot, explicitly describing his assassination by his displeased subjects;

and concludes with a very unflattering portrayal of Alexander the grouse.[6] Not only was it very well known how touchy Alexander was about any references to his father's murder, to which he tacitly consented, but Davydov's depiction of him as a deaf, stingy, and foolish bird was personally offensive: Alexander was hard of hearing and had a reputation for miserliness.

While in the Belorussian Hussar Regiment, Davydov continued to write poetry. It was during his stint there that he created the poetic image of himself as a rowdy and unruly hussar, a lover of battle, drink, pranks, and women. This is the very image to which Davydov refers in his autobiography when he describes his nonchalant behavior after the transfer from Saint Petersburg. The poems, such as "To Burtsov: Invitation to Punch" ("Burtsovu: Prizyvanie na punsh"), "To Burtsov" ("Burtsovu"), and "Hussar Feast" ("Gusarskii pir"; all written in 1804), develop this image, presenting the lyrical hero as a friend and counterpart of the notorious reveler and prankster Aleksei Burtsov (1783?–1813), at the time a lieutenant in the Belorussian Hussar Regiment. Written in a light trochaic tetrameter, the poems celebrate drinking, merrymaking, sexual adventures, and war. Burtsov is portrayed as the paragon of such behavior:

> Бурцов, ты—гусар гусаров!
> Ты—на ухарском коне—
> Жесточайший из угаров
> И наездник на войне!

[Burtsov, you are a hussar's hussar! You, on your dashing horse, are the fiercest of brawlers and the [fiercest] horseman in war!]

The lyric persona's behavior matches that of Burtsov; he also drinks and chases girls, and, most importantly, is always ready to battle:

> Саблю вон—и в сечу! Вот
> Пир иной нам бог дает,
> Пир задорней, удалее,
> И шумней, и веселее. . . .
> Нутка, кивер набекрень,
> И—ура! Счастливый день![7]

[Draw your saber and [go] into the battle! Now God gives us a different feast, a feast that is more spirited, more vigorous, and

noisier, and merrier. . . . Now, cock your shako, and—hurray!
This is a lucky day!]

Later in Davydov's life, particularly after the war with Napoleon, this uncomplicated and somewhat coarse image underwent subtle but important changes: the rowdy reveler acquired wit, sarcasm, and intelligence; he also became a regular member of friendly poetic circles and a lover not only of drunken get-togethers but also of intellectual feasts.[8] This change could be seen in both Davydov's poetry and his public behavior, and Davydov's friends, Vasily Zhukovsky and Petr Viazemsky among them, not only acknowledged and welcomed it but began to include and develop this new image in their own poetry: "The poems addressed to [Davydov] form some kind of anthology, and in this anthology the formula that is familiar to us, 'a poet and a guerrilla warrior,' is bestowed on him. [. . .] The poetic theme of a friendly feast is also firmly attached to this poetic portrait."[9] How radical this change was, however, is open to debate. True, Davydov's 1815 "Song" ("Pesnia"), alongside its profession of love for "the sword, vodka, [and] the hussar horse," expresses not just readiness for battle but also patriotic sentiments:

> За тебя на черта рад,
> Наша матушка Россия!
> Пусть французишки гнилые
> К нам пожалуют назад!
>   За тебя на черта рад,
>   Наша матушка Россия![10]

> [For you I will gladly go against the devil himself, / Our mother Russia! / Let the rotten little French / Come back! / For you I will gladly go against the devil himself, / Our mother Russia!]

Another 1815 poem, addressed to the notorious carouser, gambler, and duelist Fedor Tolstoy, though it calls for drinking, gambling, and lovemaking, also invites to the feast (along with the three Graces) "the counsel of solemn Muses."[11] At the same time, the poem concludes with the familiar invitation to drink and chase girls:

> Так время пробежит
> Меж радостей небесных,—
> А чтоб хмельнее быть,

Давай здоровье пить
Всех ветрениц известных![12]

[So the time will fly / amidst heavenly pleasures,— / And to
be even drunker / let us drink to the health / of all notorious
flirts!]

Obviously, Davydov did not completely abandon the poetic image of
a carousing hussar, and it was so convincing and long-lasting that
many years later, in the reign of Nicholas, General A. P. Ermolov,
commander-in-chief of Russian troops in the Caucasus War of 1816–27,
reportedly had to explain to the new emperor that the real Davydov
was not in fact a drunkard and philanderer. Furthermore, this reputation
is still firmly attached to Davydov's name, overshadowing his reputation as both an experienced and talented military commander and a
military historian. Most importantly, his so-called hussar poems eclipse
his other poetry, making us forget that Davydov was not a poet of one
theme or one genre: he wrote on various topics and in various genres,
including Anacreontic odes, elegies, and love poetry. Furthermore, he
was an innovator and experimenter in all these genres.[13] Pushkin, for
one, valued his novel use of poetic language and acknowledged the
influence of Davydov's poetry on his own. In an 1829 conversation with
M. V. Iuzefovich, he credited Davydov with teaching him early in his
literary career how not to be an imitator: as Iuzefovich reports, Davydov
"allowed him to sense while he was still in the Lyceum that it was
possible to be original."[14]

Davydov's military career was not irreparably damaged by his
fables, and he did not stay long in the Belorussian Hussar Regiment:
thanks to the help of his influential friend Boris Chetvertinsky, in 1806
he was transferred back to Saint Petersburg to serve in a guards hussar
regiment in the rank of lieutenant. Still, Alexander I never forgot or
forgave Davydov's satirical attacks. Whenever he could slow down the
brazen poet's career or fail to reward his impressive service, he did.
However, Mariia Naryshkina, the sister of Boris Chetvertinsky and
Alexander's mistress, was occasionally able to intercede on his behalf.[15]
In January 1807, for example, she arranged Davydov's appointment as
aide-de-camp to Lieutenant-General Petr Bagration, which took him to
East Prussia, where Bagration was commander of Russian rear-guard
forces in the war against Napoleon. While in East Prussia, Davydov
took part in the Battle of Eylau, one of the most brutal battles of the

Napoleonic wars. For the Prussian campaign he received two prestigious awards and was also promoted to the rank of staff captain of horse (*shtabs-rotmistr*, eighth class). In contrast, Davydov's outstanding service during the 1808–9 campaign against Sweden was not rewarded at all, despite Bagration's repeated recommendations. However, for his active participation in campaigns against Turkey in 1809 and 1810, Davydov was awarded the order of Saint Anna and the rank of captain of horse (*rotmistr*, seventh class).

In addition to Alexander's dislike of Davydov and the poet's persistent reputation as a carousing hussar, his independent character also interfered with his military career. It is telling that Davydov went into semi-retirement several times during the course of his career (in 1811, in 1823, in 1827, and in again in 1831, after enthusiastically participating in the suppression of the Polish uprising). Furthermore, Davydov was prone to overstepping his authority, particularly when he believed that a military situation called for action even if it was not sanctioned by his superiors. Commanders who esteemed his talents as an officer and appreciated his initiative tended to forgive Davydov his willfulness. Others were not as lenient. The most serious violation of military discipline occurred in 1813, when Davydov took Dresden on his own initiative. His commander was not amused and removed him from command. Davydov was supposed to be court-martialed, and only Kutuzov's intercession saved him. His command, however, was not returned to him. All this helps explain why his ranks and decorations did not come to him easily. Nonetheless, in October 1831, after the Polish campaign, he was promoted to the rank of general-lieutenant, "for distinguishing himself in combat."[16]

Davydov was on an extended leave between November 1826 and the Polish campaign, after which he never returned to active duty. Nonetheless, during his time on leave and in retirement, he continued to produce the occasional poem that perpetuated his image as a carousing hussar, drunkard, and philanderer. On one such poem, "To the Hero of Battles, Bivouacs, Taverns, and Whores" ("Geroiu bitv, bivakov, traktirov i bliadei"; 1830 or 1831), Davydov collaborated with Pushkin, who wrote a version of its third stanza.[17] In 1832 Davydov composed "A Hussar's Confession" ("Gusarskaia ispoved'"), which opens with lines that reconfirm his image as a hussar:

Я каюсь! я гусар давно, всегда гусар,
И с проседью усов, все раб младой привычки:

Люблю разгульный шум, умов, речей пожар
И громогласные шампанского отмычки.

[I confess! I have been a hussar since long ago, always a hussar, /
and, even with a streak of gray in my mustache, I am still a slave
of my young habit: / I love the noise of revelry, the fire of minds
and speeches, / and the thunderous uncorking of champagne.]

Davydov concludes the poem with a statement that, regardless of his
occasional attendance at high-society gatherings, he always returns to
his "hussar family."[18]

   At times, however, Davydov attempts to present himself in a somewhat different light: not as a hussar whose entire life is, as he put it in
"A Hussar's Confession," "willful play" (*udaloe razdol'e*), not even as a
poet, but as a guerilla warrior, defender of Russia, as he did in his 1826
poem "Response" ("Otvet"):

Я не поэт, я—партизан, казак.
Я иногда бывал на Пинде, но наскоком,
И беззаботно, кое-как,
Раскидывал перед Кастальским током
Мой независимый бивак.
Нет, не наезднику пристало
Петь, в креслах развалясь, лень, негу и покой. . . .
Пусть грянет Русь военною грозой—
Я в этой песни запевало![19]

[I am not a poet, I am a guerilla warrior, a Cossack. / I was on
Pindus now and then, but only on the fly; / I would pitch my
independent bivouac / by the Castalian stream only carelessly,
helter-skelter. No! It does not become a rider / to laud laziness,
luxury, and quietude, sprawling in an armchair. . . . / Let Russia
thunder with the storm of war—I am a choir leader in this song.]

The poet portrays himself as an ascetic warrior, not a merry-making
hussar. It is noteworthy that during the Patriotic War Davydov wrote
very few poems—only two in all of 1812. Remarkably, there is nothing
in his poetry of that time that reflects his guerilla experience; apparently,
he considered it a topic for serious treatment in prose. It is somewhat
unexpected therefore that in present-day cultural memory Davydov

exists not only as "the hussar poet" (*poet-gusar*) but also as "the guerilla poet" (*poet-partizan*). It seems that both the memory of his actual military career (particularly his participation in the Patriotic War) and the image Davydov created for himself as a poet who acted like a hussar both in and out of service survive in the Russian cultural imagination.

The next case is Aleksandr Polezhaev (1804–38). His service in the military was not chosen freely: Nicholas I imposed it on him as a punishment for his narrative poem *Sashka* (1825). Furthermore, his service was not even marginally successful and took several disastrous turns that contributed to his untimely death. In addition, Polezhaev's social status was marginal and ambiguous, his personality unstable, and his behavior often erratic, which likely brought on at least some of his many misfortunes. This mixture of social marginality, bad luck, questionable behavior, and Nicholas's enmity may lie behind the many inconsistencies found in accounts of Polezhaev's life. Both the events and their causes are often presented differently, and the presentation to a large extent depends on the biographer's attitude toward the imperial regime: the more hostile to it the author of a particular biographical account is, the more tragic circumstances are reported, and the less Polezhaev's own responsibility is emphasized. One interpretation originated with Polezhaev himself and was written down and made public by Alexander Herzen in his *Past and Thoughts* (*Byloe i dumy*, 1868). Herzen, who associated with Polezhaev in Moscow in 1833–34 and heard his life story from the poet himself, is known for his virulent hatred of Nicholas. His version presents Polezhaev as a victim of Nicholas's unjustifiable cruelty.[20] Other accounts—such as Polezhaev's biography in the *Russian Biographical Dictionary* (*Russkii biograficheskii slovar'*, 1896-1918)— present Nicholas's response to Polezhaev's transgressions as relatively mild and explain what happened to the poet at least partly by his own erratic behavior.

Polezhaev was a natural son of the landowner L. N. Struisky and his serf Agrafena (Stepanida in some accounts) Ivanova (or Fedorova), which circumstance determined his ambiguous social status from birth. Being the illegitimate child of a nobleman and a serf was not a rarity at the time, and illegitimate children often integrated into the social structure one way or another. Some remained serfs, others were legitimized by their fathers, still others were given a legal name and status through their mothers' marriages, actual or fake. Vasily Zhukovsky's life and successful career both as a poet and a courtier illustrates the situation well, and Polezhaev's life could have followed a similar path. Like Zhukovsky's mother, Polezhaev's mother Agrafena, manumitted by Struisky, was also married off to a man who gave her son a last name and legitimacy. The important difference, however, lay in the fact that Zhukovsky's legal father was a nobleman, whereas Polezhaev's was a merchant, which determined his adopted son's social status. Moreover, Polezhaev's stepfather disappeared several years after the marriage, and his mother returned to her former lover's estate to live with her sister's family. She died in 1810, and for the next six years Polezhaev lived with his aunt, who tended the cattle on the Struisky estate, and her husband, who was a lackey. This person was Polezhaev's first tutor, teaching him to read Russian and speak some French.

Even though biographers assert that Struisky loved his natural son, he did not legitimize him even after his stepfather's disappearance and his mother's death, and it is not clear whether he ever tried. Nonetheless, in 1816, Struisky enrolled the boy in a private boarding school in Moscow, where he spent the next four years. In 1820 Polezhaev entered Moscow University as an auditor (*vol'noslushatel'*), a student who could attend lectures and take examinations but was not formally considered a student; like all non-nobles, Polezhaev had access to a university education only in this manner. Meanwhile, Struisky murdered one of his serfs, was stripped of his rank and noble status, and was exiled to Siberia, where he died in 1825. One of Struisky's brothers then supported Polezhaev throughout his studies at the university. Polezhaev studied reluctantly and haphazardly, taking six years to graduate, rather than the usual three. Nonetheless, he eventually passed the required examinations and graduated with the degree of a so-called *deistvitel'nyi student* (actual student), which accorded him personal nobility and the right to enter service with the rank of gubernial secretary (twelfth class). It would seem that Polezhaev had finally received an opportunity to join the noble estate that was his by birth and to acquire a stable social position. However, this did not happen.

Right before Polezhaev's graduation from the university his life changed again, this time forever: through the Third Section, Nicholas I received Polezhaev's erotically and (somewhat) politically charged long poem *Sashka*. Written in the genre of mock-epic, it parodied the first chapter of Pushkin's *Eugene Onegin*, portraying not the orderly and estheticized lifestyle of a Saint Petersburg dandy but the haphazard, vulgar, and debauched behavior of a Moscow University student. Peppered with obscenities, *Sashka* described its main character's frequent drunken parties, repeated visits to whorehouses, and other unseemly behavior. The title, a nickname for Aleksandr, emphasized the autobiographical nature of the poem; the protagonist also shared the author's last name and features of his biography. Overall, the poem was a typical literary prank, or *shalost'*, widely practiced in early nineteenth-century Russia by many poets, including Pushkin.[21]

Nicholas, however, took the poem for an accurate description of actual Moscow University students' behavior and was appalled. Still shaken by the Decembrist Uprising, he decided to make an example of Polezhaev. Polezhaev was summoned to the Kremlin, where Nicholas, A. S. Shishkov (the minister of education at the time), and A. A. Pisarev (the trustee of the Moscow school district; some biographers list other names) awaited him with a beautifully copied *Sashka*. Polezhaev was ordered to read the poem aloud (or, as V. S. Kiselev-Sergenin, the author of the introduction to the 1987 collection of Polezhaev's poetry, suggests, its most egregious passages[22]), which, after an initial hesitation, he did. There is, of course, no way to know for sure how exactly the meeting unfolded, but in the end, according to Polezhaev's 1833 report to Herzen, Nicholas suggested that Polezhaev enter military service as a non-commissioned officer (*unter-ofitser*). According to Herzen, the tsar consulted the minister of education (Herzen mistakenly calls him Liven) about Polezhaev's behavior, and, having received a positive evaluation, asked Polezhaev: "'Do you want to enter the military service?' Polezhaev was silent. 'I give you a chance to rehabilitate yourself by means of military service. So, do you want to?' 'I must obey,' Polezhaev responded. The tsar came up to him, put his hand on his shoulder, and, saying 'Your fate depends on you. If I forget, you can write to me,' kissed him on the forehead."[23] Herzen presents the kiss as the sign of Nicholas's ultimate hypocrisy, almost a Judas kiss. He also claims that Nicholas's promise to help Polezhaev rehabilitate himself was fraudulent, and that he ostensibly disregarded three of Polezhaev's letters to him, which led to Polezhaev's ill-fated attempt to reach the tsar personally. In contrast, A. F. Vitberg, the author of Polezhaev's biography in the *Russian Biographical Dictionary*, argues that Nicholas actually did provide Polezhaev with a chance to rehabilitate himself, because he did not force the poet to enter the military as an enlisted man but appointed him as a non-commissioned officer, "obviously with the purpose of giving him an opportunity to receive an officer's rank as soon as possible, for which purpose his right to both the rank of twelfth class and personal nobility was preserved."[24]

Polezhaev served in the assigned regiment for about a year and then attempted to flee—or, according to his version, to go directly to Nicholas for help; he was caught—or returned to his regiment voluntarily, having realized the wrongfulness of his action. In any case, he was arrested, court-martialed, stripped of his rank and personal nobility (which made him potentially subject to corporal punishment), and forced to continue serving as an enlisted man without the right to promotion (*bez vyslugi*). Some biographers assert that it was Nicholas himself who added the clause *bez vyslugi*, thus taking away Polezhaev's right to promotion. This was, undoubtedly, a very harsh punishment.

Desperate, Polezhaev took to drink. In May 1828 he was late returning to his barracks, and when his sergeant reprimanded him, he responded with obscenities. He was arrested for insubordination and imprisoned. After many months in confinement (where, as his biographers believe, he most probably acquired his tuberculosis), Polezhaev was sentenced to run the gauntlet, but his sentence was commuted to time served because of his youth (he was still twenty-four years old) and long incarceration. Polezhaev was transferred to a different regiment, which was soon dispatched to the Caucasus. The regiment reached Groznaia Fortress (today's Groznyi) in May 1830. Polezhaev spent almost three years in the Caucasus, taking part in many dangerous military operations against the mountain people, who refused to submit to Russian imperial rule.[25] In 1831 he was promoted to the rank of non-commissioned officer and his noble status was restored. In 1832 he was recommended for promotion to the first officer's rank, that of warrant officer (*praporshchik*, fourteenth class), but the tsar rejected the recommendation.

In January 1833 Polezhaev's regiment left the Caucasus for Moscow, which it reached in the summer of the same year. Soon after that Polezhaev was transferred to a different regiment, where he served in the same rank almost until his death. An unfortunate love affair added to his misery. He drank more and more. Overstaying his leave during one of his drinking bouts, he was found and returned to his regiment. Many biographers claim that he was physically punished for this transgression, and the punishment ostensibly hastened his death from tuberculosis. Chronology contradicts this view: Polezhaev's disappearance dates from the summer of 1834, and his death, from January 1838. Other biographical accounts cite an alternative disciplinary transgression in 1837 as a reason for Polezhaev's having been physically punished: ostensibly he left the regiment without permission and drank away his uniform, for which he was flogged, despite his noble status.[26] The cruel punishment allegedly hastened his death. The fact that shortly before Polezhaev died he was finally promoted to the officer's rank of warrant officer (fourteenth class) makes the account of the flogging doubtful.

Polezhaev began writing poetry in his youth, and his first publications predate the catastrophic developments precipitated by Nicholas's discovery of *Sashka*: two of Polezhaev's early works were published in December 1825 in *Messenger of Europe* and another one in Mikhail Pogodin's almanac *Urania* (1826). In January 1826 Polezhaev recited, at a university ceremony, an ode that had been commissioned by the authorities at Moscow University. In February 1826 he was admitted to the Society of Lovers of Russian Literature affiliated with Moscow University. On July 3, 1826, his ode "Genius" ("Genii") was read at the university graduation ceremony. All this demonstrates that Polezhaev was an acknowledged rising poet.

Polezhaev's subsequent tragic and erratic life did not prevent him from continuing to write poetry. While Vissarion Belinsky argued that Polezhaev's "wild unbridled passions" ruined his talent, other critics suggested that misfortunes were in fact conducive to the full development of his Romantic idiom. As the nineteenth-century writer and critic Aleksandr Druzhinin suggested, "The crash of his private life not only didn't bring with it the crash of his significance as a poet, but rather [. . .] developed in [Polezhaev] certain poetic aspects that would not have manifested themselves without it."[27]

While the range of topics in Polezhaev's poetry is broad and diverse, the chapter will focus on works that address his being both a soldier and a poet or describe his participation in military operations. The first poem in which Polezhaev directly mentions his status as an enlisted man is an untitled 1828 poem written soon after his arrest and incarceration for the drunken confrontation with his sergeant:

Притеснил мою свободу
Кривоногий штабс-солдат:
В угождение уроду
Я отправлен в каземат.[28]

[A bowlegged staff-soldier has oppressed my freedom: to satisfy the degenerate I have been sent to the dungeon.]

While Polezhaev's superior is called "degenerate," he refers to himself as a "free singer" (*vol'nyi pevets*) and believes (mistakenly, as it turned out) that his incarceration will be short, whereas the sergeant will retain his low status forever: "Ia—pod spudom na minutu, / On—v bolote navsegda" (I am oppressed for a minute, but he is in the mire forever).[29] It is significant that in this poem, apparently written early in his incarceration, Polezhaev stresses his identity as a poet, not as a military man. Furthermore, his pride in his status as a poet allows him to disregard the catastrophic changes that have already happened to him: his having been stripped forever of his personal nobility and rank as a non-commissioned officer, changes that all but ruined his chances for a decent career befitting his education and talent.

The next poem, traditionally titled "Prisoner" ("Uznik") and written later in 1828, is not optimistic like the first one but profoundly bitter. The poem repeatedly stresses that the lyric persona (whom the reader identifies as Polezhaev himself) is not free: "I am again a prisoner and a soldier!"[30] Perhaps he is not even a poet anymore, since his poetic gift is negatively affected by this loss of freedom:

> Увы! Старинный жар стихов
> И след сатир и острых слов
> Исчезли в буйной голове,
> Как след дриады на траве.
> [. . . .]
> Поэт пленительных страстей
> Сидит живой в когтях чертей,
> Атласных <. . .> не поет
> И чуть по-волчьи не ревет.[31]

> [Alas! The olden fervor of verses and the traces of satirical and witty words have disappeared from my rebellious head, like a dryad's footprint on the grass. [. . .] The poet of captivating passions now endures the clutches of devils, he doesn't sing of satiny <. . .> and all but howls like a wolf.]

Polezhaev's lyric persona has lost his freedom not only because he is incarcerated but also because he is a soldier against his will: he is a "recruited/enlisted poet" (*verbovannyi poet*). Under the influence of the monotonous life in captivity he has lost his soul and mind (*dusha i um ubity v nem*) and he is now "a wandering automaton" and "unfeeling

soldier."[32] This poem is the most tragic portrayal of what forced enroll-
ment in the military and subsequent imprisonment did to Polezhaev as
a poet and a human being. It concludes with a disturbing description of
the lyric persona's death:

И нет ни камня, ни к<реста>,
Ни огородного шеста
Над гробом узника тюрьмы—
Жильца ничтожества и тьмы.[33]

[And there is neither a stone, nor a cross, nor a garden stake
over the tomb of the prisoner, dweller in nothingness and
darkness.]

"Prisoner" is also the most personal of all the poems in which Polezhaev
laments his fate. Other poems in which he complains of his misfortunes
or alludes to his despondency (such as "The Song of a Perishing Sea-
farer" ["Pesn' pogibaiushchego plovtsa"], "Exacerbated" ["Ozhesto-
chennyi"], "Condemned" ["Osuzhdennyi"], "Living Corpse" ["Zhivoi
mertvets"], and "Providence" ["Providenie"]—all 1828), although by
all means tragic, are far less concrete, referring to what was happening
to Polezhaev (or his lyric persona) in general terms, without ever mentioning his calling as a poet or his status as a soldier.

Polezhaev's transfer to the Caucasus changed the way he presented
himself as a soldier: instead of being a lonely stranger to his surroundings, his narrator is now a member of a victorious army bringing peace
and civilization to unreasonable and often vicious savages. (It is important to note that Polezhaev was a man of his time, and in this he was no
different from his contemporaries, including Pushkin and Lermontov.)
Imperial symbols—described with enmity in the poetry of 1828—now
receive positive treatment. He writes in the 1832 poem "Song of the
Mountain Army" ("Pesn' gorskogo opolcheniia"):

Зашумел орел двуглавый
Над враждебною рекой,
Прояснился путь кровавый
Перед дружною толпой.[34]

[The double-headed eagle roared over the hostile river, and the
bloody path cleared before the united multitude.]

The narrator here is part of the "united multitude" (*druzhnaia tolpa*)—
the Russian army advancing into the Caucasus. The rest of the poem
lauds its decisive victory over the resistant Muslim insurgents.

Polezhaev devoted two long narrative poems to the Russian army's
expeditions into the insurgents' territory, *Erpeli* (1830) and *Chir-Iurt*
(1831–32; both poems were published together in 1832, as a diptych).
The first poem describes the army's march, in late May 1830, from
Groznaia Fortress to Ghimry, the headquarters of the leader of the insurgents, the First Imam of Dagestan, Qazi Muhammad, usually called
Qazi Mulla by the Russians. The expedition's mandate was to capture
Qazi Muhammad, but the Russian commander, General-Lieutenant
R. F. Rosen, satisfied by the peace agreement offered by the insurgents,
retreated without fulfilling this task. The expedition thus turned out to
be pointless, but Polezhaev presents it as victorious and bringing lasting
peace to the region. Hostilities resumed soon after, however, and Qazi
Muhammad was eventually killed by the Russians, in October 1832.
This was also the last action in the Caucasus in which Polezhaev took
part.

Erpeli depicts in great detail the life of the soldiers during the march
toward Erpeli and their encounters with the mountain people. Its tone is
mostly informal, often chatty. However, several things are particularly
noteworthy. First is the patriotic, imperial streak visible in many parts
of the poem. For example, comfortable in their life in the camp near
Groznaia Fortress, the soldiers are initially reluctant to get ready for
the march. They first listen to Sloth (*Len'*), which tries to convince them
that their marching orders are unfair. However, Sloth is silenced by
Honor:

> «Молчать, негодная разиня!»—
> В ответ презрительно ей Честь.—
> Я—сердца русского богиня.[35]

> ["Be silent, useless oaf!" scornfully responded Honor. "I am the
> goddess of the Russian heart."]

Honor's interference transforms the soldiers, and they remain ready
to die for the Russian Empire all the way to the end of the poem. Their
enthusiasm is comparable to what Russians felt during the 1812 Patriotic
War,

Когда, готовя смерть и гром,
Они под русскими орлами
Шли защищать Романов дом.[36]

[When, preparing death and thunder [for the enemy], they
marched under the Russian eagles to defend the House of the
Romanovs.]

These sentiments are in sharp contrast to the angry epithets Polezhaev
used to describe Nicholas in "Prisoner":

Вторый Н<ерон>, Ис<кариот>,
У<дав> б<разильский> и Н<емврод>
Его [Polezhaev] враждой своей почтил
И, лобызая, удушил![37]

[This second Nero, Iscariot, Brazilian python, and Nimrod has
honored him with his enmity and stifled him with a kiss.]

It is significant that the narrator of *Erpeli* fully shares in the patriotic
feelings of his comrades.

The self-presentation of the narrator in this poem is another significant factor. In seven of the eight chapters of *Erpeli* the narrator is a
soldier, an eyewitness, and a chronicler but not a poet, even though
he obviously shares many biographical features with Polezhaev—
especially, in chapter 2 (in which the narrator presents the Caucasus
and its exotic nature to an imaginary friend who has just arrived from
Moscow, the narrator's former place of residence). The narrator even
concludes chapter 7 with a declaration that he is not a poet anymore:
"No vse ravno—ia ne poet, / A lish' ego karikatura" (But all the same, I
am not a poet, but just a caricature of one).[38]

The concluding eighth chapter begins with the narrator's jocular
conversation with his readers or listeners, who urge him to continue his
chatty account of the expedition, and the narrator obliges. Only toward
the end of the chapter is his identity as a poet revealed: the narrator
calls himself a mad poet (*poet sumasshedshii*) and an admirer of the
muses (*poklonnik muz*), and ponders how he will be remembered after
his death. Significantly, he believes that he will be remembered not as a
soldier, nor as the debaucher portrayed in *Sashka*, but as a poet:

Что ж будет памятью поэта?
Мундир?.. Не может быть!.. Грехи?..
Они оброк другого света. . . .
Стихи, друзья мои, стихи![39]

[So, how will the poet be remembered? For his uniform? It
cannot be! For his sins? They are the quitrent of another world. . . .
Poetry, my friends, poetry!]

The narrator goes on to describe the notebooks that will survive him, in
which a casual reader will find his initials and, asking what they mean,
learn the poet's name and hear the story of his life:

Ему ответят: «Полежаев. . . .»
Прибавят, может быть, что он
Был добрым сердцем одарен,
Умом довольно своенравным,
Страстями, жребием бесславным
Укор и жалость заслужил;
Во цвете лет—без жизни жил,
Без смерти умер в белом свете. . . .
Вот память добрых о поэте![40]

[They will respond: "Polezhaev. . . ." And will add, perhaps,
that he was endowed with a kind heart, a rather wayward mind;
that he had earned reproach and pity because of his passions
and inglorious lot. In the prime of his life he lived without living,
he died to the world without dying. . . . Here is what kind people
will remember about the poet!]

It is remarkable that at the end of this emphatically non-personal
poem, Polezhaev includes this portrait of himself as he wants to be
remembered, and it is the portrait of a poet.

   Chir-Iurt describes another expedition against insurgents and Qazi
Muhammad. Chir-Iurt was a strategically important village, very well
fortified, and hard to reach due to its location in the mountains. Captur-
ing it was a difficult military operation that resulted in many casualties
on both sides. Accordingly, Polezhaev uses a very different tone in this
poem; some compare it with the rhetoric of eighteenth-century solemn
odes, especially the odes dedicated to military victories. It is noteworthy

that Polezhaev emphasizes the heroic tone and subject matter by briefly acknowledging that he likes light and jocular poetry more than the serious kind.[41] Yet he returns to the heroic tone for the rest of the poem.

As in Polezhaev's other Caucasian poems, the narrator shares the heroic mood of the advancing army: "Gde tot, ch'iu dushu ne volnuet / Voiny i slavy gromkii glas?" (Where is the person whose soul is not excited by the loud voice of war and glory?)[42] Even though the narrator acknowledges his past mistakes and the resultant desolation, when he is part of historical events, he is as courageous and honorable as his comrades:

> На поле чести, в бурях брани
> Мой меч не выпадет из длани
> От страха робостной души.[43]

> [On the field of honor, in the storms of battles, my sword will not fall out of my hand because of the fear of my timid soul.]

The narrator concludes the passage with a promise of honorable service that will change his unfortunate life for the better:

> Не изменю царю и долгу,
> Лечу за честию везде
> И проложу себе дорогу
> К моей потерянной звезде![44]

> [I will not betray my tsar and my duty, I pursue honor everywhere, and I will lay a road to my lost star!]

Still, Polezhaev concludes the poem, as he usually does, with a reflection about his possible death:

> Когда воинственная лира,
> Громовый звук печальных струн,
> Забудет битвы и перун
> И воспоет отраду мира?
> Или задумчивый певец,
> Обманут сладостною думой,
> Всегда печальный и угрюмый,
> Найдет во бранях свой конец?[45]

[When will my martial lyre, the thunderous sound of its sad strings, forget battles and thunder (*perun*) and sing the joy of peace? Or will the pensive poet, deceived by sweet thoughts, always sad and gloomy, find his end in battles?]

However, Polezhaev did not die in the Caucasus, and the capture of Chir-Iurt was the last battle in which he took part; in 1833 his regiment left the region and returned to Moscow. Soon after his return, Polezhaev wrote a poem, "An Excerpt from an Epistle to A. P. L<ozovsky>" ("Otryvok iz poslaniia k A. P. L<ozovskom>u"), in which he expresses satisfaction that he has left the Caucasus:

> И нет их, нет! Промчались годы
> Душевных бурь и мятежей,
> И я далек от рубежей
> Войны, разбоя и свободы. . . .
> И я без грусти и тоски
> Покинул бранные станицы.[46]

[They are gone, gone! The years of internal turmoil and rebellion have flown by, and I am far away from the lines of war, plunder, and freedom. . . . And I have left the martial settlements without sadness and grief.]

And yet, the time in the Caucasus was the best in Polezhaev's military career; it was the time when he achieved a modicum of service success, having been restored to his rank as a non-commissioned officer and the status of a nobleman. It was also apparently a time when he felt less lonely and marginalized—a time when he saw himself as a participant in important events, accepted, and ready for heroic deeds. For once, his military service not only made some sense to him but also served as a source of poetic inspiration. As soon as Polezhaev left the Caucasus and combat, his pessimism and sense of non-belonging became overwhelming. He seems to say as much in his poem "To My Genius" ("K moemu geniiu"; 1836–37?):

> И я, как жрец, на поле битвы
> Курил мой светлый фимиам,
> И благодетельное слово
> В устах правдивого судьи,

Казалось, было уж готово
Изречь: «Воскресни и живи!»
Я оживал. . . . Но ты, мой гений,
Исчез, забыл меня, а я
Теперь один, в цепи творений
Пью грустно воздух бытия. . . .[47]

[I also, like a priest, burned my bright incense in the battlefield,
and the beneficent word on the lips of the righteous judge, it
seemed, was ready to pronounce: "Rise and live!" I was coming to
life. . . . But you, my genius, disappeared, forgot me, and now I am
alone, in the chain of being I sadly drink the air of existence. . . .]

It is not quite clear what the narrator regrets: the life in the Caucasus,
dangerous but heroic, or the fact that he has survived it and now has to
continue a life he never wanted and could not escape; retirement from
military service was not in his power. Only death would free him from
his service obligations.

Like Polezhaev, Mikhail Lermontov began his education at Moscow
University. He passed the entrance examinations and, on September 1,
1830, was accepted to study in the "moral-political" department. In the
spring of 1832, however, he requested a transfer to Saint Petersburg
University. Russian scholarly tradition cites Lermontov's disappointment in the level of instruction, but Lermontov could also have been in
direct conflict with his professors, at least two of whom complained that,
while the 1831 exams demonstrated Lermontov's general erudition,
they also showed that "he did not know the course material."[48] Lermontov himself, as was customary, alluded to family circumstances in his
application for the transfer. He was allowed to leave Moscow University,
but his plan to continue his education in Petersburg proved unsuccessful: the university refused to give him credit for the courses he had taken
in Moscow. Not wanting to repeat his first year of studies, Lermontov
decided to go into the military and applied to the School of Ensigns of
the Guard and Cavalry Junkers. He passed the entrance examinations
and began his studies on November 14, 1832, in the rank of a non-
commissioned officer (*unter-ofitser*). He spent two years in the school,
graduating on November 22, 1834, with the rank of subaltern lieutenant

(*kornet*, twelfth class in cavalry guards regiments). He was assigned to serve in the prestigious Life-Guards Hussar Regiment stationed in Saint Petersburg.

Lermontov apparently was not entirely happy in the military school, but exactly how miserable he was is hard to ascertain. He did call his years at the school *"deux années terribles"* ("two terrible years") in his letter to M. A. Lopukhina of December 23, 1834, but it is not possible to discern how serious he was: this complaint about the school seems to be the only one to be found in his correspondence.[49] The school's curriculum, although understandably oriented toward military training, also included mathematics, history, philology, jurisprudence, and French, and some of the professors were good enough to engage Lermontov intellectually.[50] The military training was also good, and Lermontov graduated as "an educated officer, with a broad outlook, knowledge of military history, and the basics of military art."[51]

The new milieu, rather than the curriculum or military training, was apparently what made Lermontov feel uncomfortable, and not just in the school but also in Saint Petersburg in general. He was an outsider both in the capital and among his high society classmates. At least initially, he felt his loss of social status painfully. Most importantly, Lermontov was not sure whether military service would be conducive to his career as a poet, both because he did not know how to reconcile writing poetry with his image as an officer and because his new comrades were not particularly interested in literature.[52] Nonetheless, he did his best to assimilate, learning to drink and carouse as was customary among his classmates. Eventually, he made some friends at the school, including N. S. Martynov, who would become Lermontov's victorious opponent in his last, fatal duel.

In his second year at the school Lermontov also participated in a clandestine manuscript magazine, *The School Dawn* (*Shkol'naia zaria*), published by the cadets, to which he contributed a number of poems, most of them obscene. For several years after his graduation, he was known as the author of unprintable verse, a poet whose poetry was unsuitable for young female readers.

Lermontov passed his first years of service rather pleasantly in Saint Petersburg. His service obligations, in addition to the usual military training and parades, also required attendance at court balls, which pleased the young officer. In February 1837, however, Lermontov was arrested for writing a poem on Pushkin's death in a duel, in which he accused high society and the court of abetting d'Anthès in the poet's death. In a week, by Nicholas's order, Lermontov was transferred to active duty in a non-guards regiment stationed in the Caucasus. His rank remained the same, which was effectively a demotion, since the guard ranks had more value. The Caucasus, of course, was a second Siberia, where at that time many of the Decembrists were serving to atone for their participation in the December 14, 1825, uprising.

Thanks to his influential grandmother's intercession, Lermontov spent only a short time in the Caucasus. Furthermore, although he "participated in a few minor skirmishes," his time there "amounted to an extended vacation through the southern regions of the empire."[53] Notably, it was around this time that Lermontov first began to think about leaving the military and immersing himself in literature.[54]

On October 11, 1837, Lermontov was transferred to a hussar regiment stationed in Novgorod. During his short time in this regiment, Lermontov was on leave in Saint Petersburg twice, and in April 1838 he was transferred to the Life-Guards Hussar Regiment stationed in Tsarskoe Selo near Saint Petersburg. Lermontov joined the regiment in May of that year, still hoping to retire soon.[55] Meanwhile he continued to serve, both fulfilling his service obligations and participating in pranks as was customary among the elite youth, military and civil alike.[56] Thus, in September 1838, Grand Duke Michael ordered Lermontov arrested for appearing at a parade wearing a sword that was far shorter than regulations required. Lermontov spent three weeks under arrest for this prank. Nonetheless, in December 1839 he was promoted to the rank of lieutenant (ninth class in cavalry guards regiments).

On February 18, 1840, Lermontov fought a duel with the son of the French ambassador.[57] About a month after the duel (in which he was slightly wounded), Lermontov was arrested and court-martialed. On April 13, as a punishment, he was transferred to an infantry regiment stationed in the Caucasus. He left Saint Petersburg in early May and arrived in Stavropol (the headquarters of the army commander) on June 10. Lermontov stayed in the Caucasus for about a year, this time taking part in several significant military operations. One of the most serious was the July 11 battle near the river Valerik in Chechnya. During this battle, Lermontov was charged with supervising the advancing detachment and, according to his superiors, "fulfilled the commission with which he was entrusted with exceptional valor and composure and broke into the enemy's fortifications with the first group of the most courageous soldiers."[58] In October he replaced the wounded commander of the squad of volunteer horsemen, the so-called flying hundred. For the rest of the month, Lermontov and his squad took part in several dangerous operations. Until December 1840, when he received a two-month leave of absence, he continued to participate in expeditions into Chechnya. His superiors recommended Lermontov for several awards, one of them a golden saber with the engraving "For Courage," but the tsar declined to follow the recommendations.

On January 14, 1841, Lermontov set out from Stavropol for Petersburg, where he arrived in early February. During his stay in the capital, he attempted to resign his commission, but his request was refused. Furthermore, around April 11, he was abruptly ordered to leave Petersburg for the Caucasus in forty-eight hours. On the way back to his regiment, he stopped in Piatigorsk to stay at the famous local spa on account of his poor health. While there, Lermontov quarreled with Nikolai Martynov, his classmate from military school. The question of who was at fault is still being debated, but at any rate, they fought, and Lermontov was killed on the spot. He was twenty-six years old.

Lermontov entered military school somewhat reluctantly, under pressure of circumstances: he could not continue his education at the university of his choice, and he detested the very idea of civil service. In addition, while some of his family members (including his grandmother, who raised him) strongly advised against entering the military school, others supported his decision.[59] It is, of course, impossible to say how his career as a writer would have turned out if he had stayed at the university, but it is possible to consider how military service shaped him as a person and a writer, by assessing how his military affiliation affected his literary production and the way he positioned himself on the contemporary literary scene, as well as by tracing the military thematic in his oeuvre.

Significantly, Lermontov virtually stopped writing lyric poetry upon entering military school: "He wrote more than three hundred lyrics in the four years from 1829 to 1832 but fewer than ten during the following four years," possibly doubting his "future as a poet."[60] Instead of lyrics, Lermontov turned to narrative genres, both in prose (*Vadim*, 1832–34?) and verse (*Khadzhi Abrek*, 1833), which allowed him to explore the idea of action.[61] It should be noted that some of Lermontov's narrative poems, the first of which was *Circassians* (*Cherkesy*, 1828), predate his time at military school; they too are also full of action, and many of them take place in the Caucasus, known to the young Lermontov both from the literary tradition and from personal experience, thanks to two trips to Piatigorsk. In the absence of lyrical production, however, the "action" works certainly acquired more weight.

Despite his doubts about himself as a poet in the military, Lermontov continued to write, and by 1837 he had obviously matured as a writer. In 1835–36 he worked on his narrative poem *Sashka* (the dates are still being disputed among the Lermontov scholars) and wrote his best drama, *Masquerade*. In 1837 he returned to writing lyric poetry in earnest and also wrote the first of the novellas that would become part of his most significant prose work, *A Hero of Our Time* (1837–40). Lermontov's "Death of the Poet" was a turning point in his biography as a poet and a man: not only did it make him an instant celebrity but it also crystalized his early dreams of heroism into a more serious and comprehensive concept of bravery on the battlefield as well as confrontation with high society.[62]

Lermontov's time in the military was undoubtedly essential for his poetic self, and his literary production, both in prose and in verse, testifies to that. At the same time, as early as his first exile to the Caucasus Lermontov began to consider resigning his commission and devoting himself to literature. His several subsequent attempts to abandon military service suggest that, at least occasionally, Lermontov, unlike Davydov, regarded it as an impediment to his writing. In this respect, his situation was more like that of Polezhaev, who likewise wanted to retire but could not. It is not unlikely that Lermontov felt some affinity with Polezhaev, and this may be the impetus behind his narrative poem *Sashka*, which shares with the original not only its title and eponymous main character but also some themes, such as visiting a brothel and consorting with a prostitute. In addition, the Caucasus and the Caucasian War were major themes for both Polezhaev and Lermontov. Finally, another point of similarity is that regardless of the fact that Lermontov was a more successful military officer whose behavior was much less disorderly than that of Polezhaev, he also was strongly disliked by Nicholas and, apparently, for a similar reason: what Nicholas perceived as the lack of a moral center. The tsar wrote to his wife about *A Hero of Our Time*: "[It shows] a pitiful talent that points to the perverted mind of the author."[63]

At the same time, Lermontov's narrators (or lyric personas) in his works about the Caucasian War, unlike Polezhaev's, do not exhibit obvious autobiographical features. The first-person narrator that resembles Lermontov most closely is that of *A Hero of Our Time*, but even in this novel whatever autobiographical features that can be detected are ironically distorted. In the three poems that directly depict the Caucasian War, "Valerik," "The Bequeathal" (both 1840), and "The Dream" (1841), the lyric personas become increasingly disconnected from Lermontov's personality and biography. Paradoxically, to achieve this freedom from his biographical self, Lermontov seems to have needed to use a lyric persona who was, like himself, a military man.[64]

"Valerik" is written in the form of a letter to a woman whom the lyric persona loved in the past and perhaps still continues to love. It describes his everyday life in the regiment stationed in the Caucasus, and this description resembles similar passages in Polezhaev's two Caucasian narrative poems, *Erpeli* and *Chir-Iurt*; it is, however, more succinct and streamlined. The poem's structure is also more balanced, almost symmetrical: it begins and ends with an address to the former beloved. Its central episode is the battle of Valerik, which is contrasted to the usual small skirmishes as a much more serious and even tragic episode. The description of the most violent fighting, which takes place in the waters of the river, resembles Achilles's *aristeia*, that is, his finest moment in the battle against Trojans in the *Iliad*. Like the Scamander River where Achilles fought, the Valerik is choked with bodies, dead and alive, and its waters run red with blood:

> И два часа в струях потока
> Бой длился. Резались жестоко
> Как звери, молча, с грудью грудь,
> Ручей телами запрудили.
> Хотел воды я зачерпнуть . . .
> (И зной и битва утомили
> Меня), но мутная волна
> Была тепла, была красна. (2:71)

[For two hours in the currents of the stream the battle lasted. [The fighters] cut each other fiercely like beasts, in silence, breast against breast; [they] choked the creek with bodies. I wanted to scoop up some water . . . (the heat and the battle had tired me), but the cloudy wave was warm, was red.]

It is noteworthy that the wording of the original does not distinguish between the battling enemies: in the clauses that describe the fight, the verbs have no grammatical subject.

The lyric persona, of course, is the character whose voice the reader hears and through whose eyes he or she sees the battle, but he is not the central figure of the poem; rather, it is the dying captain surrounded by his grieving troops, described about halfway through the poem. Even though the lyric persona takes part in the fight (see the passage quoted above), his main role is to reflect on what takes place: he offers a way to judge the actions of both sides. Notably, he equates them, referring to them in the most general terms:

Я думал: жалкий человек.
Чего он хочет! . . небо ясно,
Под небом места много всем,
Но беспрестанно и напрасно
Один враждует он—зачем? (2:172)

[I thought: man is pitiful. What does he want? . . The sky is clear, there is enough space for everyone under the sky, but he alone feuds incessantly and vainly—for what?]

The phrase "man is pitiful" applies both to Russians and Caucasians. It is remarkable that it is a local man, a peaceful *(mirnòi,* that is, not fighting the Russian invasion of the Caucasus) Caucasian, who interrupts the lyric persona's musings, likening the Valerik, perhaps unwittingly, to the Styx:

Галуб прервал мое мечтанье,
Ударив по плечу; он был
Кунак мой: я его спросил,
Как месту этому названье?
Он отвечал мне: Валерик
А перевесть на ваш язык,
Так будет речка смерти: верно,
Дано старинными людьми. (2:172)

[Galub interrupted my dreaming, having slapped me on the shoulder. He was my *kunak* ["friend"]. I asked him what this place was called. He responded: *The Valerik,* and to translate it into your tongue, it would be river of death. Surely it [the name] was given by people of olden times.]

Galub's explanation implies that war is an eternal activity, known from ancient times and to be continued as long as people exist.

The lyric persona shares a few characteristics with the author of the poem: like Lermontov, he is an officer fighting at the Valerik; like

Lermontov, he has also experienced unhappy love; like Lermontov, perhaps, he contrasts the heroic behavior of warriors to the indifference of the poem's addressee. But this is all; the similarity is too general to tie the lyric persona to Lermontov the man (as was possible with Davydov and, especially, Polezhaev). Notably, this lyric persona is not a poet: he writes a letter, not a poem.

The lyric persona of "The Bequeathal" ("Zaveshchanie") is also a warrior and an unlucky lover, and he is even less a poet than the lyric persona in "Valerik." The poem is a dying officer's last wish, which he is conveying to his comrade. He knows that death is near, and asks his interlocutor, if he happens to visit his home, to conceal his death from his parents in order not to upset them, but not to spare a young lady who lives nearby. He does not believe that she will be seriously affected:

> Ты расскажи всю правду ей,
> Пустого сердца не жалей;
> Пускай она поплачет. . . .
> Ей ничего не значит! (2:175)

[Tell her the whole truth, do not spare her empty heart. Let her cry. . . . This is nothing to her!]

The officer's beloved is even more heartless than the addressee of "Valerik," whom the lyric persona of the poem imagines reacting to his letter, albeit with misunderstanding: "And you will quietly say, 'Odd fellow'" (*I tikho molvite: chudak!*; 2:173). While, like the author, the lyric persona in "The Bequeathal" has experienced an unhappy love, the similarity between them ends here: the lyric persona has parents who raised him (Lermontov's mother died when he was a toddler, and his father was estranged and then died when Lermontov was ten years old). Furthermore, his social background is very different from that of Lermontov: he is obviously a middling provincial nobleman, in sharp contrast to the well-off and well-educated Lermontov, who, through his service, had become a Saint Petersburg high-society man.

The last poem to be discussed, "The Dream" ("Son"), is also about a dying warrior and a distant beloved. The poem is symmetrical, even circular: the lyric persona lies fatally wounded in a valley in Dagestan and dreams about an evening party in his homeland, where young and beautiful women merrily talk about him—all but one, who daydreams and sees the lyric persona dying in a valley in Dagestan. Again, the lyric persona is a soldier in love, but not a poet: over time, Lermontov kept moving the "I" of his lyrics about war farther and farther from his biographical self.

The three poets discussed in this chapter served in the military for different reasons, with different level of success, and with different degrees of enthusiasm. Their poetic personas were also dissimilar: Davydov created a poetic "I" that shared some superficial but recognizable features with the author (both were hussars) but behaviorally and psychologically was quite different from his creator, who was not only a successful military man and a serious military historian but also (mostly) a devoted family man.[65] Polezhaev, especially in his poetry about war, did little to separate the lyric persona from the authorial figure. Furthermore, he makes it easy for the reader to recognize this similarity by frequently using his first and last names to mark his lyric persona. Lermontov was known for his transparently biographical lyric persona in his early poetry, but as he matured, he moved away from obvious biographism toward more subtle methods of lyrical expression.

What appears to be similar among the three poets is that being a poet in the military curtailed their creative freedom. Even though writers in civil service were not completely free of state control, all three of these examples of poets in the military seem to demonstrate, albeit to different degrees, the existence of a far harsher state control over military men engaged in literary pursuits. Davydov was temporarily transferred to a less prestigious regiment for writing three fables that offended Alexander I. Even though he was allowed to return and serve in the regiments and places where he wanted to serve, his (mostly successful) career was affected by this youthful misstep. Polezhaev was most directly hurt by his service in the military: regardless of what some scholars say, Nicholas's order that Polezhaev enter military service was a punishment for writing Sashka. Polezhaev was never free, never truly forgiven, even after he wrote his fairly patriotic narrative poetry. Likewise, Lermontov, despite his graduation from a prestigious military school and serving in a Life-Guards regiment, was not simply reprimanded or transferred for writing his poem "The Death of the Poet" but arrested and investigated for sedition. He also apparently was not permitted to retire when he wanted to.[66] Nonetheless, Lermontov managed to use his—perhaps unwelcome—service in the military and participation in the Caucasian War to work out a unique poetic voice, free from direct connections with his biographical persona and thus more universal and expressive.

5

Service Ranks
in Dostoevsky's Life and Fiction

A writer, a poet. It seems strange somehow. . . . When has a
poet made his way in the world, risen to high rank? They're
only scribbling fellows after all, not to be relied upon.

Fedor Dostoevsky, *The Insulted and Injured*

Dostoevsky had very little personal experience with the hierarchy
of ranks and no investment in it; therefore, the worlds of both military
and, especially, civil service were alien to him and interested him
mostly as material for his writing. In particular, Dostoevsky developed
as a writer by responding to Gogol's representation of civil servitors—
either continuing, playing with, or, more often, disagreeing with it.
Gogolian low-ranking clerks and their exaggerated poverty and mental
deficiencies repeatedly reappear, revised and reshaped, in Dostoevsky's
works, from his first publications to *A Writer's Diary*. As a rule, his low-
ranking clerks are more complex and often less likable characters than
Gogol's originals. Furthermore, they tend to be more aggressive and
sometimes sinister. Even the most likable of them (such as Makar Devushkin of *Poor Folk*) contain the seeds of aggression and the ability to
behave badly, whereas Foma Opiskin of *Selo Stepanchikovo*, the underground man, and, especially, Fedor Karamazov of *Brothers Karamazov*
are truly aggressive and bad. It is indeed (as is often argued) a short
step from Dostoevsky's sinister clerks to Fedor Sologub's Ardalion
Peredonov of *Petty Demon*. At the same time, Dostoevsky also develops
the potentially sympathetic traits of Gogol's characters; despite all his

faults, Marmeladov, in *Crime and Punishment*, for example, inspires pity in both the characters and the readers alike.

In Gogol's tales, low-ranking clerks often clash with their high-ranking superiors, "generals" or "Their Excellencies," and come to grief. Dostoevsky repeatedly revisits this situation and revises it. Like his titular councilors, his generals are not as flat as their Gogolian originals: they can display compassion toward their low-ranking subordinates or show the capacity to take a high moral stand, but they can also fall flat on their faces while attempting to be compassionate and humane. The most complex of these generals is Ardalion Ivolgin of *The Idiot*. A liar and buffoon, he is nonetheless portrayed so that his death following a confrontation with a lower-ranking clerk is perceived as tragic and rehabilitates him in the eyes of those around him as well as the reader. Dostoevsky thus develops Gogol's legacy of depicting civil servants in different, sometimes opposite, directions. He complicates both Gogol's characters and the situations in which he places them. In some cases, he retains and increases the absurd element inherent in Gogol's characters; in others, he problematizes it, uncovering traces of humanity in flawed, comical, and sinister figures.

Although his service experience was limited, Dostoevsky did serve, twice. His first stint in the military began in January 1838, when he was accepted into the third "conductor" grade at the Chief Engineering School, which trained military engineers.[1] How eager he was to enter a military school is difficult to ascertain, and it is possible that it was his father, M. A. Dostoevsky, who chose it, in hopes of securing a decent service position for his son. In any case, Dostoevsky studied conscientiously, receiving good grades in most classes. However, he disliked drills and military discipline. His brother Mikhail wrote to their father on January 29, 1838: "He looks great in his uniform! Regulations [or drills, *front*] are the only thing that oppress him, because one has to stand at attention for every officer!"[2] Consequently, his grade for drills was low. Dostoevsky's lack of aptitude for drawing further reduced his grade point average. He also got into a conflict with his mathematics teacher, who, according to Dostoevsky, lowered his grade as payback. As a result, at the end of his first school year, Dostoevsky was not promoted to the next grade, a failure that caused him to become ill and to be hospitalized in the school's infirmary (49, 52–54).

In July 1839 Dostoevsky was finally promoted to the second "conductor" grade. On November 29, 1840, the rank of non-commissioned officer (*unter-ofitser*) was conferred on him "for good behavior and knowledge of drills and regulations" (64). The next month, he was promoted again, to the rank of ensign (*portupei-iunker*, 70). In August 1841 Dostoevsky was promoted to the rank of warrant officer (*praporshchik*, fourteenth class) and transferred to the lowest officer class to continue his studies (71, 74). In August 1842, after successfully passing all his yearly examinations, he was promoted to the highest officer class and made second lieutenant (*podporuchik*, thirteenth class; 79).

Dostoevsky graduated in August 1843 with the rank of second lieutenant and, after a short leave, began service at the Chief Engineering Administration.[3] However, within a year, in August 1844, Dostoevsky submitted a letter of resignation, citing "family reasons." The resignation was accepted, and, as was customary, he was promoted to the next rank, that of lieutenant (*poruchik*, twelfth class), and discharged in October of the same year (89–93). In addition to his apparent general dislike for service and his growing interest in literature, Dostoevsky offered two other, contradictory reasons for his resignation. In a letter to his brother-in-law P. A. Karepin written shortly after he submitted his resignation, Dostoevsky cites the upcoming "detached duty to the fortress <. . .> in Orenburg or Sevastopol or even someplace farther away" (90, brackets in original). According to Dostoevsky's physician S. D. Ianovsky, however, later, in May 1846, Dostoevsky gave a different explanation, which Ianovsky conveyed to the literary historian O. F. Miller by letter in 1882. According to Ianovsky, Dostoevsky told him the following story:

> When I was finishing my course of study in the Engineering school, I had <. . .> to submit a project on an assigned topic. I completed this assignment, and, having been inspected and approved by the [school] council, it was sent for final approval to the Emperor Nicholas Pavlovich <. . .> As soon as the emperor took one glance at my drawing, he immediately saw that the fortress I had designed did not have a single gate! My mistake, which had not been noticed by anyone including the director, was seen by the emperor at once, and he wrote on my drawing: "What kind of a fool drew this?" This inscription was presented to me in the original; I saw it [. . .] and immediately decided to leave an office where this nickname obviously would have stayed with me all my life.[4]

The compilers of the *Letopis' zhizni i tvorchestva* have been unable to find such a drawing in the Chief Engineering School's archive. Furthermore,

Dostoevsky begins the story with a reference to Chatsky's words in A. S. Griboedov's *Woe from Wit*: "I'd be glad to serve, it is servility that revolts me" (*"Sluzhit' by rad, prisluzhivat'sia toshno,"* 117), which heightens the story's fictional flavor.[5]

Dostoevsky's second stint in the military began in early 1854, after his release from Siberian prison camp. As part of the sentence he received for participating in the Petrashevsky Circle required, he was enlisted as a private in the Siberian Seventh Line Battalion stationed in Semipalatinsk (191–92, 194, 196). He served there until the spring of 1859, when his petition to retire for health reasons was accepted, and he was released from service with the rank of second lieutenant (255–58) and allowed to live in the European part of the Russian Empire, first in Tver and soon after in Saint Petersburg. These five years in the military, especially before he was promoted, in 1855, to the rank of non-commissioned officer and, in 1856, to that of warrant officer (fourteenth class), were quite difficult for Dostoevsky. For the first month or so, he was stationed in the barracks with the rest of the enlisted men, after which his company commander allowed him to live in private quarters (198). If Dostoevsky was shielded somewhat from the hardships of the soldier's life (as A. E. Vrangel reports in his memoir), the privileges he received were not significant; the writer often complained in his letters to Mikhail Dostoevsky about the difficulties of his service.[6]

Dostoevsky resumed writing while in Semipalatinsk, and he was able to reenter literary life soon after his return from Siberia. At that time, he wrote actively, gave public readings of his old and new works, began publishing again, and, in 1861, together with his brother Mikhail, founded the journal *Time* (*Vremia*). From that time on, Dostoevsky led the life of a professional writer, supporting himself and his family on honoraria and never considering the possibility of returning to state service.

Dostoevsky thus had no personal experience with the world of civil service and was not familiar with the workings of the Russian bureaucracy firsthand. Nonetheless, as is well known, his early writings—in particular, *Poor Folk*, *The Double*, and "Mr. Prokharchin" (all published in 1846)—feature civil clerks as protagonists: Makar Devushkin of *Poor Folk* and Iakov Goliadkin of *The Double* are titular councilors serving in unnamed Saint Petersburg offices; Semen Ivanovich Prokharchin's rank is not named but is described as "small" (*melkii*).[7] It is likely, however, that his rank is also titular councilor: as G. M. Fridlender points out in his commentary to the story, Prokharchin's name, Semen

Ivanovich, is the name of the deceased clerk replaced by Goliadkin Jr. in *The Double*.[8] Since Goliadkin Jr. is a titular councilor, it is likely that the clerk he replaces had the same rank. Furthermore, the Semen Ivanovich replaced by Goliadkin Jr. shares with Prokharchin not only a first name and patronymic but also a secret passion for hoarding money (1:149).

As chapter 3 demonstrates, it was Nikolai Gogol who created the titular councilor as a literary type in his "Notes of a Madman" and "The Overcoat," and in his first portrayals of titular councilors, Dostoevsky is working not so much with the reality of state service in Russia as with the literary tradition originated by Gogol. In all three stories, Dostoevsky frequently refers to Gogol's works. In *Poor Folk*, not only does Makar Devushkin, like Akaky Bashmachkin, have a funny-sounding last name, but he is also a copyist proud of his handwriting (1:71). Furthermore, just like Akaky, he is concerned with the poor state of his clothing (1:74)—notably, his overcoat (1:76)—and footwear—notably, the soles of his boots (1:76). Like Gogol's Poprishchin, Makar reads trashy literature; and, as Varenka points out, has "uneven" writing (*slog*) (1:70).

Iakov Petrovich Goliadkin, of *The Double*, also has the kind of "speaking name" so common in Gogol's characters: according to Dahl's dictionary, the words *goliada* and *goliadka* derive from *gol'* and *golyi*, which mean not only "naked" but also "destitute."[9] More significantly, Goliadkin seems to be a quintessential Gogolian titular councilor: meek, awkward, and destined to meet with disaster. Like Poprishchin, he has designs on the daughter of a higher-ranking official, State Councilor Olsufy Berendeev ("His Excellency"). As in Akaky's case, Goliadkin's ruin begins when he encounters a group of servitors while attending a party. The group represents the entire Table of Ranks, from collegiate registrar (fourteenth class), to lieutenant (twelfth class), to collegiate councilor (sixth class), to state councilor (fifth class). In Goliadkin's view, however, they all look higher-ranking than they actually are: the collegiate registrar "looked more like a state councilor than a [collegiate] registrar" (1:129); the collegiate councilor "seemed to be something else. [. . .] He was higher!" (1:129). Most significantly, Goliadkin's rival in love, a collegiate assessor (eighth class), looks "more like an elder [*starets*] than a youth—speaking in a favorable sense" (1:129-30). This distorted perspective is similar to Poprishchin's misjudgment of the status of his rival *kammerjunker* Teplov, whom he believes to be as high-ranking as a general. Confronted with higher-ranking officials,

Goliadkin—whose insanity, like Poprishchin's, creeps up on him over the course of the story—completely loses his mind and is eventually taken to an insane asylum.

In "Mr. Prokharchin," Dostoevsky also evokes Gogol's works, beginning with his character's name, which derives from *prokharchit'sia*, "to eat away, spend everything." This, of course, is not true in the case of Prokharchin, who, on the contrary, stashes away as much money as he possibly can. Nonetheless, he appears destitute, as is proper for Gogolian low-ranking clerks. Furthermore, like Poprishchin, Prokharchin goes mad in the course of the story; and like Akaky, he dies at the end. In addition, he has boots that are worn out and unusable, and among the old trash found in his chest after his death are "old soles and boot tops," which makes him kin to Akaky's "father, grandfather, and even brother-in-law," all of whom wore boots, "only changing the soles three times a year."[10] Finally, Prokharchin himself refers to Gogol's story "The Nose," babbling in his delirium: "They'll bite off your nose, you won't even notice it and will eat it yourself with bread" (1:255).

Dostoevsky thus makes it clear that he wants his works to be read in the context of Gogol's stories about poor clerks. At the same time, Dostoevsky experiments with Gogol's characters, making them not necessarily more able as civil servants, but infinitely more psychologically complex.[11] In *Poor Folk*, he asks what happens if the likes of Poprishchin and Bashmachkin were to be given self-awareness, if they could look at themselves analytically, as Makar Devushkin does? This self-awareness allows Makar, while reading "The Overcoat," to recognize himself in Akaky and to disagree with Gogol's disparaging treatment of him (1:62–63). Furthermore, Dostoevsky endows Makar with something resembling honor and dignity, which makes him sensitive to what he considers to be Gogol's gratuitous exposure of Akaky's (and, by extension, his own) poverty and weakness. As a result, Makar is not as one-dimensional as Akaky: his character has complexity and, moreover, ambiguity. Carol Apollonio goes so far as to claim that "he is an extraordinarily complex figure." And not all this complexity is good: Makar turns out to have a dark side to him that, in Apollonio's words, "prefigures the most complex and sinister figures of Dostoevsky's later fiction."[12] If Akaky's shy and grotesque sexuality, while unmistakably present, cannot really harm anyone except himself, Makar's seemingly fatherly behavior toward Varenka has a shade of the predatory about it. Poprishchin is, of course, sexually more aggressive, but he too only dreams of entering Sophie's bedroom and is no threat to her marriage.

By contrast, Makar, while ostensibly acting on Varenka's behalf, in fact goes a long way toward ruining her reputation and interfering with her impending marriage—which, as Apollonio contends, is the only chance she has to live a decent life.[13] In Dostoevsky's rendition a titular councilor may be not a meek and harmless "insignificant man," a victim of the corrupt social environment, but (at least potentially) a cunning oppressor in his own right. It is not incidentally, therefore, that Dostoevsky mentions, in passing, that the despicable Fedor Karamazov retired in the rank of titular councilor (15:93).

In *The Double*, Dostoevsky explores what happens if the likes of Poprishchin and Bashmachkin were to possess interiority, an interiority Dostoevsky explores by having Goliadkin's thoughts "bleed" into his third-person narrative.[14] Dostoevsky's narrator "plunges" readers "into Golyadkin's world," making them experience Goliadkin's inner life.[15] The effect is surprisingly negative: the reader feels awkward and uneasy being exposed to Goliadkin's inner self and is relieved when the titular councilor is finally taken to the insane asylum. Significantly, in his October 8, 1845, letter to his brother Mikhail, Dostoevsky ascribes his difficulties completing *The Double* to his character's malice: "*Iakov Petrovich Goliadkin* holds his own entirely. He is a terrible scoundrel and there's no approaching him; he absolutely refuses to move forward, claiming [*pretenduia*] that he is not ready yet, that for the time being he is on his own [*sam po sebe*], that he is all right [or 'he is nothing,' *nichego*], as sober as a judge [*ni v odnom glazu*], but if, perhaps, if it comes to this, he also can, why not, why ever not? After all, he is like everyone else, he is just nothing out of the ordinary [*tak sebe*], but is like everybody else. What does he care [*chto emu*]! A scoundrel, a terrible scoundrel!" (28:1:113). The story's stubborn refusal to move forward, as described in this letter, closely resembles (or parodies, in Bakhtin's words) Goliadkin's vacillation before entering the party at his superior's in chapter 4 of *The Double*.[16] Many expressions used in the letter can also be found in the novella: "he, ladies and gentlemen, is all right [or 'nothing,' *nichego*]," "he is on his own [*sam po sebe*]," "But this is all right [*nichego*] that he stands here, he is nothing out of the ordinary [*on tak sebe*]." Like the novella, Goliadkin can also move forward, if he wishes: he "can also come in . . . why not come in?" (1:131). The character's behavior thus determines the narrative technique, affecting not only Dostoevsky's ability (or rather inability) to write but also his narrator's voice. This allows the reader to experience Goliadkin's unpleasant inner world firsthand.

It is notable that when Dostoevsky attempted to revise *The Double* in the early 1860s, he planned to ascribe to Goliadkin Sr. the dream of becoming Napoleon.[17] However, it is Prokharchin who, despite his low status, obvious lack of ability, and seeming meekness, is Dostoevsky's first Napoleonic figure. Prokharchin has a goal in life and the firmness of character to achieve it: after his death it turns out that by strictly controlling all his expenses and leading a life of extreme self-deprivation, he has accumulated 2,497 rubles and 50 kopecks—an enormous sum, given his low pay. His roommates sense this unusual ability in him even before the money is found and are offended by it. Furthermore, they detect Prokharchin's Napoleonic ambitions: "'So what are you?' finally thundered Mark Ivanovich, jumping out of the chair on which he had just sat down to rest, and running up to [Prokharchin's] bed, in utter excitement, in a frenzy, shaking with chagrin and rage. 'What are you? You dolt! [You have] nothing [*ni kola, ni dvora*]. Are you the only one in the world? Is the world made just for you? Are you, perhaps, some Napoleon? What are you? Who are you? Are you Napoleon, eh? Napoleon or not?! Tell me, sir, [are you] Napoleon or not? . .'" (1:256–57). The mortally ill Prokharchin does not answer this question, but after his death, a *napoleon d'or*, that is, a golden coin stamped with Napoleon's profile, is found among his hoarded money, answering Mark Ivanovich's question in the affirmative.

Dostoevsky's experimentation with titular councilors put him not only in a dialogue with Gogol but also in disagreement with contemporary critics, most importantly, with Vissarion Belinsky, who was the first to dub Gogol's characters "insignificant men" and to praise Gogol for looking at them with sympathy.[18] In Dostoevsky's presentation, these insignificant men turn out not to be defenseless or harmless. It is noteworthy that Belinsky misunderstood and disliked the innovative narrative technique Dostoevsky used to portray his characters—a technique that allowed him to present them as complex, ambiguous, and often unpleasant personalities. If upon reading *Poor Folk* Belinsky famously exclaimed, "A new Gogol has been born," *The Double* did not quite satisfy him: the critic found "monstrous deficiencies" in the novella's style.[19] But it was "Mr. Prokharchin" that truly annoyed him. In his essay "View on Russian Literature in the Year 1846," he writes: "In the tenth issue of *Notes of the Fatherland* the third work of Mr. Dostoevsky appeared, the tale 'Mr. Prokharchin,' which made all admirers of his talent unpleasantly amazed. The sparks of great talent do glisten in it, but they glisten in such a dense darkness that their light does not allow the reader to see anything. . . . It seems to us that it was not inspiration, not free and naïve creativity that engendered this tale, but something like . . . how should we put it? Either smart-aleckry [*umnichan'e*] or pretentiousness. . . . Perhaps we are mistaken, but why then does [this tale] have to be so affected, mannered, incomprehensible?"[20] Belinsky goes on to criticize what he believes to be the unnecessary repetitions in Dostoevsky's narrative. Significantly, he concludes his analysis by comparing Dostoevsky's manner of writing unfavorably to that of Gogol: "Let us remark in passing that Gogol does not use such repetitions. Of course, we cannot require from Mr. Dostoevsky's works the perfection that Gogol's works have, but we nonetheless think that a big talent would benefit from following the example of a bigger one."[21] Belinsky obviously did not appreciate Dostoevsky's innovations—innovations that allowed Dostoevsky to complicate Gogol's one-dimensional characters and which would eventually allow him to create his greatest works. Perhaps Belinsky also misread Gogol, who was, after all, the writer whose narrative tradition (including unnecessary repetitions and other stylistic "deficiencies") Dostoevsky was both mimicking and developing.

After Dostoevsky's return to literature in the late 1850s, his representation of servitors continued to engage the literary tradition created by Gogol, and in one of the first works written at that time, this engagement acquired a particularly caustic and personal character. As is well known, the central figure in *The Village of Stepanchikovo and Its Inhabitants: From the Notes of an Unknown* (*Selo Stepanchikovo i ego obitateli: Iz zapisok neizvestnogo*, 1859; also translated as *The Friend of the Family*), Foma Fomich Opiskin, is a parody of Gogol's personality and his works, especially his last book, *Selected Passages from Correspondence with Friends*.[22] However, the novella also refers to other works by Gogol, including "The Overcoat" and the second volume of *Dead Souls*.[23] The connection with "The Overcoat" is particularly interesting, because it links *The Village of Stepanchikovo* with Dostoevsky's own *Poor Folk* and *The Double*. One such connection is the figure of "His Excellency" (*Ego prevoskhoditel'stvo*) that appears in all four works.[24] It is also possible to detect similarities between the characters of Foma and Goliadkin (especially if Goliadkin Sr. and Goliadkin Jr. are one person): like Goliadkin, Foma is at once insolent and cowardly. Although Foma is rather successful in concealing his cowardice, it is still evident in many episodes of the novella. By referring in the *Village of Stepanchikovo* to his earlier "Gogolian" works, Dostoevsky makes the novella's connections to Gogol both more visible and more complex. In fact, in *The Village of Stepanchi-kovo* Dostoevsky formally announces his departure from the Gogolian literary tradition—a tradition with which he had already begun to disagree in his early works.[25]

The setting and content of *The Village of Stepanchikovo* are, of course, very different from both Gogol's *Petersburg Tales* and Dostoevsky's first novellas, also set in Petersburg. For one thing, none of the characters is in service at the time of the events described: all are retired and live in the countryside, on the estate owned by the main positive character, Colonel Egor Il'ich Rostanev.[26] Yet the ranks of most characters are not only mentioned repeatedly, but their relative importance is frequently stressed. In fact, the hierarchy of ranks determines the relations among the characters, even family members. For example, one character inimical to Rostanev reminds him that as the wife/widow of a general, *general'sha*, Rostanev's mother outranks her son (3:11).

It may rightly be argued that service hierarchy structured relations in Russian society during the Imperial period, a situation commonly reflected in literary works, including Dostoevsky's *The Village of Stepanchikovo*. What is unusual and thus noteworthy in Dostoevsky's novella is that, on the one hand, Foma Opiskin seems to be outside this structure and, on the other, he subverts and uses the hierarchy of ranks to his advantage. The reader learns early on in the novella that Foma used to serve ("They said [. . .] that at some point in time he had served somewhere") and that his service was not successful (3:7). In criticizing Foma's insolent behavior, the landowner Bakhcheev remarks, "Would that it were so [*i ved' dobro by*] that he had some unusually [high] rank [. . .] then he could have been forgiven because of his rank; but he doesn't even have a decent little rank [*a to ved' i chinishka-to net*]; I know for sure that he doesn't" (3:26–27). It is not quite clear from Bakhcheev's remark whether Foma never received any rank despite his time in service, or whether his rank was simply so low that it was not worth mentioning. In any case, it is obvious that Foma's rank is negligible: he is a nobody in that system. It is the more remarkable, therefore, that Foma discounts the system and asserts his own importance independent of rank. First, while conversing with Rostanev's peasants, he claims that rank is irrelevant and does not define a person's place in society or value to the state. When one peasant asks about the pay Foma received while in service, Foma bristles, and another peasant tries to calm him by suggesting that he might have had a significant rank: "Perhaps you are a major, or a colonel, or even Your Excellency [*vashe siiatel'stvo*],—we

don't know how to title [*velichat'*] you" (3:16).[27] Foma, however, rejects
the honor: "There is pay and there is pay [*zhalovan'e zhalovan'iu roz'*],
you blockhead [*poskonnaia golova*]. Somebody can have a general's rank
but not receive anything—which means that he doesn't deserve it, isn't
of any use to the tsar. And I received twenty thousand [rubles] when I
served under the minister, and didn't accept [the pay] anyway, because
I served for honor [*iz chesti*] and had my own income" (3:16). Foma
seems to connect his putative pay with merit, not rank, implying that his
service was valuable despite his low rank (or even the absence of rank)
and disregarding the fact that one's place in the system of ranks normally
defined one's pay.[28] Foma's obviously mendacious bragging recalls
both Khlestakov's lying about his ostensible importance in the service
hierarchy and Gogol's own not quite truthful reports on his service
success, discussed in chapter 3.

Not only does Foma hugely exaggerate his service accomplishments,
but he also attempts to subvert the entire hierarchy of ranks by demanding that Rostanev call him "Your Excellency" (*Vashe prevoskhoditel'stvo*),
an address appropriate only for persons with ranks from the fifth to
third classes.[29] Foma demands to be addressed with this honorific to
punish Rostanev for paying respect to his former superior, General
Rusapetov. In contrast to Gogol's heartless general in "The Overcoat,"
General Rusapetov is, at least in Rostanev's presentation, "the most
noble person [. . .] shining with virtues and a grandee to boot! He was
good [*oblagodetel'stvoval*] to his sister-in-law, he married off one orphan
to a wonderful young man [. . .] in a word [he was] a general among
generals!" (3:55). Despite the comical ring of Rostanev's praise, General
Rusapetov's good deeds connect him both to "His Excellency" in *Poor
Folk*—who compassionately gave Makar Devushkin money to mend his
old, torn uniform—and to "His Excellency" Berendeev in *The Double*—
who is repeatedly called a "beneficent person" (*blagodetel'nyi chelovek*)
and "benefactor" (*blagodetel'*).

Offended by Rostanev's preparing a lavish dinner for the general
(which the general eventually skipped), Foma insists that the only way
for Rostanev to show his repentance is to address him as "Your Excellency." At first Rostanev refuses on the grounds that this is improper
from the standpoint of the Table of Ranks: "Foma Fomich, [. . .] but how
is this possible? How can I have the heart to do so? Can I, do I have the
right to promote you to [the rank of] general? Think, who promotes
people to [the ranks of] generals? How can I say to you 'Your Excellency'? [. . .] A general is a decoration to the fatherland: a general has

gone to war, he has spilled his blood on the field of honor! How can I say to you 'Your Excellency'?" (3:56). Foma rejects Rostanev's argumentation and persists in his demand. He stops speaking to Rostanev for a week to emphasize his displeasure. Furthermore, he maintains that he wants Rostanev to use the title only for his own good: "I resolved to demand the general's title from you exclusively to enlighten your mind, to develop your morality [nravstvennost'], and to shower [oblit'] you with the rays of new ideas. I wanted precisely that you not henceforth consider generals to be the highest luminaries on the entire globe; I wanted to prove to you that rank is nothing without magnanimity and that you had no reason to rejoice over your general's visit—when, perhaps, there are people standing near you on whom virtue shines [ozarennye dobrodetel'iu]!" (3:87). After a while Rostanev gives up and reluctantly says: "Well [Nu], Your Excellency." But this does not satisfy Foma, and he demands not only a more respectful address but the appropriate body language: "No, not 'Well, Your Excellency,' but simply 'Your Excellency'! I am telling you, colonel, change your attitude! I hope you will not be offended if I suggest that you should bow slightly and, at the same time, bend your body forward. One speaks with a general bending his body forward, expressing his respect this way and his readiness, so to speak, to hurry to fulfill his commissions. I myself used to be in the society of generals and know all this. . . . So, 'Your Excellency'" (3:88, emphasis in the original). Rostanev finally submits. What is noteworthy in this episode is that, in his craving to be addressed as a general, Foma is remarkably similar to Gogol—not only to the young Gogol who, in his correspondence with his family and friends, simultaneously displayed disregard for the system of ranks along with keen desire to succeed within it, but particularly to the mature Gogol, who, in his *Selected Passages from Correspondence with Friends*, adopted the posture and tone of someone who, because of his virtue, has the right to instruct, censure, and even command—that is, the posture of a high-ranking person, a general of sorts. In *The Village of Stepanchikovo* Dostoevsky parodies Gogol's tone and uses the Table of Ranks to demonstrate its inappropriateness—not only from a social point of view but also from a writerly point of view. As Kristin Vitalich puts it (using Lacanian terminology), "In parody the up-and-coming author (the subject) calls into question the status of the established author (the master signifier) whose work has become synonymous with literature, specifically, the ability of his style to serve as a stamp (or, rather, a literary master signifier) for a given cultural and historical moment."[30] With *The Village of*

Stepanchikovo, Dostoevsky thus rejects Gogol's writerly stance at the time he wrote *Selected Passages*, the genealogy suggested by Belinsky's exclamation, "A new Gogol has been born!," and the advice to emulate Gogol's style that he gives Dostoevsky in his essay "A View on Russian Literature in the Year 1846." By parodying Gogol, Dostoevsky was both announcing his artistic freedom from him and formulating his own stance as a writer—a stance he would follow thereafter: that of someone who would never impose his views on the reader, often using hesitant and humble narrators to give readers the freedom to interpret what they read for themselves.

Certainly, Dostoevsky did not entirely reject Gogol as a writer and he did not stop valuing and referring to his works. On the contrary, Gogol's presence in Dostoevsky's writings never disappeared. It was the veneration Gogol received as the alleged head of the most influential literary movement of Dostoevsky's time (an attitude reflected in the title of a series of articles Nikolai Chernyshevsky wrote in the mid-1850s, *Sketches of the Gogol Period of Russian Literature*) that Dostoevsky rejected, a rejection that gave him more freedom to play with Gogolian themes and images. Significantly, the title of general is applied to the protagonist-narrator in *The Insulted and Injured*, a work written soon after *The Village of Stepanchikovo*; first, Nikolai Ikhmenev mockingly refers to the narrator as a general after his first successful novel (3:190), and second, Masloboev somewhat sarcastically yet seriously calls the narrator, his schoolmate who made it as a writer, a "general in literature" (*literaturnyi general*, 3:261, 272). Both times, the narrator rejects the title. In his role as a writer, the narrator is a somewhat autobiographical figure, and Dostoevsky's use of the title of general to indicate the narrator's writerly success demonstrates the complexity and ambiguity of his attitude toward Gogol even after the publication of *The Village of Stepanchikovo*. By calling him a general, Dostoevsky suggests that the narrator is "the new Gogol," thus acknowledging the narrator's and, by extension, his own indebtedness to Gogol; by making him refuse the rank, Dostoevsky reconfirms his discomfort with Gogol's figurative assumption of a general's mantle in *Selected Passages*.

In his next work, the story "A Nasty Business" ("Skvernyi anekdot," 1862; also translated as "A Nasty Story" and "A Nasty Anecdote"), Dostoevsky recasts an encounter between a low-ranking clerk and "His Excellency," this time as a painful conflict, in which "His Excellency" is bested far more shamefully than Gogol's general when accosted by Akaky's ghost. Crucially, however, in this work the reader is allowed access to "His Excellency's" point of view and is thus forced to experience his shame firsthand. The fact that the lowly clerk is clearly unlikable makes the situation even less straightforward. The presence of two characters—the lowly clerk's mother who stands outside the hierarchy of ranks, and Akim Petrovich, a desk chief serving under "His Excellency" who is an insider—both of whom are capable of kindness and a genuine understanding of the situation, problematizes the stock scenario, laying bare the artificiality of its main actors' behavior. Since "A Nasty Business" is framed as a discussion about the Great Reforms of the early 1860s, complicating a situation borrowed from Gogol allows Dostoevsky to express his skepticism toward the over-optimistic expectations regarding the social changes the reforms were supposed to precipitate.

In "A Nasty Business," Ivan Il'ich Pralinsky, a newly minted actual state councilor (fourth class), attempts to act as a kind and beneficent "His Excellency." Ostensibly inspired by the spirit of the Great Reforms—and also by the excessive dose of champagne he consumes in the company of two other generals—he declares to his drinking companions that it is important to treat one's subordinates "humanely": "In my view, humaneness is the most important thing [*pervoe delo*], humaneness toward subordinates, remembering that they are humans too [*chto i oni cheloveki*]" (5:8). The same evening, he acts upon his declared convictions by appearing uninvited at the wedding reception of one of his subordinates, Collegiate Registrar Pseldonimov (fourteenth class). Pralinsky expects that his appearance at the party will be perceived as a great honor for the other guests. He imagines how he will be seated next "to the most important guest, some titular councilor or a relative, a retired staff-captain with a red nose." Significantly, he recalls that "Gogol described these originals nicely" (5:14).[31]

Pralinsky's sudden decision to act humanely toward Pseldonimov is particularly unexpected because prior to the described episode he had already attempted to do so, and he had failed because of Pseldonimov's supposedly unpleasant facial expression. Pralinsky planned to imitate "His Excellency's" kind behavior toward Makar Devushkin in Dostoevsky's *Poor Folk*: he noticed the sorry condition of Pseldonimov's uniform and considered giving him ten rubles to supplement his pay. While standing in front of Pseldonimov's home, Pralinsky recalls the episode and the reason for his failure to help him out, namely, his unpleasant appearance: "He now recalled a very young man, with a long hooked nose, with whitish and straggly hair, sapless and undernourished, in an impossible uniform and indecently impossible pants [*nevyrazimye*]. He remembered that at that moment he had had a thought: shouldn't he allocate [*opredelit'*] the poor sot [*bedniaku*] ten rubles for the holiday to mend his clothes [*dlia popravki*]? But since the face of this poor sot was too sour, and his stare utterly unattractive, even eliciting disgust, the kind thought somehow evaporated all by itself, so that Pseldonimov remained without a reward" (5:12). Pralinsky should have heeded his memory; indeed, Pseldonimov is not an agreeable person; he is so unpleasantly surprised by his superior's unexpected visit that he barely finds the strength to greet Pralinsky, as seen in his stuttering address to him: "Yyyy-our Excel-lency" (5:16).

Pralinsky's dream of humane behavior swiftly turns into a nightmare: nobody at the wedding is happy to see him or appreciates his "humane" attention. Embarrassed, he gets dead drunk and disgustingly sick in the bed prepared for the newlyweds. He leaves his subordinate's home in the morning crushed by his disgrace. The only uplifting memory he retains is that of Pseldonimov's mother, the only one at the party who treats him kindly. First she greets Pralinsky cordially when no one else does, which makes him a little more comfortable in a situation that was becoming increasingly awkward: "But she had such a kind ruddy Russian face, so open and round, she smiled so goodheartedly, bowed so simply that Ivan Il'ich was almost consoled and even began to hope" (5:21). In the morning, when Pralinsky shamefacedly prepares to leave Pseldonimov's home secretly, the mother again treats him kindly, suggesting that he wash his face before leaving: "He wanted to steal out quietly. But suddenly the door opened, and old Pseldonimova came in with an earthenware basin and a pitcher. A towel hung on her shoulder. She put down the pitcher and declared without wasting any words that he definitely [*nepremenno*] had to wash his face. 'Now, dear sir, wash your face, you cannot go without washing.' And in this moment Ivan Il'ich realized that, if there was one creature in the world before whom he now could not be ashamed and [of whom he could not] be afraid, it was precisely this old woman. He washed his face" (5:42). The passage that follows is an almost precise quotation from Gogol's "The Overcoat," from the famous episode that describes Akaky's young colleague's sudden realization that Akaky was human. He was supposedly affected for life by this experience: "And for a long time afterwards, during his gayest moments, he would see that stooping figure with a bald patch in front, muttering pathetically: 'Leave me alone, why do you have to torment me?' In these piercing words, he could hear the sound of others:

'I am your brother.'"[32] The old woman's kindness seems to change Pra-linsky in a somewhat similar way, and Dostoevsky describes this change in language that clearly recalls Gogol's: "And for a long time afterwards, during difficult moments of his life, he would remember, among other pangs of conscience, all the circumstances of this waking up, and this earthenware basin with the faience pitcher full of cold water [. . .] and the old woman with a linen [*kamchatyi*] towel on her left shoulder" (5:42–43). Yet, unlike Akaky's colleague, Pralinsky, as the story's con-clusion suggests, does not necessarily become more humane. Is this just a commentary on Pralinsky's inability to change, or does Dostoevsky use Gogol's passage to cast doubt on the young clerk's transformation as well? The latter is likely. It is important to recall Boris Eikhenbaum's reading of this passage from "The Overcoat," in his article "How Gogol's 'Overcoat' Is Made" (1919), as rhetorically alien to the rest of Gogol's story, as "an unexpected [stylistic] intrusion into the general style that is based on word-play." This stylistic incongruity, Eikhenbaum argues, undermines the veracity of the young clerk's moral transformation.[33] By referring so openly to this passage in "The Overcoat," which is not only stylistically out of place but also obviously exaggerates the young clerk's reaction to Akaky's words, Dostoevsky signals that a transfor-mation is as unlikely for Pralinsky as it was for Gogol's supposedly warm-hearted official.

Indeed, Pralinsky's inability to feel genuine remorse (as opposed to the shame he does feel) is evident in the concluding episodes of the story, where Akim Petrovich, his desk chief, reports that Pseldonimov has asked to be transferred out of the department of which Pralinsky is head. Instead of feeling uneasy, Pralinsky asks Akim Petrovich to tell Pseldonimov that he, Pralinsky, is ready to forgive him. Pralinsky is then amazed by Akim's—quite appropriate—reaction: "But suddenly Ivan Il'ich stopped short, looking in bewilderment at Akim Petrovich's strange behavior. [. . .] Instead of listening to him—and listening to the end—he suddenly blushed like mad and began bowing in a quick and unseemly manner, with small bows, and at the same time walking backward toward the doors. His entire appearance expressed his desire to sink into the earth or, to put it better, to get to his desk as soon as possible. Left alone, Ivan Il'ich rose in confusion from his chair. He looked in the mirror and didn't see [*ne zamechal*] his face" (5:44–45). The reader is thus prompted to think that Pralinsky finally "gets it." But the last paragraph of the story indicates that he most probably did not, a least not entirely: "'No, we need strictness, only strictness and strictness!'

he whispered to himself almost unconsciously; and suddenly bright color appeared on his face. He had never felt so ashamed, so uneasy, not even in the most unbearable moments of his eight-day illness" (5:45).[34] "Aha!" the reader thinks, "At last!" But, like Raskolnikov until the last pages of the novel's epilogue, Pralinsky is obviously ashamed not of his behavior at Pseldonimov's wedding but of the fact that he could not do what he set out to do, namely, act "humanely" toward a lowly clerk: "'I couldn't withstand it!' [*ne vyderzhal!*], he said to himself and sat down powerlessly" (5:45).[35] The story seems to imply that the humanistic ideals first formulated by Belinsky and his generation and ostensibly implemented by the Great Reforms remain just that—ideals. They do not effect an immediate change in relations between people, especially between members of the service hierarchy. Importantly, it is the supposedly meek Pseldonimov who resists the change and rejects Pralinsky's friendship, however awkwardly and tactlessly offered. Pralinsky does not learn from his experience, remaining as haughty and heartless as before.[36]

The main character and narrator in Dostoevsky's next work featuring a clerk, *Notes from the Underground* (*Zapiski iz podpol'ia*, 1864), is a retired collegiate assessor. Despite his higher rank (eighth class) and resemblance to a "superfluous man," he retains connections to Gogol's—as well as to Dostoevsky's own—"insignificant" titular councilors and collegiate registrars. Like Makar Devushkin, the underground man lives "in a corner" (*v uglu*, 5:101); like Poprishchin, he dislikes going to the office (5:125) and entertains the possibility of ending up in an insane asylum "as 'the king of Spain'" (5:126). Furthermore, like Poprishchin, who complains that everything good in this world goes to generals and *kammerjunkers*, the underground man is annoyed by his former classmate Zverkov's intimacy with "generals, colonels, and even *kammerjunkers*" (5:144). Like Akaky, he is concerned with the state of his overcoat and borrows money to mend it from his desk chief, Anton Antonych Setochkin, who has the same name as Goliadkin's desk chief (5:131). Finally, like Prokharchin, the underground man has Napoleonic dreams (5:133–34).

Nonetheless, the underground man is a much more complex character than either Gogol's or Dostoevsky's previous titular councilors, and, even though he possesses some traits that may move the reader to sympathy (or at least pity), he is even more difficult to like. Most importantly, the reader is given direct access to his inner world: writing in the first person, the underground man is shamelessly, even aggressively open and over-sincere in reporting about himself. The reader's discomfort with the narration is heightened by the fact that, unlike Goliadkin, the highly self-aware underground man is intellectually the reader's peer. He therefore is capable of inducing self-awareness in readers, thereby forcing them to identify with him. If Akaky is not acknowledged by his colleagues as "brother" because they cannot see him as their equal, the underground man, by contrast, makes readers reluctant to accept him as their brother because they are all too aware of his uncomfortable similarity to them.[37]

Dostoevsky returns to the image of the "insignificant" titular councilor in his next major work, *Crime and Punishment* (*Prestuplenie i nakazanie*, 1866). The often drunk Marmeladov, dismissed from service—the first time ostensibly due to staff reductions, the second because of his drinking—is perhaps the most morally ambivalent of all Dostoevsky's titular councilors. The consequences of Marmeladov's drinking are devastating for his family; his consumptive wife does everything in her power to care for her young children properly, while his daughter, Sonia, becomes a prostitute to feed them. When in need of money for drink, Marmeladov steals from his wife and begs Sonia for handouts, shamelessly taking the money she earns by selling her body. All this hardly endears him to the reader. Yet Marmeladov is entirely self-aware; he clearly understands the baseness of his behavior and takes responsibility for it. Whether his repentance—which he expresses in a buffoonish, almost jeering way—redeems him is debatable. Nonetheless, when he is run over by a carriage, Sonia, Rodion Raskolnikov, and even his embittered and half-mad wife show great care for him. Most importantly, in witnessing Marmeladov's death and helping his family, Raskolnikov takes a step toward his own eventual redemption.

In his next novel, *The Idiot* (*Idiot*, 1868–69), Dostoevsky continues to explore and develop the figure of the titular councilor bequeathed by Gogol. To begin with, like Akaky Akakievich Bashmachkin, Prince Myshkin arrives in Saint Petersburg "wearing a light cloak and shivering in the winter cold." His supposed idiocy is several times indicated by other characters using the word *togo* (which can serve as a euphemism for madness) that in Gogol's story illustrates Akaky's actual idiocy. Like Akaky, Myshkin is also a talented copyist.[38] By ascribing the features of a barely human Gogolian character to his "positively beautiful human being," Dostoevsky thereby changes our attitude toward Gogol's pitiful original.[39]

In *The Idiot*, Dostoevsky also creates another confrontation between a low-ranking clerk and a general. In this novel, however, the power balance is reversed, and the situation is incomparably more complex. From the novel's outset, the clerk, Luk'ian Lebedev, is presented as someone who knows a lot about social hierarchies and who is capable of using that knowledge to manipulate others and benefit himself. Though he sometimes pretends to be meek, feebleminded, and powerless, he is independent, clever, and strong. By contrast, the retired general Ivolgin is an inherently tainted character; a drunkard and liar, he clearly retired in disgrace. General Ivolgin steals Lebedev's wallet in order to sustain his drinking and support his mistress. Lebedev teases the general mercilessly until he secretly returns the wallet. Yet Lebedev continues to tease him and, to stress his distrust in everything the general says, he also refuses to accept Ivolgin's claim that, as a young boy, he served as Napoleon's page. To ridicule the general's lie, Lebedev concocts his own ludicrous claim, that "in 1812, still being a child, he lost his left leg and buried it at the Vagankovo cemetery in Moscow" (8:411). Exposed as both liar and thief, tormented by Lebedev and, even more severely, by his conscience and shame, the general has a stroke and, after a brief illness, dies.[40]

While the main elements of the Gogolian situation are present in *The Idiot*, it is the clerk who is arguably the aggressor here. Whether he is simply cruel or, tired of the general's lies, is trying to teach him a lesson, the medicine is too strong; reversing the original situation (in which the low-ranking clerks, Poprishchin and Bashmachkin, suffer), Dostoevsky has the general die, and, despite his obvious guilt and his unbearably buffoonish character, his death is tragic, almost Shakespearean. At the same time, the episode retains a modicum of the original situation's comic quality; even the thoughtful and kind Prince Myshkin cannot refrain from laughing after hearing the general's story of his service to Napoleon (the prince, of course, restrains his merriment until after the general has left). Nonetheless, the general's affliction positively affects everyone who had previously laughed at or rejected him, including Lebedev himself. Marmeladov and General Ivolgin are the only instances in which Dostoevsky treats his Gogol-inspired characters with genuine compassion, and therefore their deaths have a curative effect.

Dostoevsky next refers to the Table of Ranks in *A Writer's Diary* (*Dnevnik pisatelia*, 1873–81). Most significantly, in his 1876 piece "The Best People" ("Luchshie liudi"), he offers for the first and only time his general view of the system of ranks, which he presents as both good and not so good for Russia. He begins with a sarcastic description of Peter's 1722 law: "But suddenly there appeared a radical change in the organization of our best people as well: by decree of the state, all the best people were sorted out into fourteen categories called classes, one higher than the other in a kind of ladder, so that we had precisely fourteen categories of human valor, each with a German name" (23:154).[41] In subsequent analysis, Dostoevsky criticizes the rigidity of the Table of Ranks, which allowed the pre-Petrine upper classes to retain their superiority, yet he also acknowledges the law's two positive outcomes. First, the Table allowed the most talented people from the non-noble classes to join the cultural elite, bringing with them new views and new, fruitful ideas: "But this change did achieve its aim in part because it considerably expanded the limits of the old barriers. There came an influx of fresh forces from the depths of society—democratic forces, by our terminology—and from the rank of the seminarians in particular. This influx brought much that was vivifying and productive into the group of the best people, for there appeared people with talents, with new outlooks, and with education that was unprecedented at the time" (665; 23:155). Second, the Table of Ranks encouraged education and introduced the idea of honor: "One must also point out, however, that these 'best' people who settled themselves in place so solidly also set up some very fine rules to live by—the virtual *obligation* to acquire some education, for example—so that this whole caste of best people at the same time made up the bulk of Russia's educated class, the guardian and the bearer of Russian enlightenment, such as it was then. It goes without saying that this class was also the only guardian and bearer of the code of honor, but entirely on the European model, so that the letter and the form of the code at last entirely overcame any genuine feeling in its content: there was a lot of honor, but ultimately there were not such a lot of honorable people" (666; 23:155, emphasis in the original). While Dostoevsky's attitude to the idea of honor borrowed from the West is ambivalent, he nonetheless acknowledges its value.[42]

Elsewhere in the *Diary* Dostoevsky continues to refer to Gogol's portrayals of the service hierarchy. Unsympathetic critics pointed out that the *Diary*'s form resembles Gogol's "Notes of a Madman" and its author was as mentally deranged as Gogol's protagonist. Dostoevsky responded to these allegations in his story "Bobok" (first published as part of the "Diary of a Writer" column in *The Citizen* [*Grazhdanin*] in 1873), where he playfully acknowledged and reinforced its narrator's similarity to Poprishchin. Dostoevsky even makes the narrator of "Bobok" aware of this similarity: he talks about his own purported madness, his deteriorating style, and his increasingly frequent hallucinations. He also shares with the reader a Spanish joke about an insane asylum.[43] Dostoevsky returns to "Notes of a Madman" and its protagonist later in the *Diary*, in the sketch "An Outline of a Denunciatory Tale from Modern Life" ("Plan oblichitel'noi povestii iz sobremennoi zhizni," published in *A Writer's Diary* in 1877), and there his references to Gogol's story are more direct. Unlike the rest of the *Diary*, which pays little attention to rank, these two pieces are full of such references. Like Gogol's story, both, different as they are, deal with the characters' sense of self, vis-à-vis the hierarchy of ranks, which is sometimes inadequate, sometimes superior. At the same time, Dostoevsky continues to revise Gogol's view of the supposed injustice of the service hierarchy.

Dostoevsky introduces the theme of rank early in "Bobok," as soon as the narrator arrives at the cemetery for the funeral of a distant relative, a collegiate councilor. Dostoevsky does not tell what the narrator's rank is, but it is clearly lower than that of the deceased, whose family shuns him as socially inferior: "They kept apart from me and looked down their noses," remarks the narrator (172; 21:43). By mentioning his old worn-out uniform ("My uniform coat really is rather shabby," 172; 21:43), the narrator reminds the reader of poorly dressed titular councilors—most obviously, Gogol's Akaky Bashmachkin and Dostoevsky's Makar Devushkin—and suggests that the narrator may also be a titular councilor.

The narrator emphasizes the theme of social hierarchy by mentioning the differently priced shrouds and burial plots (categories or *razriady*). Remaining at the cemetery after his relative's burial, he dozes off and hears the voices of the recently buried dead, who are often identified by the ranks they bore when they were alive. They also behave in accordance with their former ranks. The narrator notes that "His Excellency," Major-General Pervoedov (fourth class) speaks in a "very weighty and authoritative" voice, and what he says is "presumptuous" (174; 21:45). His speech thus reflects his high rank and seems to follow Gogol's presentations of "their excellencies," in both "Notes of a Madman" and "The Overcoat," as arrogant and haughty. By contrast, the narrator characterizes the voice of a former court councilor (seventh class) as "soft and saccharine," even "obsequious" (174; 21:45). Shortly thereafter the owner of the voice justifies the narrator's characterization by introducing himself thus: "I am only Court Councilor Lebeziatnikov" (179; 21:49). His Gogolian tag name also reflects his behavior as it derives from the verb *lebezit,'* to fawn. His use of the qualifier "only" [*vsego tol'ko*] stresses the relative insignificance of his rank. His name is also the same as that of a rather unpleasant character in *Crime and Punishment*—Mr. Lebeziatnikov (*gospodin Lebeziatnikov*). The earlier Lebeziatnikov redeems himself, however, after Petr Luzhin slips a banknote into Sonia's pocket and then accuses her of stealing it. Indignant at the hypocrisy he witnesses, Mr. Lebeziatnikov exposes Luzhin. Dostoevsky's early fawner thus exemplifies the possibility of moral transformation, a critically important theme in both *Crime and Punishment* and "Bobok."

As the narrator of "Bobok" listens, other former servitors join the fray: a nameless state councilor (fifth class) and finally, a higher-ranking "His Excellency," Privy Councilor Tarasevich (third class). Tarasevich, the highest-ranking in this company of the dead, speaks, as is proper for his rank, in "a fussy, lisping voice," which had something "capriciously imperious" in it (179; 21:48). Tarasevich thus displaces Pervoedov from the highest rank in the underworld. For a while, the usual subordination defines the way the dead servitors interact: Lebeziatnikov is fawning, Tarasevich puts on airs and refuses to make Pervoedov's acquaintance, and Pervoedov is hurt but tries to preserve his pride. The incongruity of these out-of-place hierarchical relations seems Gogolian in spirit. However, when the cynical Petr Klinevich challenges the hierarchical order by pointing out that the hierarchy of ranks is no longer relevant to the deceased and therefore should be discarded, Dostoevsky mounts a comic defense of the system. Since Klinevich rejects the service hierarchy not in the name of human equality, but in the name of moral nihilism, the general's refusal to accept Klinevich's immoral egalitarianism and his insistence that his rank still matters as a sign of his past honorable service to the state become significant. Despite Klinevich's attacks, the general defends the principle: "I served my emperor . . . I have a sword" (184; 21:53). Klinevich laughingly dismisses Pervoedov's argument: "Your sword is fit only for killing mice; and besides, you've never drawn it from its scabbard," to which Pervoedov firmly responds, "All the same, I was a part of the whole" (184; 21:53). Moreover, after other dead join in mocking him and his sword, Pervoedov exclaims: "A sword, my dear sir, signifies honor!" (184; 21:53). It is important that the general's claim anticipates Dostoevsky's own opinion of the rank system (quoted earlier in this chapter) as artificial but nevertheless morally significant. It also resembles his view of the sword's symbolism as expressed in his 1875–76 notebook for *A Writer's Diary*. There Dostoevsky directly connects the sword and the idea of honor, both service honor and personal honor: "And the duel is not at all silly. [. . .] Generals who

claimed that the sword had been given to them to protect their fatherland did not know or kept forgetting that those who drew it for the
protection of their honor were also the ones who could stand up against
the enemy" (24:102). Granted, the general in "Bobok" seems to be exactly
the type of general who forgets about the importance of personal honor
for the overall integrity of the service nobility. Nonetheless, he is the
only dead servitor who defends the sword's honor against nihilism and
debauchery. In this he agrees with the narrator: both reject moral nihilism, and do so in similar terms. The general interrupts the dead who
are discussing plans for moral disrobing ("Let us bare ourselves [*Zago-
limsia i obnazhimsia*]!"; 183; 21:52): "'I protest! I protest with every ounce
of my strength!' said General Pervoedov forcefully" (184; 21:52); and
the narrator twice exclaims "No, I cannot put up with this!" (178;
21:48, 54).[44] Furthermore, the agreement between "His Excellency" (the
general) and the narrator (possibly a titular councilor) demonstrates
that a character's moral judgment is neither proportional nor inversely
proportional to rank: both generals and titular councilors can be morally
sound.

Dostoevsky's next work in the tradition, "An Outline of a Denunciatory Tale from Modern Life," reimagines Gogol's "Notes of a Madman"
in a new social situation. This tale is also Dostoevsky's last rendition of
a confrontation between "His Excellency" and a low-ranking clerk. This
new Poprishchin, although Dostoevsky portrays him as more intelligent
than Gogol's character ("To exemplify a type, I would rather present a
person who is a bit cleverer than average rather than stupider," 25:132),
shares much with the original. Like Poprishchin, he has difficulties
succeeding in his service career: "And so the young man enters, let's
suppose, the service. He doesn't possess stature, doesn't 'possess wit,'
and has no connections" (25:132). Like Poprishchin, he believes that he
is a good writer and even contemplates a career in literature: "Why
should I serve, [only] misfits [*meshki*] serve, my career [*poprishche*] is literature," 25:132; note the word "*poprishche*" here, a reference to Gogol's
Poprishchin). After failing as a writer, he succeeds in attaching himself
to his superior—he manages to do what Dostoevsky calls *primostit'sia*,
"to find a situation." Here Dostoevsky directly connects his imaginary
careerist to Poprishchin: "And Poprishchin in Gogol also began by distinguishing himself in sharpening quills and was summoned for this
purpose to the apartment of 'His Excellency,' where he saw the director's
daughter, for whom he sharpened two quills. But Poprishchin's time
has passed, and quills are not sharpened anymore; and our hero cannot

transform his character [*izmenit' svoemu kharakteru*]: it is not quills that are on his mind but the most daring dreams. To be brief, in the shortest time he is already convinced that he has captivated the director's daughter, and she is pining for him" (25:133). Here Dostoevsky makes his character even less likable than the original: if Gogol's Poprishchin seems to be sincerely in love with the director's daughter, Dostoevsky's imitator wants to use her to advance his career. "'So, here is my fortune [*vot i kar'era*],' he thinks; 'And what would be the use of women, if a clever man couldn't make a career through them [*cherez nikh*]: this is the gist of the woman question, if you really consider it. And above all, it is not shameful: who didn't [*malo li kto*] find their path through women?'" (25:133). The last sentence clearly alludes to Poprishchin's list of historical examples regarding a sudden elevation in social standing: "See how many examples there are in history: some commoner, not even a gentleman but a tradesman [*meshchanin*] or even a peasant—and all of a sudden it turns out that he is some grandee [*vel'mozha*] or even a sovereign [*gosudar'*]."[45] Dostoevsky's character, however, refers to a particular method of social climbing common in Russia in the eighteenth century, the so-called *sluchài*, advancement through a love affair with the empress.

Like Gogol's Poprishchin, Dostoevsky's character is mistaken about the director's daughter's tender feelings: "But—but at this time there appears [*podvertyvaetsia*], as in Poprishchin's case, an aide-de-camp!" (instead of the *kammerjunker* in Gogol's story; 25:133). Unlike Poprishchin, however, Dostoevsky's character does not go mad from unrequited love but writes an anonymous letter denouncing his beloved: "O! How he locks himself in his little room [to hide] from his landlady, how he trembles in fear that he will be seen! But he scribbles, scribbles [*strochit*], changing his handwriting, creates four pages of slander and offenses, rereads [everything] with delight and, having sat up all night, at sunrise seals the letter and addresses it to the bridegroom, the aide-de-camp. He has changed his handwriting, he is not afraid. Now he counts the hours; now the letter should have arrived—this is [the letter] to the bridegroom about his bride—O! of course he will refuse [to marry her], he will be scared, because this is not a letter but a 'masterpiece' [Dostoevsky uses the mockingly distorted *shedëvr* instead of the normal *shedevr*]!" (25:133–34). The letter does not work: the aide-de-camp weds the director's daughter anyway. However, Dostoevsky's character cannot stop: "Our hero has happened to find [*napal na*] his career, so to speak. He was seized by some kind of illusion [*mirazh*], like Poprishchin"

(25:134). He now begins to write anonymous letters denouncing his superior, the general: "He finds out [*vyvedyvaet*] everything about his general, he figures out, he pours everything that has accumulated in him during all the years of unsatisfying [*neudovletvorennoi*] service—peeved ambition [*samoliubie*], bile, jealousy. He criticizes all the general's actions, he ridicules him in the most merciless way—and this [he does] in several letters, a whole series of letters. And how he likes it at first! The general's deeds [*postupki*], and his wife, and his mistress—everything, everything he depicted in his letters" (25:134). He is so proud of himself that he even addresses one of the letters to a minister, proposing radical state reforms. He believes that when his authorship of the letters becomes known, the minister will be so impressed that he will make the letter known to the emperor (25:134). Thus his "illusion," like Poprishchin's delirium, is supposed to elevate him—if not to royal rank, then to a position that would bring him close to the royal person.

For a while Dostoevsky's character enjoys his new occupation, but then his intelligence trips him up and he realizes the true nature of what he is doing: "Some time passes in this manner, but . . . but suddenly a strange idea dawns on him, namely: that he is Poprishchin, no better than [*ne bolee kak*] Poprishchin, the very same Poprishchin, but a million times baser; and all these stealthy lampoons [*paskvili iz-za ugla*], all this anonymous power is in fact an illusion and nothing else, and the most disgusting [*gaden'kii*] illusion, even worse than the dream about the Spanish throne" (25:134). Furthermore, he also cannot keep his secret, shares some minor details of his clandestine occupation with one of his fellow clerks, and suddenly comes to the terrifying conclusion that everyone knows about his letter-writing. This conclusion drives him close to insanity ("in a word, he nearly goes insane," 25:135). Unable to contain himself, he confesses to "His Excellency," hoping that his noble honesty will not only bring him forgiveness but will heighten his status:

> Of course, because of his illness, of course, because of his suspiciousness [*mnitel'nost'*], but *most of all because*—even in a funk, humiliated and blaming himself—he still dreamed as before, like a fool intoxicated by self-conceit, that perhaps His Excellency, having listened to him and nonetheless, so to speak, been stricken by his genius—will open his arms/hands [*ruki*], with which he signs so many papers for the benefit of the fatherland, and will embrace him: "Is it possible, he would say [*deskat'*], you have been driven to this, unfortunate but gifted young man! O!

> It is I who am to blame, I haven't noticed [*prosmotrel*] you! I take
> all the blame. O Lord, this is what our talented youth is forced to
> do because of our old ways and prejudices! But come, come to
> my bosom and share my [service] position with me, and we . . .
> and we will turn the department around!" (25:135–36, emphasis
> in the original)

"His Excellency," however, does not embrace the new Poprishchin but kicks him out of his office—and the department. This time, Dostoevsky's titular councilor does not resemble a defenseless clerk in the least: he is an ignoble and aggressive social climber. Dostoevsky's imaginary scenario is a commentary on changed mores—but also on the unrealized potential for evildoing that exists in Gogol's Poprishchin.

Dostoevsky concludes his sketch with an open nod to Gogol: "In a word, it seems to me that the type of the anonymous spitter is a pretty good theme for a tale. And it is serious. Of course, it would be nice to have Gogol for this [*tut, konechno, by nuzhen Gogol*], but . . . I am glad that at least I came across the idea by chance" (25:136). This not quite complimentary nod serves to emphasize Dostoevsky's disagreement with Gogol rather than his dependence on him. Dostoevsky's Poprishchin in fact resembles his own Goliadkin—who also thinks that the general's daughter is in love with him and who also goes mad, but who is far more aggressive and sinister than Gogol's character. The conclusion of Dostoevsky's sketch ("Perhaps I will indeed try to put it into a novel," 25:136) could thus be a tongue-in-cheek reference to his own earlier work—which he valued greatly although it was so shortsightedly underappreciated by critics, including Belinsky.

Despite Dostoevsky's short stint in the Chief Engineering Administration in his youth and perhaps because of his forced service in the Siberian Seventh Line Battalion after his release from prison camp, military service is represented rather sketchily in his literary writings. He portrays military servitors much less frequently than clerks, and when he does depict them, they usually appear in the context of affairs of honor. In dealing with the military hierarchy and conflicts over honor, Dostoevsky also depends more on the preexisting literary tradition than on firsthand knowledge of actual customs.

In discussing the code of honor, Dostoevsky repeatedly cites the example of Gogol's Lieutenant Pirogov, whose name appears throughout his work: in *Notes from the Underground*; *The Idiot*; Dostoevsky's critical essay "A Number of Articles about Russian Literature"; the article "Something about Lying," published in 1873 in *A Writer's Diary*; and the notes for the *Diary* (see 5:128, 8:385, 18:59 and 124–23; 24:79 and 102; 25:241). In each case, Pirogov, who is flogged by the locksmith Schiller and does not retaliate, is presented by Dostoevsky as the epitome of ignominy.[46]

Even though, according to the code of honor, Pirogov has no acceptable recourse against his offender, a German artisan, Dostoevsky seems to believe that in cases like Pirogov's even raw violence is better than inaction. In *Demons (Besy*, 1871–72), he portrays a nameless second lieutenant who, after a public reprimand, bites his superior officer on the shoulder (10:269). The chronicler of the novel presents him as a radical and a madman, and it is tempting to agree with him. However, Iliusha Snegirev of *The Brothers Karamazov (Brat'ia Karamazovy*, 1880), who bites Alesha Karamazov's finger to avenge his father's dishonor, is a noble character in the eyes of both Alesha (14:183 and 187) and, especially, his father, the retired staff-captain Nikolai Snegirev (14:186).[47] Granted, according to the honor code, Snegirev should have challenged his offender, Dmitry Karamazov, regardless of the possibility that his death in a duel would have left his large and infirm family destitute. Iliusha's actions, however, absolve his father's otherwise dishonorable behavior. By staging many conflicts across ranks, Dostoevsky suggests that physical offences render the hierarchy of ranks irrelevant. The reluctance of Gogol's Pirogov to cross class boundaries to punish Schiller forever dishonors him in Dostoevsky's eyes. The nameless second lieutenant (thirteenth class), who cannot challenge his superior to a duel, avenges his honor by unconventional means. While Dmitry Karamazov and Snegirev are equals and thus able to duel, it is the unranked child Iliusha who resolves the conflict of honor. Iliusha's youthful approach demonstrates that convention can rigidify and harm human relations.

Throughout his work, Dostoevsky suggests that the right to defend one's honor is a universal human right, unregulated by the Table of Ranks. His challenge to Gogol's rigid (albeit fantastic, as is argued in chapter 3) hierarchy of ranks ultimately amounts to the same idea: like the code of honor, rank does not define the person. "His Excellency" can show kindness, whereas a low-ranking clerk can be mean and aggressive. Dostoevsky believes neither in the honor code entirely regulating a person's behavior nor in reducing him to his rank. Personality and morality trump conventions and institutions.

Conclusion

Beyond Rank

The tradition at the center of inquiry in this book essentially ends with Dostoevsky: in many ways, he was the last writer for whom the system of rank mattered. Although it had little appeal to him as a means of career-building, it was a frequent theme in his works; it was a device he used to voice his opinion about Russian literary tradition and to define his own place in it; it was also a cultural phenomenon that factored into his assessment of the Russian nobility and its values—an important question for him ever since he was stripped of his own noble status as part of the punishment for his involvement in the Petrashevsky Circle. However, rank never defined who Dostoevsky was as a member of Russian society.

The diminished worth of rank for mid-nineteenth-century writers of noble status reflects both the gradual fading, in the second half of the nineteenth century, of the Table of Ranks' importance as a career tool and the new view of the value of writing versus that of service. While the Table of Ranks maintained its relevance in Russian society up until 1917, it lost its unique power to define a nobleman's status vis-à-vis his peers—the power that Peter the Great intended it to have and that lasted throughout the eighteenth and the first third of the nineteenth centuries. Later in the nineteenth century, however, a greater divergence among writers of noble status in their relation to service emerged: some continued to use it to build their careers, others served out of necessity (to support themselves financially, for example), yet others completely lost interest in service and did not serve. Several factors contributed to this change. One was the nobility's becoming, in the reign of Nicholas I, far less willing to cooperate with the government and thus more reluctant to serve.[1] Nicholas's strict supervision of the literary sphere surely increased this reluctance among writers. In addition, the professionalization of literature that was finally happening in earnest in the second half of the century made serving the state both less attractive and less necessary. Lastly, different ways to be socially important became available and acceptable to both nobles and non-nobles, such as the ability to influence public opinion through the written word, including literature, criticism, and journalism.

Vissarion Belinsky is a good example of a person who never held a rank and who earned such a lofty reputation as a literary critic that his opinions still continue to be relevant in Russia today. Belinsky was a typical *raznochinets*: his father was born to a priest's family, became a physician, and in 1830 gained hereditary nobility through his service rank.[2] Vissarion, however, was confirmed as a hereditary noble only in 1847, shortly before his untimely death from tuberculosis. Notably, although undoubtedly intelligent and able, Belinsky missed the chance to become ennobled through his own rank, which he would have been able to do if he had graduated from the university and served (as Nikolai Chernyshevsky and many other *raznochintsy* did): even though he studied at Moscow University in 1829–32, not only did he not receive a degree but he was never even promoted to the second year of studies, spending all three years repeating the first-year program. Belinsky was eventually expelled, for reasons of "poor health" and "limited abilities."[3] Nonetheless, he launched a strikingly successful career as a literary critic: in 1834 he began publishing in Nikolai Nadezhdin's journals *Telescope* and *Rumor* (*Molva*), where his first important critical essays appeared, including the 1834 "Literary Reveries" ("Literaturnye mechtaniia"), the essay that marked the beginning of his fame as a critic. Both journals were closed in 1836, after Petr Chaadaev's first "Philosophical Letter" was published in *Telescope*; Nadezhdin was sent into exile, and Belinsky was questioned by the police but released for lack of evidence. He survived their closure by unofficially editing *The Moscow Observer* (*Moskovskii nabliudatel'*), where he continued to publish his critical essays. In 1839 he became the leading critic in Andrei Kraevsky's influential *Notes of the Fatherland* (*Otechestvennye zapiski*). During his years with *Notes of the Fatherland*, Belinsky gained an enormous authority among Russian readers and writers. It was he who announced that Dostoevsky's *Poor Folk* qualified him as "the new Gogol" and thus launched Dostoevsky's literary career. For his polemical zeal and refusal to compromise, Belinsky's admirers nicknamed him "the furious [*neistovyi*] Vissarion" (after the title character in Ludovico Ariosto's *Orlando Furioso*). In 1847 Belinsky moved to *The Contemporary*, whose editorship Nikolai Nekrasov and Ivan Panaev assumed that year. He continued to publish his increasingly influential essays there until his death in 1848. It speaks for itself that Belinsky's 1847 public letter to Gogol criticizing his *Selected Passages from Correspondence with Friends* acquired the status of a political manifesto both among its readers and in the eyes of state authorities. When the members of the Petrashevsky Circle were arrested in 1849, they were accused, among other things, of reading and passing along this letter, and, as is well known, the punishments they received were uncommonly severe. After Belinsky's death his influence did not diminish: it lasted throughout the nineteenth century, and even though it faded somewhat in the era of modernism (the modernists did not share his sociological approach to literature), it grew again during the Soviet period. Furthermore, even now, fairly or not, Belinsky is still considered to be "the father of Russian criticism." As the literary scholar Boris Egorov writes in his entry on Belinsky in *Russian Writers, 1800–1917*, "The role of Belinsky in Russian criticism is similar to Pushkin's role in literature."[4] Curiously, according to the Russian Wikipedia article on Belinsky, in 2013, 478 streets, squares, and alleys in Russian cities were named after him.[5]

The development of different ways of making a name also caused some nobles not to serve and yet to enjoy a high status among their peers. The case of Belinsky's contemporary and frequent opponent, the leading Slavophile Konstantin Aksakov (1817–60), is illuminating. One of the founding members of the Slavophile movement, a member of the famous Aksakov family,[6] Konstantin was a talented and well-educated man: he graduated from Moscow University with the degree of candidate (*kandidat*), which involved passing further examinations in addition to those required for the degree of actual student (*deistvitel'nyi student*). He subsequently also earned a master's (*magisterskaia*) degree, again passing examinations and writing a long and serious research paper on Lomonosov, which was published in 1846. Nonetheless, Konstantin never launched a formal career as a scholar or educator: offered a teaching position at Kiev University, he found himself unable to leave his family household in Moscow and declined the offer. Instead, he chose to lead the life of a private person, writing and publishing poetry, literary criticism, and historical treatises. And yet, his prestige among his comrades the Slavophiles, as well as among his opponents the Western-izers, was extraordinarily high. Similarly to Belinsky's, it was based entirely on his writings and his personal reputation as a passionate and uncompromising exponent of his chosen ideology, Slavophilism.

Not everyone followed Konstantin Aksakov's example: service was still a common occupation for young noblemen. However, nineteenth-century writers increasingly viewed it as a serious impediment to their writing. Ivan Panaev (1812–52)—a writer, critic, and journalist, and beginning in 1847, the co-owner and coeditor, with Nekrasov, of *The Contemporary*—considered service a nuisance that interfered with his literary pursuits for the duration of his employment, from 1831 to 1844; he retired early, despite the likelihood of making a brilliant career. As Chernyshevsky wrote in his obituary for Panaev, he "left the service and never regretted that he neglected his service career for literature."[7] In contrast, Ivan Aksakov (1823–86), Konstantin's younger brother, began service with genuine enthusiasm, only to change his attitude when faced with the reality of the Russian bureaucracy. In his youth, apparently keen on improving the functioning of the Russian legal sys-tem, he chose to attend the elite Petersburg law school (Imperatorskoe uchilishche pravovedeniia) and in 1842 eagerly began his service in the Moscow Criminal Department of the Senate. He was soon disappointed (as his satirical *Life of a Bureaucrat* [*Zhizn' chinovnika*], 1843, attests), but continued to serve, conscientiously—even after he was held under arrest for five days in 1849 on suspicion of participating in a political conspiracy—until 1851, when his supervisor forcefully suggested that the poetry he wrote was incompatible with his being a civil servant. Instead of giving up poetry, Aksakov resigned his service position. He briefly returned to service in 1855, during the Crimean War (he con-sidered it to be his duty to serve in time of war), and retired for good in 1857, in the rank of court councilor (seventh class). The difference be-tween Ivan Aksakov's relatively short stint in service and Panaev's was in Aksakov's earnest initial desire to be a useful state official. However, his decision to retire when faced with the choice between service and writing is as indicative of the changing views of the relative value for noblemen of these two activities as was Panaev's choice to abandon service.

Leo Tolstoy was also eager to serve as a young man—in his case, in order to improve his social standing (not only was his family not very prominent, despite being titled, but in addition Tolstoy did not finish his university education, which left him without a rank and made his

entering the service and thus achieving appropriate status more difficult). Tolstoy's early diaries reflect his anxiety about having no rank.
While in the Caucasus, where one of his older brothers served, he
passed an examination that gained him the rank of ensign (1851). About
two years later, Tolstoy was promoted to the first officer's rank of warrant officer (fourteenth class), and when the Crimean War broke out, he
requested to be transferred first to the Danube Army fighting against
Turkey, and then to Crimea, where he served with distinction. While
in Crimea, he wrote his *Sevastopol Sketches* (1855), which brought him
fame as a writer. Tolstoy lost interest in a service career and began
thinking about retirement soon after the sketches' publication, when he
realized that literature was an occupation that could bring him not only
satisfaction but also social standing. On March 11, 1855, he wrote in his
diary: "A military career is not for me, and the sooner I get out of it [*iz
neia vyberus'*] in order to devote myself completely to a literary one, the
better."[8] He retired in 1856, in the rank of lieutenant (twelfth class).

Tolstoy was not particularly interested in the Table of Ranks as a
topic in his writings. Granted, he understood the rank system well, and
his literary works depict characters in service. The society described in
War and Peace is a society of servitors. In *Anna Karenina*, it is important
to realize the difference between Konstantin Levin (who does not
serve), Aleksei Karenin (who is a high-ranking civil servant and the
executor of imperial policies), and Stiva Oblonsky, Karenin's protégé
(he received his service position thanks to Karenin), who serves for
status and income. It is noteworthy, however, that when Stiva needs to
increase his income, he prefers more lucrative private employment to
state service; for him, wealth trumps the prestige of serving the state, and
this is important for understanding his character—particularly in contrast to Levin, who considers such employment dishonorable. Finally,
it is crucial to realize how much Aleksei Vronsky loses when he sacri-
fices his service career to be with Anna: he becomes a nobody in the
eyes of members of his circle. And yet, even though it is an important
part of Tolstoy's characters' lives, state service as such almost never
becomes the focus of his attention. One exception, perhaps, is his 1886
novella *The Death of Ivan Ilyich (Smert' Ivana Il'icha)*, whose title character
is concerned with the success of his service career (he is a high-ranking
bureaucrat), only to discover, when facing death, that it is irrelevant.

Other writers of noble status served for the duration or large parts of
their careers as writers, and they balanced their service and writerly
careers in various ways. Ivan Goncharov (1812–91) was in service from

1834 to 1860 and then again from 1862 to 1867. Born to a family of merchants (*iz kupecheskikh detei*: this is how the service record compiled at the time of his retirement defines his origins[9]), Goncharov was first educated in the Moscow Commerce School (Moskovskoe kommercheskoe uchilishche) but eventually convinced his mother to allow him to enter Moscow University, from which he graduated in 1834. He began his service in his native Simbirsk, as a secretary in the chancellery of the governor. Dissatisfied with both Simbirsk and the service, he moved to Saint Petersburg and in May 1835 began to serve in the Ministry of Finance in the position of translator (Goncharov knew three foreign languages). His first rank was that of gubernial secretary (twelfth class). He was poorly paid and, like Akaky Bashmachkin, worried at times about the condition of his overcoat. He supplemented his income with private tutoring.

Goncharov stayed at the Ministry of Finance until 1852, when he was invited to join Admiral Putiatin's expedition to Japan. By that time Goncharov was in the rank of collegiate assessor (eighth class). Upon his return from Japan, he was promoted to the rank of court councilor (seventh class) and continued to serve in the Ministry of Finance in the position of a desk chief. In July of the same year he was promoted to the rank of collegiate councilor (sixth class) and in December, to the rank of state councilor (fifth class; as his service record indicates, Goncharov was promoted "against the rules," *vne pravil*, to recognize his special service, *osobye zaslugi*, as secretary to Admiral Putiatin). In 1856 Goncharov transferred to the Ministry of Education and assumed the position of censor in the Saint Petersburg Censorship Committee. He served in this position until his temporary retirement, in February 1860. Goncharov returned to service in 1862, to the Ministry of Internal Affairs, and for about a year served as the editor-in-chief of the government newspaper *The Northern Mail* (*Severnaia pochta*). In June 1863 he resigned his editorial position and was appointed a member of the Council of the Minister of Internal Affairs for Book Printing. Simultaneously, Goncharov was promoted to the rank of actual state councilor (fourth class); this was the rank in which he retired.[10]

It is difficult to ascertain how Goncharov combined service and writing, except for the fact that it took him over ten years to finish *Oblomov* and that the last push to conclude the novel came during one of his prolonged leaves of absence abroad. The only work of his that directly refers to the state service and its relation to writing is his first novel, *A Common Story* (*Obyknovennaia istoriia*, 1847). Its two protagonists,

Aleksandr Aduev and his uncle, Petr Aduev, both serve, the former just beginning his service at the opening of the novel, the latter successfully climbing the ladder of ranks (when the reader meets him, he is in the rank of state councilor, fifth class). It is often suggested that the character of Aduev Jr. is autobiographical: like Goncharov, he arrives in Saint Petersburg from the provinces and begins his service at the bottom. Somewhat ironically, it is Aduev Sr.'s career that anticipates Goncharov's own eventual service success: at the end of the novel he is in the rank of actual state councilor—the very same rank in which Goncharov would conclude his service. The coincidental similarity ends here: unlike Goncharov, Aduev Sr. is about to be promoted to the rank of privy state councilor but decides to resign for the sake of his wife's health. Aduev Sr. also owns two factories—that is, he is both a state servitor and a businessman. Particularly noteworthy in *A Common Story* is Aduev Sr.'s idea that while service and business can go together, service and poetry cannot.[11] As he tells his nephew (who at that time is still very much absorbed in writing poetry), "I am a state councilor by rank and a manufacturer by trade; but if you were to offer me the title of first among poets instead, by God, I would not accept it!"[12] Gradually, Aduev Jr. arrives at the same conclusion.

It is noteworthy that Goncharov himself, while continuing to write prose, served quite willingly. His characters in *A Common Story* likewise do not show any dislike of civil service. In contrast, Mikhail Saltykov (1826–89; his pen name was Shchedrin, and he is commonly referred to as Saltykov-Shchedrin), who also served for most of his life, was far more ambivalent in his attitude toward service. After his graduation in 1844 from the Imperial Alexander Lyceum (originally the Lyceum in Tsarskoe Selo, Pushkin's alma mater; it was renamed and moved to Saint Petersburg in 1843), he began his service in the chancellery of the Ministry of Defense in the rank of collegiate secretary (tenth class). Even though Saltykov-Shchedrin entered the state service somewhat reluctantly (reportedly, he wanted to continue his education at a university), it was a good beginning to a promising career. In 1847 Saltykov-Shchedrin was promoted to the rank of titular councilor (ninth class), but the next year his writing interfered with his career progress: Nicholas I found dangerous ideas in Saltykov-Shchedrin's early novella *A Complicated Affair* (*Zaputannoe delo*, 1848), and the writer was arrested and exiled to Vyatka, where he continued to serve, first in the provincial (*gubernskaia*) chancellery and then in the capacity of an official on special assignment (*chinovnik po osobym porucheniiam*) to the Vyatka governor.

He was recommended for a promotion to the rank of collegiate assessor (eighth class) in 1850 but did not receive it until 1852, due to Nicholas's distrust of him. In 1854, still in Vyatka, he was made a court councilor (seventh class). After Nicholas's death in 1855, Saltykov-Shchedrin was allowed to return to Saint Petersburg. Beginning in January 1856, he resumed his service in the Ministry of Internal Affairs, this time as an official on special assignment. It seems that the same year Saltykov-Shchedrin was promoted to the rank of collegiate councilor (sixth class): in her letter of 1856, his mother, who disapproved of his marriage, scornfully calls him and his wife "a collegiate councilor and his indigent lady [*goloi barynei*]."[13] In 1858 Saltykov-Shchedrin was transferred to Ryazan to take up the position of vice-governor. It is likely that at that time he was promoted to the rank of state councilor (fifth class). His attempts to improve the way the provincial offices worked caused conflicts with the Ryazan governor, and in 1860 Saltykov-Shchedrin requested a transfer to Tver, where he served for another two years in the same position, causing the same problems, until his first retirement in 1862. In 1864, however, he found it necessary to return to service, this time to the Ministry of Finance.[14] For the next four years he served in the provinces in the position of head of the treasury department, first in Penza, then in Tula, and then in Ryazan. During this stint in service, Saltykov-Shchedrin was promoted to the rank of actual state councilor (fourth class; the promotion took place in 1866). Head of the treasury department was a powerful position, and by many accounts Saltykov-Shchedrin used this power aggressively to enforce finance revision policies in the guberniyas in which he served, and this again caused conflicts with the respective governors and thus repeated transfers. Despite the support of his classmate Mikhail Reitern, who was the Minister of Finance at the time, Saltykov-Shchedrin was forced to retire in July 1868.

As is evident from this short description of Saltykov-Shchedrin's service career, he both attempted to participate in service conscientiously and resented it. A zealous official trying to fulfill his duties, he was also a vehement critic of the system. He criticized bureaucracy in his journalistic essays, such as "More Tooth-Gnashing" ("Eshche skrezhet zubovnyi," 1860) and "Well-Meant Speeches" ("Blagonamerennye rechi," 1876); he portrayed it caustically in his literary works, such as *The History of a Town* (*Istoriia odnogo goroda*, 1869–70) and *Pompadours and Pompadouresses* (*Pompadury i pompadurshi*, 1863–74). In Saltykov-Shchedrin's fiction, the world of bureaucracy, often portrayed allegorically, is an ugly and nonsensical world, in which the reality of state service is not only satirized but grotesquely distorted. At the same time, Saltykov-Shchedrin was one of very few state servants who—when he was in service, however reluctantly—attempted to reform the Russian bureaucracy. It is for this reason that the Russian biographer of Saltykov-Shchedrin, V. V. Prozorov, aptly calls him "one of the strangest officials in Russian history."[15] His prolonged service apparently also made him one of the most idiosyncratic Russian writers. In 1882 the historian and editor of the journal *Russian Antiquities* (*Russkaia starina*) Mikhail Semevsky wrote up Saltykov-Shchedrin's service history as told to him by the writer. According to Semevsky's report, the writer concluded his description of his service career with the following declaration: "In general, I repeat: I try to forget the time of my service. And you shouldn't publish anything about it. I am a writer, this is my calling." In response, Semevsky pointed out that "if he hadn't gone through all the stages of service [. . .] then, perhaps, he wouldn't have become who he is now [as a writer], that is, wouldn't know Russia [*Rus'*] and all its bureaucracy as he does." Semevsky reports that Saltykov-Shchedrin agreed with his assessment that his service experience made him the writer he was.[16]

Nonetheless, Saltykov-Shchedrin did see service as interfering with his writing—or, at least, not coexisting with it harmoniously. In 1887 he wrote a short autobiography for Semevsky's collection *Acquaintances* (*Znakomye*), mockingly describing the relationship between his service and his writing: "When I was ten, I entered the Moscow Noble Institute, and then was transferred to the Lyceum in Tsarskoe Selo. There I began writing poetry, for which I was often punished; there I also began publishing it. [. . .] After graduation from the Lyceum (in 1844), I didn't write poetry any more. Then I served and wrote, wrote and served until 1848, when I was exiled to Vyatka for the novella *A Complicated Affair*. I lived there for almost eight years and served, but didn't write. In 1856 I returned to literature with *Provincial Sketches* [*Gubernskie ocherki*] and up to 1868 wrote and served, served and wrote. In 1868 I left service for good and devoted myself entirely to literature."[17] Saltykov-Shchedrin presents the relationship between service and writing as incongruous and slightly comical. Before him, looking at these relations from a different perspective, Ivan Panaev likewise found them incongruous and comical. He included a minor character, an elderly countess, in his 1840 novella *Delirium Tremens* (*Belaia goriachka*). The old lady is outraged by a non-serving and thus rankless poet and contrasts him unfavorably with the high-ranking Derzhavin: "How come he only twiddles his thumbs [*b'et baklushi*] and writes his little verses? <. . .> In our time the leading poets were also important state officials [*gosudarstvennye liudi*]. The late Gavrila Romanovich [Derzhavin] was a minister and actual privy councilor, a man who was in favor [*pol'zovalsia milost'iu*] throughout three reigns."[18] Of course, Derzhavin's service career was not as smooth as the countess is presenting it, but what is noteworthy here is not so much her ignorance but Panaev's (or his narrator's) ridicule of the very idea that it is good for a poet to serve and climb the ladder of ranks.

The pinnacle of this kind of ridicule of a writing government official is the persona of Kozma (*Koz'ma*) Prutkov, bureaucrat and graphomaniac, created in 1854 by a group of writers: the three brothers Zhemchuzhnikov (Aleksandr, 1826–96; Aleksei, 1821–1908; and Vladimir, 1830–84) and their better-known first cousin, A. K. Tolstoy (1817–75).[19] In the 1884 sketch "Biographical Information about Kozma Prutkov" ("Biograficheskie svedeniia o Koz'me Prutkove"), the surviving creators provide details about his service career. They begin his biography with the declaration that he was a lifelong state servitor: "*Kozma Petrovich Prutkov* spent all his life, except for the years of his childhood and early boyhood, in state service, first in the military, and then in the civil branch."[20] They continue: "In 1820, he entered the military service, just for the sake of the uniform [*tol'ko dlia mundira*], and spent just slightly over two years in this service, as a hussar."[21] After having a prophetic dream (entirely nonsensical and impossible to interpret), he retired and took up the civil service. The sketch quotes Kozma's purported explanation of his decision to retire: "The same morning, having barely awakened, I decided to leave the regiment and sent in my resignation; and when the resignation was granted, I immediately obtained a service position in the Ministry of Finance, at the Assay Office, where I would remain forever!" And, as the sketch informs us, he did: "Indeed, having joined the Assay Office in 1823, he stayed there until his death, that is, until January 13, 1863. Superiors distinguished and rewarded him. Here at the Assay Office, he was honored by having been awarded all civil ranks, including actual state councilor, and the highest position, that of chief of the Assay Office."[22]

Kozma Prutkov's career as a writer was not long: as the authors of the biography point out, he began writing in 1853 only to stop in 1854, and then returned to writing again in the 1860s. As they put it, "he acted openly [*glasno*] as a writer [*na literaturnom poprishche*] for only five

years."[23] Before that he published anonymously or under pseudonyms—
just like some of the serving poets of the late eighteenth century. Despite
his short literary career, Kozma Prutkov wrote prolifically and in various
genres: poetry, prose, drama, and journalism. He is particularly famous
for his fables and aphorisms; these genres conveniently allowed his
creators to portray him as nonsensical, pompous, and utterly hackneyed.
He is also known for his "Project: Concerning the Introduction of Like-
Mindedness in Russia" ("Proekt: O vvedenii edinomysliia v Rossii,"
published in *The Contemporary* in 1863). This parodic representation of a
writing bureaucrat was so successful that many quotations from his
works have entered the common parlance and are used by educated
Russians to this day.

It is noteworthy that all the creators of Kozma Prutkov served for
significant parts of their lives, and their attitude toward service was
mostly unenthusiastic (with the possible exception of Aleksandr Zhemchuzhnikov). Aleksei Tolstoy served from 1834 to 1861. He began his
service as a diplomat but in 1840 transferred to the second division of
His Imperial Majesty's Chancellery, which was in charge of legal affairs.
He received the title of *kammerjunker* in 1843. Tolstoy served in the
chancellery until 1855, when he transferred to a rifle regiment in the rank
of major (eighth class), with the intention of participating in the Crimean
War. He fell ill with typhus, and did not get a chance to take part in
combat. On the day of Alexander II's coronation, he was appointed
aide-de-camp to the emperor, an appointment he accepted only reluctantly. Disliking court service, he managed to receive an indefinite
leave of absence in 1859, and in 1861 he was allowed to retire. In a letter
to Alexander II of August or September 1861, he wrote, explaining his
reasons for retiring: "*Service and art are incompatible*, one hurts the other,
it is necessary to choose."[24]

Aleksandr Zhemchuzhnikov served for the longest time among the
group, from 1851 to 1885, in various positions, including vice-governor
of Pskov (1870–73; he received the rank of actual state councilor during
this appointment), as an official on special assignment (1873–82), and,
in 1882–85, as governor of Vilna (today's Vilnius). There are no indications that his long and successful service career vexed him or interfered
with his literary pursuits. An occasional writer, Aleksandr was the one
who initiated the persona of Kozma Prutkov by writing the fables
ascribed to him; he also continued to write in Prutkov's style long after
the others had abandoned the game or died (his last work in the style of

Kozma Prutkov was published in 1907). Aleksei Zhemchuzhnikov, who was Ivan Aksakov's classmate at law school, served from 1841 to 1858. His service career was successful: he was made a *kammerjunker* in 1844 and received the rank of state councilor in 1854. He retired at the age of thirty-seven, apparently having grown to resent the state bureaucracy. The fact that Aleksei was a much more prolific writer than either of his brothers could also have influenced his decision to retire early.

Vladimir Zhemchuzhnikov served on and off from 1854 to 1882, in different ministries and departments, including a stint in the military during the Crimean War (he did not participate in combat due to illness and retired in 1857 in the rank of lieutenant). The biographers cite Vladimir's honesty and adherence to principles as the reason for his frequent transfers. Upon retirement, Vladimir expressed his dislike of service in a letter to the literary historian A. N. Pypin, written in January 1883, calling it "servitude" (*kabala*) and rejoicing that he had escaped it.[25] Regardless of his dissatisfaction, his service can be called quite successful: he was made actual state councilor in 1877. Vladimir's literary pursuits were limited to his contributions to Kozma Prutkov's oeuvre. For example, he was the author of the "Project: Concerning the Introduction of Like-Mindedness in Russia."

At least partly, Kozma Prutkov's persona reflected his creators' lukewarm attitude to service and their collective preference for writing over serving. And yet, service could still be perceived as a useful tool for improving one's social standing. The life choices of Afanasy Fet, one of the greatest nineteenth-century Russian poets, demonstrate the lasting appeal of service as a status-making mechanism. At the same time, the Table of Ranks did not work for Fet as he hoped it would: he was unable to gain the hereditary nobility he craved through advancing in rank. He acquired it, one might say, fraudulently, thanks to Alexander II's finally taking pity on him and allowing him, without the support of proper documentation, to assume the last name and noble status of his stepfather, A. N. Shenshin. Paradoxically, Fet's failure to be ennobled through service and his becoming a nobleman of ancient standing (*stolbovoi dvorianin*) by deceit caused him to become an almost irrational admirer of rank, a fiery defender of landowners' privileges, and a fierce hater of *raznochintsy*. It is ironic that—like Gogol's Poprishchin of "Notes of a Madman," unsure of his status as a nobleman—he claimed that only noblemen could write well. In a letter to Grand Duke Konstantin (who published his poetry under the pen name K. R. and whose friendship was Fet's pride and joy), he writes: "Doesn't the reason that the muse of our poetry has gained universal respect—while nobody cares about our art—lie in the fact that the former visits [only] the highest estate, and the muse of plastic arts chooses at random [*kogo popalo*]?"[26]

One must admit that Fet's life was tragic. While pregnant with him, his mother left her husband, Darmstadt court official Johann Wilhelm Foeth, and fled with a Russian nobleman, Afanasy Shenshin, to his estate in the Orel guberniya. The future poet was born there in the fall of 1820 and baptized Afanasy Shenshin. His mother and stepfather married two years later, in September 1822, after obtaining a divorce from Foeth. According to newly published documents, Fet's stepfather did not plan to continue deceiving the authorities about the boy's legitimacy,[27] but nonetheless he was raised believing that he was Afanasy Shenshin, a Russian nobleman. When he was fourteen years old, he was admitted under this name to a private school in Verro (today's Võru, in Estonia), and only there was he informed that in fact his real name was Foeth, that he was not Russian, and was not a nobleman. It was extremely devastating news for the young Fet.[28] He must have suffered deep trauma over this sudden loss of identity.

In 1838, after successfully passing the entrance examinations, Fet entered Moscow University as a foreign subject. He graduated in 1844 with the title of actual student. At this point, he decided that the only way to restore his status as a Russian subject and a hereditary noble was to enter the military service: according to the Table of Ranks, the first officer's rank, that of the fourteenth class, would have brought him hereditary nobility. Accordingly, in April 1845 he entered a provincial cuirassier regiment as a non-commissioned officer. In February 1846 he was sworn in as a Russian subject and in March promoted to the first officer's rank, that of cornet (fourteenth class). Unfortunately for Fet, Nicholas I's manifesto of June 11, 1845, made gaining hereditary nobility in the military much more difficult: it was to be granted only to officers who acquired the rank of the eighth class. However distressing this new rule should have been for Fet, he persevered. In 1851 he was already in the rank of staff captain of horse (*shtabs-rotmistr*, tenth class). In May 1853 Fet found a way to transfer to a guards regiment, which made climbing the ladder of ranks easier (it also allowed him to spend summers near Saint Petersburg and thus establish connections in literary circles, which helped him continue building the career as a poet he had begun while he was a Moscow University student). In January 1854 Fet was confirmed in the rank of lieutenant (the equivalent of staff captain of horse and the ninth class in the guards regiments). His goal had almost been achieved: the next promotion would have placed him in the eighth class and thus accorded him hereditary nobility. Alas, on December 9, 1856, Alexander II issued a manifesto that made it necessary for military officers to gain the rank of the sixth class in order to qualify for hereditary nobility. This ended Fet's quest: he first took a year-long leave of absence, then an indefinite (*bessrochnyi*) leave, and finally retired on January 27 1857, apparently in the same rank of staff captain of horse.

The fact that by that time Fet was a well-known poet could have contributed to his decision to retire. For one thing, beginning in 1854, Fet's income as a publishing poet allowed him to stop worrying about money.[29] However, toward the end of the 1850s, his popularity as a poet began to diminish: his lyrical poetry was not "civic" enough for progressive journals like *The Contemporary*, and it was too nontraditional, and thus hard to understand, for conservative journals like *The Russian Messenger* (*Russkii vestnik*).[30] It is noteworthy that in the face of his purported failure as a poet Fet decided to return to his original plan: to become a nobleman—if not legally, then at least de facto. He decided to buy land and live as a nobleman, on an estate. Accordingly, he bought land in his native district of Mtsensk, built a house there, and began the life of a landowner. For several years he eagerly pursued this lifestyle, even publishing articles on agriculture and estate management. Still, the dream of regaining both his noble status and his original name did not fade away, and in 1873 Fet petitioned the tsar to acknowledge him as the hereditary nobleman Shenshin. Although he could not provide the required supporting documentation (he explained that the documents had been lost in the fifty-three years that had passed since his birth), Alexander II allowed him to assume the name of Shenshin and regain "all the rights and privileges that were due to his birth and heritage [*po rodu i naslediiu*]."[31] As B. Ia. Bukhshtab points out, friends and acquaintances were perplexed by Fet's actions. Ivan Turgenev wrote to him: "As Fet, you had a name; as Shenshin, you have only a surname."[32]

Toward the end of 1870, due to the rebirth of interest in poetry in Russia, Fet's status as a poet began to rise, as did his productivity. He began to publish again, both his original poetry and translations (he eventually translated virtually the entire corpus of Latin poetry). Signs of public recognition followed: on January 1, 1885, he was awarded the Order of Saint Anna, first class, for his literary achievements; and on December 29 of the same year he was elected a corresponding member of the Academy of Sciences (literature division). And yet, Fet's vanity was not satisfied. He was furious when he learned that a fellow poet,

Apollon Maikov (1821–97), was given the rank of privy councilor (third class) to mark his fifty years of literary work.[33] Fet wanted to be similarly distinguished, and he began to seek the court title of *kammerherr*. His low service rank made his quest difficult, but his friendship with K. R. apparently helped, and in 1889 he was made *kammerherr*. His contemporaries found Fet's action distasteful. The critic N. N. Strakhov wrote to Leo Tolstoy: "I will complain to you about Fet, who has defiled himself in my eyes, and not only mine."[34] The poet and translator P. A. Kozlov wrote an epigram (one of many):

> Под старость ключ украсил фалды Фета;
> Вполне заслужен им такой почет.
> Имеет важный смысл награда эта:
> Кто без ключа стихи его поймет?[35]

> [In his old age a key decorated Fet's coattails. He has fully earned this honor. This award has an important meaning: who can understand his poetry without a clue?]

Fet died in November 1892, still an unhappy man, despite his seeming success at gaining the social status he craved: even though he apparently died of a heart attack, right before his death he attempted to commit suicide.[36]

Fet's reputation as a great poet deservedly eclipsed his dubious actions as a person. And yet, his story is a fitting conclusion for a history of the nearly two-hundred-year-long interaction of literature and the rank system in Russia. It is ironic that it begins with Sumarokov's anxiety over his service rank and ends with Fet's almost insane obsession with it. Granted, Fet was an exception; granted, his adolescent trauma and his two failures to gain nobility on his own contributed to this obsession, but it is important that the Table of Ranks was there to give form to and support this obsession. It still had the power to shape writers' lives and could even seem more important to some of them than their literary work and literary success.

This book concludes with the case of Fet, that is, in 1892, rather than in 1917; although the Table of Ranks continued to exist and many Russians (including some writers, such as Innokenty Annensky, 1855–1909, and Vasily Rozanov, 1856–1919, both of whom were educators) continued to serve, it is fair to say that for writers service and ranks lost their importance. Rank remained a topic in such works as Andrei Bely's

Petersburg, but its presence in this novel is accounted for by the author's thematization of the nineteenth-century literary tradition: *Petersburg* is quintessentially a "Petersburg tale," a genre initiated by Gogol and Pushkin, and developed by Dostoevsky; and by definition any Petersburg tale has to include ranking officials. For Andrei Bely and his contemporaries, rank had become a literary topos, not a working mechanism to define their own status.

Appendix: The Table of Ranks

The table is simplified and reflects the most significant changes introduced between 1722 and 1917.

Class	Civil ranks	Military ranks	Court ranks	Form of Address
I.	Chancellor Actual Privy Councilor, First Class (beginning in the late eighteenth century)	General Field Marshal General Admiral	none	Your High Excellency
II.		General of Infantry (before 1763, after 1798) General of Cavalry (before 1763, after 1798) General-in-Chief (en chef) (1730–98) General of Artillery (since 1798) Admiral	Grand *Kammerherr*	Your High Excellency
III.	Privy Councilor	Lieutenant General (before 1741, after 1798) Vice Admiral	Marshal of the Court Master of the Court	Your Excellency
IV	Actual State Councilor	Major General Lieutenant-Colonel of the Guard Rear Admiral	*Kammerherr* (1737–1809)	Your Excellency
V.	State Councilor	Brigadier (1722–96) Captain-Commodore (1707–32, 1751–64, 1798–1827) Premier Major of the Guard (1748–98)	Master of Ceremonies *Kammerjunker* (1742–1809)	Your High Ancestry
VI.	Collegiate Councilor	Colonel Captain First Rank (Navy) Second Major of the Guard (1748–98)	*Kammer-Fourrie* (until 1884) *Kammerherr* (until 1737) *Kammerjunker* (1737–42)	Your High Honor
VII.	Court Councilor (from 1745)	Lieutenant Colonel Captain of the Guard Capitan in Cavalry Guard (*rotmistr*) Captain Second Rank (Navy)	none	Your High Honor

Continued on next page

The Table of Ranks — Continued

Class	Civil ranks	Military ranks	Court ranks	Form of Address
VIII.	Collegiate Assessor	Premier Major and Second Major (1731–98) Major in infantry (1798–1884) Captain in Infantry (since 1884) Captain in Cavalry (*rotmistr*) (since 1884) Staff Captain of the Guard (since 1798) Captain Third Rank (Navy) (1722–64)	Titular *kammerherr* (1722–1809)	Your High Honor
IX.	Titular Councilor	Captain in Infantry (1722–1884) Staff Captain in Infantry (since 1884) Lieutenant (*poruchik*) of the Guard (since 1730) Captain in Cavalry (*rotmistr*) (1798–1884) Staff Captain in Cavalry (*shtabs-rotmistr*) (since 1884)	*Kammerjunker* (until 1737) Court *Fourrier*	Your Honor
X.	Collegiate Secretary	Captain-Lieutenant in Infantry (1730–97) Staff Captain in Infantry (1797–1884) Second Captain in Cavalry (*sekund-rotmistr*) (1730–97) Staff Captain in Cavalry (*shtabs-rotmistr*) (1797–1884) Lieutenant (*poruchik*) (since 1884) Second Lieutenant (*podporuchik*) of the Guard (since 1730)	none	Your Honor
XI.	Ship Secretary (1764–1834)	Ship Secretary (Navy) (1722–64)	none	Your Honor
XII.	Gubernial Secretary	Lieutenant (*poruchik*) (1730–1884) Second Lieutenant (*podporuchik*) in Infantry (1730–1884) Cornet in Cavalry (since 1884) Warrant Officer (*praporshchik*) of the Guard (1730–1884)	none	Your Honor

Continued on next page

The Table of Ranks—Continued

Class	Civil ranks	Military ranks	Court ranks	Form of Address
XIII.	Provincial Secretary (1722–75) Senate Registrar (from 1764) Synod Registrar (from 1764)	Second Lieutenant (*podporuchik*) in Infantry (1730–1884) Warrant Officer (*praporshchik*) in Infantry (since 1884, only at wartime) Midshipman (*gardemarin*) (Navy) (1860–82)	none	Your Honor
XIV.	Collegiate Registrar	Warrant Officer (*fendrik*) in Infantry (1722–30) Warrant Officer (*praporshchik*) in Infantry (1730–1884) Cornet in Cavalry (1730–1884) Ensign (*michman*) (Navy) (1732–96)	none	Your Honor

Notes

Introduction

1. For Raeff's view, see his *Origins of the Russian Intelligentsia: The Eighteenth-Century Nobility* (New York: Harcourt Brace Jovanovich, 1966), 8; on the advantages of using the term "elite," see, for example, E. N. Marasinova, *Vlast' i lichnost': Ocherki russkoi istorii XVIII veka* (Moscow: Nauka, 2008), 95–98.

2. A. A. Kara-Murza argues that the most important aspect of Russia's transition under Peter "from Tsardom to Empire" was in "the profound transformation in the principles of how the Russian elite was composed"; see his "Ot Tsarstva k Imperii: Formirovanie novoi elity," in *Chelovek mezhdu Tsarstvom i Imperiei: Sbornik materialov mezhdunarodnoi konferentsii*, ed. M. S. Kiseleva (Moscow: Institut cheloveka Rossiiskoi Akademii Nauk, 2003), 72. Others emphasize continuity; see, for example, Lindsey Hughes, *Russia in the Age of Peter the Great* (New Haven, CT: Yale University Press, 1998), 172. For a classic work that examines the process of post-Petrine nobility formation, see S. M. Troitskii, *Russkii absoliutizm i dvorianstvo v XVIII veke: Formirovanie biurokratii* (Moscow: Nauka, 1974); for a recent discussion of this topic, see "Ocherk I: Za izuchenie XVIII veka," in Marasinova, *Vlast' i lichnost'*, 9–75.

3. Even though the Table of Ranks did provide a way for gifted commoners to enter the noble estate, Hughes rightly warns against ascribing to the Table of Ranks "such modern concepts as equality of opportunity." She stresses that the Table was designed first and foremost to serve the state, rather than to help talented people advance. At the same time, she agrees that Peter did value merit and acknowledges that when a commoner served the state well, he had a good chance of being promoted. See her *Russia in the Age of Peter*, 182–85 (quotation on 184).

4. Raeff, *Origins of the Russian Intelligentsia*, 8–9.

5. For an excellent discussion of this change, see I. I. Fediukin, "'Chest' k delu um i okhotu razhdaet': Reforma dvorianskoi sluzhby i teoreticheskie osnovy politiki v 1730-e gg.," in *Gishtorii Rossiiskie, ili Opyty i razyskaniia: K iubileiu Aleksandra Borisovicha Kamenskogo*, ed. E. B. Smilianskaia (Moscow: Drevlekhranilishche, 2014), 83–142. Fediukin argues that one of the reform's

main purposes was to create a noble class that would be more enthusiastic about service and let the non-enthusiastic or incompetent nobles retire.

6. See Raeff, *Origins of the Russian Intelligentsia*, 112–13; Iu. M. Lotman, *Roman A. S. Pushkina "Evgenii Onegin": Kommentarii* (Leningrad: Prosveshchenie, 1980), 49–51, esp. 49n1; Marasinova, *Vlast' i lichnost'*, 227–30. Michaël Confino argues that Raeff's (and, by extension, Lotman's and Marasinova's) assertions that the majority of noblemen stayed in service are based on incomplete data and reflect only the attitudes of the upper crust of the nobility; see "Histoire et psychologie: A propos de la noblesse russe au XVIIIe siècle," *Annales: Economies, Sociétés, Civilisations* 6 (1967): 1163–1205. Nicholas V. Riasanovsky, in his *A Parting of Ways: Government and the Educated Public in Russia, 1801–1855* (Oxford: Clarendon Press, 1976), looking at the problem from a different perspective (namely, the nobility's willingness to cooperate with the government and thus to serve), dates the decline of this cooperation from "around 1840" (249).

7. Raeff discusses the tension and its causes in chapter 3 of his *Origins of the Russian Intelligentsia*, esp. 53–59. On the existence of different groups within the eighteenth-century noble estate and the frictions that developed among them, see also E. N. Marasinova, *Psikhologiia elity rossiiskogo dvorianstva poslednei treti XVIII veka (po materialam perepiski)* (Moscow: ROSSPEN, 1999), 10–14.

8. See Fediukin, "'Chest' k delu.'"

9. The Table of Ranks gave military service preference over the other two types (civil and court): as its subtitle declares, "military ranks are higher than others [*voinskie chiny vyshe protchikh*]"; see A. A. Preobrazhenskii and T. E. Novitskaia, eds., *Zakonodatel'stvo Petra I* (Moscow: Iuridicheskaia literatura, 1997), 393. It was customary to begin in military service and switch to civil service later in life, gaining a rank or two thanks to the transfer; see David L. Ransel, "Bureaucracy and Patronage: The View from an Eighteenth-Century Russian Letter-Writer," in *The Rich, the Well-Born, and the Powerful: Elites and Upper Classes in History*, ed. Frederic Cople Jaher (Urbana: University of Illinois Press, 1973), 155.

10. Here and throughout, brackets around ellipses indicate omissions from the original text. Suspension points that appear in the original are not bracketed.

11. A. P. Sumarokov, "K tipografskim naborshchikam," in his *Polnoe sobranie vsekh sochinenii: V stikhakh i proze*, 2nd ed. (Moscow: V universitetskoi tipografii u N. Novikova, 1787), 4:315. On clerks as Sumarokov's "constant satirical target," see Marcus C. Levitt, "The Barbarians among Us, or Sumarokov's Views on Orthography," in his *Early Modern Russian Letters: Texts and Contexts* (Boston: Academic Studies Press, 2009), 255n15.

12. A. S. Pushkin, *Polnoe sobranie sochinenii v 16-ti tomakh* (Leningrad: AN SSSR, 1937–59), 12:159.

13. Cf. also Nekrasov's and Turgenev's rude and insulting 1846 poem "Belinsky's Epistle to Dostoevsky" ("Poslanie Belinskogo k Dostoevskomu"),

in which Dostoevsky's less-than-polished behavior at a high-society gathering is ridiculed. For a discussion of this episode, see William M. Todd III, "Dostoevskii kak professional'nyi pisatel': Professiia, zaniatie, etika," *Novoe literaturnoe obozrenie* 58 (2002): 22. An added irony is the fact that Belinsky also owed his nobility to his father's service rank and, furthermore, wasn't confirmed as noble until 1847.

14. It is known, however, that Tolstoy criticized Dostoevsky's writing style as lacking elegance and even good grammar. One of his criticisms (dated from December 1890) was written down by A. V. Zhirkevich: "Dostoevsky [has] rich content, a serious attitude toward his work [*k delu*], and bad [*durnaia*] form." See Zhirkevich, "Vstrechi s Tolstym," in *L. N. Tolstoi v vospominaniiakh sovremennikov*, vol. 2 (Moscow: Khudozhestvennaia literatura, 1978), 7. It is worth considering to what degree this "bad form" was for Count Leo Tolstoy a consequence of Dostoevsky's non-aristocratic origins.

15. See A. M. Panchenko, *Russkaia stikhotvornaia kul'tura XVII veka* (Leningrad: Nauka, 1973), esp. the chapter titled "Prikaznaia shkola," 34–76.

16. See D. M. Bulanin, "Drevniaia Rus'," in *Istoriia russkoi perevodnoi khudozhestvennoi literatury: Drevniaia Rus', XVIII vek*, vol. 1, *Proza*, ed. Iu. D. Levin (St. Petersburg: Dmitrii Bulanin, 1995), 70–72. Bulanin singles out the clerks of the *Posol'skii prikaz* (Foreign Office) as the most active group of translators of fiction.

17. In the works of these writers, literature still cannot be separated from theology or the religious moralizing typical of medieval literature; see A. M. Panchenko, "O smene pisatel'skogo tipa v Petrovskuiu epokhu," *XVIII vek* 9 (1974): 113. However, the genres they used were no longer medieval.

18. See Gary Marker, "Literacy and Literacy Texts in Muscovy: A Reconsideration," *Slavic Review* 49 (1990): 74–89. Marker concludes that the most optimistic estimates suggest that "rudimentary literacy rates [. . .] were well below 10 percent for the entire population," with the number of those who could write at about 3 percent. Less optimistic estimates give 3 to 5 and 1 to 2 percent, respectively (89).

19. Hughes, *Russia in the Age of Peter*, 174.

20. L. Stone and J. C. F. Stone, *An Open Elite? England 1540–1880* (Oxford: Oxford University Press, 1984), 262–66. See also the chapter titled "Literacy" in *Gentry Culture in Late Medieval England*, ed. Raluca Radulescu and Alison Truelove (Manchester: Manchester University Press, 2005), which documents how the ability to write gained prestige among the fifteenth-century English gentry. In *The World of Christopher Marlowe* (London: Faber and Faber, 2004), David Riggs devotes a chapter to the social composition of the student body at Cambridge during the late sixteenth century. Among other groups, he mentions the young gentlemen, who usually spent a year or two at the university, rarely taking degrees, since their purpose was "to get such learning as may serve for delight and ornament" (66). It is noteworthy, however, that they did go to the university to attain such learning.

21. Domna Stanton, *The Aristocrat as Art: A Study of the* Honnête Homme *and the* Dandy *in Seventeenth- and Nineteenth-Century French Literature* (New York: Columbia University Press, 1980), 48. See also chapter 8 in Ellery Schalk, *From Valor to Pedigree: Ideas of Nobility in France in the Sixteenth and Seventeenth Centuries* (Princeton, NJ: Princeton University Press, 1986).

22. Jonathan Dewald, *Aristocratic Experience and the Origins of Modern Culture: France, 1570–1715* (Berkeley: University of California Press, 1993), 174.

23. See Raeff, *Origins of the Russian Intelligentsia*, esp. the chapter "Home and School"; see also Brenda Meehan-Waters, *Autocracy and Aristocracy: The Russian Service Elite of 1730* (New Brunswick, NJ: Rutgers University Press, 1982), 39–47.

24. See Hughes, *Russia in the Age of Peter*, 174–75, for details on "compulsory education for nobles" under Peter. See also Fediukin, "'Chest' k delu,'" 94, 99, 102–3.

25. A. G. Tartakovskii, *Russkaia memuaristika XVIII–pervoi poloviny XIX v.* (Moscow: Nauka, 1991), 244–70.

26. Dewald, *Aristocratic Experience*, 174–75.

27. Hughes, *Russia in the Age of Peter*, 172–79.

28. See Panchenko, "O smene pisatel'skogo tipa," 123–25.

29. See W. Gareth Jones, "The Russian Language as a Definer of Nobility," in *A Window on Russia: Papers from the V International Conference of the Study Group on Eighteenth-Century Russia, Gargnano, 1994*, ed. Maria Di Salvo and Lindsey Hughes (Roma: La Fenice Edizioni, 1996), 293.

30. See Marcus C. Levitt, "Aleksandr Petrovich Sumarokov," in *Early Modern Russian Writers: Late Seventeenth and Eighteenth Centuries*, ed. Marcus C. Levitt, Dictionary of Literary Biography 150 (Detroit, MI: Gale Research, 1995), 372–73.

31. See Viktor Zhivov, "Pervye russkie literaturnye biografii kak sotsial'noe iavlenie: Trediakovskii, Lomonosov, Sumarokov," *Novoe literaturnoe obozrenie* 25 (1997): 55. Zhivov quotes statistical data on the participation of the nobility in literature provided in Vladimir Nahirny, *The Russian Intelligentsia: From Torment to Silence* (New Brunswick, NJ: Transaction Books, 1983), 28.

32. For an overview of the eighteenth-century Russian patronage system in general, see Ransel, "Bureaucracy and Patronage," 154–78; for a brief discussion of patronage relations in the literary milieu, see William Mills Todd III, *Fiction and Society in the Age of Pushkin: Ideology, Institutions, and Narrative* (Cambridge, MA: Harvard University Press, 1986), 51–52; for a useful analysis of the term "Maecenas" (*metsenat*) in eighteenth-century poetry, see N. D. Kochetkova, "Obraz metsenata v predstavleniiakh russkikh pisatelei XVIII veka," in *A. M. Panchenko i russkaia kul'tura: Issledovaniia i materialy* (St. Petersburg: Pushkinskii dom, 2008), 87–97. It is remarkable that an aversion to patronage first emerged in the context of literary production; as Marasinova indicates, used for career

advancement, patronage remained an acceptable and desirable system to the end of the eighteenth century (and beyond); see her *Vlast' i lichnost'*, 314–18.

33. See Raymond Williams, *The Sociology of Culture* (New York: Schocken Books, 1981), 41.

34. Alain Viala, *Naissance de l'écrivain: Sociologie de la littérature à l'âge classique* (Paris: Editions de Minuit, 1985), 51–57.

35. Irina Reyfman, *Ritualized Violence Russian Style: The Duel in Russian Culture and Literature* (Stanford, CA: Stanford University Press, 1999), 132–33, discusses several early nineteenth-century occasions when Russian officers attempted to challenge members of the imperial family. Such challenges clearly demonstrated that the challenging officers were attempting to establish an equal relationship (that of fellow noblemen) between themselves and the imperial family.

36. Derzhavin not only helped his career as a poet by writing his ode "Felitsa," addressed to Catherine, but also served as her secretary; Murav'ev and Zhukovsky tutored members of the imperial family; Karamzin accepted the position of court historiographer in order to be able to write his *History of the Russian State*, and Pushkin returned to state service to be able to work in state archives.

37. See A. S. Collins, *The Profession of Letters: A Study of the Relation of Author to Patron, Publisher, and Public, 1780–1832* (London: George Routledge, 1928), 7; T. Grits, V. Trenin, and M. Nikitin, *Slovesnost' i kommertsiia: Knizhnaia lavka A. F. Smirdina* (1929; repr., Moscow: AGRAF, 2001), 73; Zhivov, "Pervye russkie literaturnye biografii," 24; Todd, "Dostoevskii kak professional'nyi pisatel'." Viala argues that the field of literature differs from any other artistic field because, unlike in visual arts, theater, or music, there are no schools that teach writing. The writer's craft is therefore not professional; see his *Naissance de l'écrivain*, 2n2. The existence of the Literary Institute in Russia and creative writing courses in American colleges and universities—to name but two examples— challenges this view.

38. See G. A. Gukovskii, "Lomonosov, Sumarokov, shkola Sumarokova," in his *Russkaia poeziia XVIII veka* (1927), reprinted in Gukovskii, *Rannie raboty po istorii russkoi poezii XVIII veka*, ed. V. M. Zhivov (Moscow: Iazyki russkoi kul'tury, 2001), 40–71. For an overview of how eighteenth-century Russian writers confronted the idea of professionalism, see André Meynieux, *La littérature et le métier d'écrivain en Russie avant Pouchkine*, Cahiers d'études littéraires 2 (Paris: Librairie des cinq continents, 1966).

39. In France, the book market emerged in the seventeenth century (Viala, *Naissance de l'écrivain*, 8); in England, in the 1730s (Collins, *The Profession of Letters*, 17–18; Barbara M. Benedict, "Readers, Writers, Reviewers, and the Professionalization of Literature," in *The Cambridge Companion to English Literature, 1740–1830*, ed. Thomas Keymer and Jon Mee [Cambridge: Cambridge University

Press, 2015], 3–23, chapter DOI http://dx.doi.org/10.1017/CCOL0521809746
.001). For an overview of the history of European book markets, see Ernst Fischer,
"The Book Market," *European History Online (EGO)* (March 12, 2010), http://
www.ieg-ego.eu/fischere-2010-en (accessed June 9, 2015), esp. 11–25.

40. For a thorough examination of entertainment literature, see David
Gasperetti, *The Rise of the Russian Novel: Carnival, Stylization, and Mockery of the
West* (DeKalb: Northern Illinois University Press, 1998); Paola Castagna, "*Imitatio*
or Plagiarism: A Quest for Literary Metamorphosis in the Russian Chivalric
Romance *Bova Korolevich*" (PhD diss., Columbia University, 2008). On the two
groups of eighteenth-century readers, see Gasperetti, *Rise of the Russian Novel*,
ch. 2, esp. 54–59. For a discussion of the book market for this group, see Grits et
al., *Slovesnost' i kommertsiia*, ch. 1, 11–46.

41. Pat Rogers, *Hacks and Dunces: Pope, Swift and Grub Street* (London:
Methuen, 1980). It is Pope whom Collins considers "founder in England of the
profession of letters" (*The Profession of Letters*, 17).

42. Gary Marker, *Publishing, Printing, and the Origins of Intellectual Life in
Russia, 1700–1800* (Princeton, NJ: Princeton University Press, 1985), 58, 85. See
also Grits et al., *Slovesnost' i kommertsiia*, ch. 2, 47–71.

43. Marker, *Publishing, Printing*, 105–34; on Novikov, see 122–34.

44. See V. A. Zapadov, "Problema literaturnogo servilizma i diletantizma i
poeticheskaia pozitsiia G. R. Derzhavina," *XVIII vek* 16 (1989): 68–73; Marasinova, *Vlast' i lichnost'*, 351, esp. n2.

45. V. P. Stepanov, "Sumarokov Aleksandr Petrovich," in *Slovar' russkikh
pisatelei XVIII veka*, ed. N. D. Kochetkova et al., 3 vols. (Leningrad/St. Petersburg: Nauka, 1988–2010), 3:184.

46. P. A. Nikolaev, ed., *Russkie pisateli, 1800–1917: Biograficheskii slovar'*, 5
vols. to date (Moscow: Sovetskaia entsiklopediia, 1989–), 3:329. V. A. Manuilov,
ed., *Lermontovskaia entsiklopedia* (Moscow: Sovetskaia entsiklopediia, 1981) has
a detailed entry on Lermontov's military service, 87–90. It does not cite his service
record, however.

47. Nikolaev, *Russkie pisateli*, 4:269.

48. Ibid., 2:596. The supplement speaks of "educated classes," and not just
the nobility, because secular education, beginning at the gymnasium level,
opened state service to all estates.

49. See A. A. Del'vig (and E. A. Baratynskii), "Pevtsy 15-go klassa," in
Del'vig's *Polnoe sobranie stikhotvorenii*, the section titled "Kollektivnye stikhotvoreniia" (Leningrad: Sovetskii pisatel', 1959), 225–27; for their opponents' response, which uses the same play on the Table of Ranks, see ibid., 335.

Chapter 1. To Serve or to Write?

1. Viala's terms, "institutions de la vie littéraire" and "institutions littéraires," which, as he argues, mark the formation of the field of literature in

seventeenth-century France (see his *Naissance de l'écrivain*, 10), are also useful for the analysis of the eighteenth-century Russian situation. As for the Russian Academy, it did issue the six volumes of the dictionary, *Slovar' Akademii Rossiiskoi*, in 1789–94.

2. Archbishop Avvakum was the first major writer of this type; see A. N. Robinson, *Zhizneopisaniia Avvakuma i Epifaniia: Issledovanie i teksty* (Moscow: AN SSSR, 1963). However, his *Life* wasn't known outside the community of Old Believers until it was published in 1861. It therefore couldn't have influenced the formation of the new concept of authorship in the eighteenth century.

3. N. M. Karamzin, *Selected Prose*, trans. and intro. Henry M. Nebel Jr. (Evanston, IL: Northwestern University Press, 1969), 194.

4. This reluctance concerned only literary works. Writers hesitant to publish literature did not hesitate to publish other kinds of works: philosophical, pedagogical, economic, or religious.

5. See, for example, V. P. Stepanov, "K voprosu o reputatsii literatury v seredine XVIII v.," *XVIII vek* 14 (1983): 105–20. Stepanov arrives at his conclusion in a rather convoluted way: he begins by reiterating Panchenko's idea that the post-Petrine emphasis on service turned literary activity into an optional and thus private occupation. Stepanov then argues that in the second third of the century the emphasis on the importance of useful literature created according to rules allowed writing nobles to lay claim to professionalism (understood as calling, not as publishing for a living). By the end of the century, however, noblemen increasingly began to use service success to assert their independence from the state, relegating writing to the private sphere. In Stepanov's view, the predominance of noblemen among Russian writers made dilettante writing the norm.

6. V. A. Zapadov, "Problema literaturnogo servilizma i diletantizma." Marasinova supports this viewpoint, emphasizing the general contempt among the nobility for writers producing poetry to order and accepting patronage; see her *Vlast' i lichnost'*, 370–73.

7. See Svetlana Boym, *Common Places: Mythologies of Everyday Life in Russia* (Cambridge, MA: Harvard University Press, 1994), 73–88. In Boym's useful overview of the history of these concepts in Russia from the seventeenth to the late twentieth century the emphasis is on differences from the West and their causes. For a more balanced analysis of these notions in a Russian eighteenth-century context, see Andreas Schönle, "The Scare of the Self: Sentimentalism, Privacy, and Private Life in Russian Culture, 1780–1820," *Slavic Review* 57 (1998): 723–46.

8. See Maks Fasmer, *Etimologicheskii slovar' russkgo iazyka*, trans. O. N. Trubachev, ed. B. A. Larin (Moscow: "Progress," 1986), 3:362, 399. Both words entered the Russian vocabulary from Polish.

9. The first Russian law that guaranteed individual rights (those of the nobility) was Peter III's 1762 edict allowing nobles not to serve; Catherine II's

1785 Charter to the Nobility added other rights, most importantly, to property and to physical inviolability. Only gradually were these rights extended to other estates. The laws, however, were not consistently enforced. For the nobles' use of dueling to protect their private space from both their peers and the state, see Reyfman, *Ritualized Violence Russian Style*.

10. See, for example, *Akademik: Filosofskaia entsiklopedia na Akademike*, where *privatnost'* is defined, not quite consistently, as "a sphere of life interests, daily living, emotions, or attachments of a particular human being, private personality, or individual, which is separated from other social spheres" (http://dic.academic .ru/dic.nsf/enc_philosophy/8928/ПРИВАТНОСТЬ). Curiously, the only sphere where the word's meaning is close to the right to remain undisturbed is that of the Internet.

11. Schönle, "The Scare of the Self," 735.

12. Pushkin, "Puteshestvie iz Moskvy v Peterburg," in his *Polnoe sobranie sochinenii v 16-ti tomakh*, 11:249.

13. For a discussion of Sumarokov and professionalism, see Marcus Levitt, "The Illegal Staging of Sumarokov's *Sinav i Truvor* in 1770 and the Problem of Authorial Status in Eighteenth-Century Russia," *Slavic and East European Journal* 43 (1999): 299–300, reprinted in his *Early Modern Russian Letters*, 190–217. Further citations to this work refer to the latter publication.

14. G. P. Makogonenko, ed., *Pis'ma russkikh pisatelei XIII veka* (Leningrad: Nauka, 1980), 86 and 87. All subsequent references to this edition are given parenthetically in the text. The Chancellery was the general assembly of all academicians and adjuncts, and the Conference was the assembly of all Academy members with collegiate rank; see V. P. Stepanov's commentary to Sumarokov's letters, in Makogonenko, *Pis'ma*, 193n10. Obviously, Sumarokov implies that his superior rank as a brigadier gives him the right to join the Academy without leaving the military service for the civil one.

15. It is not quite clear what Sumarokov meant by "second or third brigadier": there were no grades within the rank. It is possible that Sumarokov means the order of promotion to the rank of brigadier, that is, that only one or two people were promoted to this rank earlier than he.

16. For Elizabeth's decree, see *F. G. Volkov i russkii teatr ego vremeni: Sbornik materialov* (Moscow: Izdatel'stvo Akademii Nauk SSSR, 1953), 144–45.

17. Levitt, "Aleksandr Petrovich Sumarokov," 376–77.

18. *Bova the King's Son* is one of the chivalric romances adapted in Muscovite Russia and extremely popular among lowbrow eighteenth-century readers.

19. See Levitt, "Illegal Staging," 211, for his analysis of the place the notion of honor had in Sumarokov's view of authorship.

20. On Sumarokov's participation in the patronage system, see Todd, *Fiction and Society*, 53–55.

21. For more on Sumarokov's insistence in his correspondence that writing equals service, see Marasinova, *Vlast' i lichnost'*, 374–75.

22. See Zhivov, "Pervye russkie literaturnye biografii," 54–55.

23. Thomas Newlin detects "existential panic" in these formulations; see his *The Voice in the Garden: Andrei Bolotov and the Anxieties of Russian Pastoral, 1738–1833* (Evanston, IL: Northwestern University Press, 2001), 223n13.

24. Mikhail Lomonosov, *Polnoe sobranie sochinenii* (Moscow: Izdatel'stvo Akademii Nauk SSSR, 1957), 10:545.

25. Thomas Newlin, "Andrei Timofeevich Bolotov," in Levitt, *Early Modern Russian Writers*, 38.

26. Ibid., 37.

27. Newlin, *Voice in the Garden*, 8–10, and esp. ch. 2.

28. Andrei Bolotov, *Zhizn' i prikliucheniia Andreia Bolotova, opisannye samim im dlia svoikh potomkov* (Moscow: Terra, 1993), 1:399–400. Bolotov calls his commander "the little old man" (*starichok*).

29. Bolotov, *Zhizn' i prikliucheniia*, letter 63, http://az.lib.ru/b/bolotow_a_t/text_0080.shtml.

30. Ibid., letter 64.

31. Bolotov, *Zhizn' i prikliucheniia*, 2:157.

32. Newlin comments on the correlation between gardening and writing for Bolotov—his two favorite occupations while in the country. See Newlin, *Voice in the Garden*, 115 and 231n38. On Bolotov's gardening projects, see Andreas Schönle, *The Ruler in the Garden: Politics and Landscape Design in Imperial Russia* (New York: Peter Lang, 2007), 116–63. Schönle also comments on the analogy between Bolotov's gardening activities and his writing (124).

33. Bolotov, *Zhizn' i prikliucheniia*, 2:214.

34. Ibid., 2:303.

35. Ibid., 3:470.

36. Newlin, *Voice in the Garden*, 29–32.

37. I. Vladimirova [Irina Reyfman], M. Grigor'ev [Mark Altshuller], and K. Kumpan, "A. A. Blok i russkaia kul'tura XVIII veka," in *Nasledie A. Bloka i aktual'nye problemy poetiki*, ed. D. E. Maksimov et al., Blokovskii sbornik 4 (Tartu: Tartuskii gosudarstvennyi universitet, 1981), 84.

38. Alexander Levitsky, "Aleksei Andreevich Rzhevsky," in Levitt, *Early Modern Russian Writers*, 344.

39. See N. A. Murzanov, ed., *Slovar' russkikh senatorov 1711–1917 gg.: Materialy dlia biografii* (St. Petersburg: Dmitrii Bulanin, 2011), 369.

40. See ibid. and K. Iu. Lappo-Danilevsky, "Rzhevskii Aleksei Andreevich," in Kochetkova, *Slovar' russkikh pisatelei*, 3:242–43.

41. Levitsky, in his "Aleksei Andreevich Rzhevsky," 346, points out that Rzhevsky's service success "paralleled his rise in degrees in Masonic lodges in the 1770s." It may be surmised that the diminishment in his writing activities had to do with his involvement in Masonic affairs. Many eighteenth-century writers of noble status were Masons, and in many (but not all) cases this was an important factor shaping both their literary and service careers. This topic, however, lies outside this inquiry.

42. Levitsky, "Aleksei Andreevich Rzhevsky," 346 and 344.

43. See G. A. Gukovskii, "Rzhevskii," in his *Rannie raboty*, 157–83. For a discussion of Rzhevsky's poetry, see Irina Reyfman, "Alexey Rzhevsky, Russian Mannerist," in *Rank and Style: Russians in State Service, Life, and Literature* (Boston, MA: Academic Studies Press, 2012), 229–44.

44. Quoted in N. D. Kochetkova, "Bogdanovich Ippolit Fedorovich," in her *Slovar' russkikh pisatelei*, 1:106.

45. I. F. Bogdanovich, *Dushen'ka*, in his *Stikhotvoreniia i poemy* (Leningrad: Sovetskii pisatel', 1957), 45.

46. Quoted in I. Z. Serman, Commentary to *Dushen'ka*, ibid., 225.

47. See Kochetkova, "Bogdanovich Ippolit Fedorovich," 106–8; Joachim Klein, "Bogdanovich i ego 'Dushen'ka,'" in his *Puti kul'turnogo importa: Trudy po russkoi literature XVIII veka* (Moscow: Iazyki slavianskikh kul'tur, 2005), 476–77.

48. As Thomas Barran emphasizes, "This persona does not agree with the biographical facts. Bogdanovich adopted an authorial pose in the preface to *Dushen'ka* that may have provided the impetus for the rewriting of his biography"; see his "Ippolit Fedorovich Bogdanovich," in Levitt, *Early Modern Russian Writers*, 33.

49. Nikolai Karamzin, "O Bogdanoviche i ego sochineniiakh," in his *Izbrannye stat'i i pis'ma* (Moscow: Sovremennik, 1982), 118. The quote is from Barran's translation, "Ippolit Fedorovich Bogdanovich," 33.

50. Quoted in Kochetkova, "Bogdanovich Ippolit Fedorovich," 108–9.

51. See Ia. K. Grot, "Rukopisi Derzhavina i N. A. L'vova," *Izvestie II-ogo Otdeleniia Akademii Nauk* 8, no. 4 (1859); V. I. Novikov, "L'vov v literaturnom okruzhenii G. R. Derzhavina," in *Genii vkusa: Materialy nauchnoi konferentsii, posviashchennoi tvorchestvu N. A. L'vova*, ed. M. V. Stroganov (Tver: Tverskoi gosudarstvennyi universitet, 2001), 328–31.

52. See V. P. Stark, "L'vov i Pushkin: Neskol'ko sblizhenii," in Stroganov, *Genii vkusa*, 334–37.

53. See K. Iu. Lappo-Danilevskii, "O literaturnom nasledii N. A. L'vova," in *Izbrannye sochineniia*, by N. A. L'vov, ed. K. Iu. Lappo-Danilevskii (St. Petersburg: Akropol', 1994), 15.

54. Anna Lisa Crone, *The Daring of Derzhavin: The Moral and Aesthetic Independence of the Poet in Russia* (Bloomington, IN: Slavica, 2001), 25–26, 41–42.

55. See Joachim Klein, "Poet-samokhval: 'Pamiatnik' Derzhavina i status poeta v russkoi kul'ture XVIII veka," in his *Puti kul'turnogo importa*, 516–20; Tat'iana Smoliarova, *Zrimaia lirika: Derzhavin* (Moscow: Novoe literaturnoe obozrenie, 2011), 548–49. Ironically, Derzhavin was dismissed from his last position for "overzealous service" (V. A. Zapadov, "Derzhavin Gavrila Romanovich," in Kochetkova, *Slovar' russkikh pisatelei*, 1:257).

56. G. R. Derzhavin, "Zhizn' Zvanskaia," in his *Stikhotvoreniia* (Leningrad: Sovetskii pisatel', 1957), 334.

57. Crone, *The Daring of Derzhavin*, 11. In Crone's representation, however, service, as eventually understood by Derzhavin, becomes ministry, that is, a

higher kind of service, to the fatherland (not the state) and mankind (see ibid., 11–12, 122–28, 219). This view of writerly activity lies beyond the scope of this book.

58. I. I. Dmitriev, Letter to A. F. Merzliakov of 1805, in his *Sochineniia*, ed. A. A. Floridov (St. Petersburg: Ia. Sokolov, 1895), 2:191.

59. Dmitriev, "Vzgliad na moiu zhizn'," in his *Sochineniia*, 2:65.

60. M. N. Murav'ev, *Stikhotvoreniia* (Leningrad: Sovetskii pisatel', 1967), 245; the date is unknown.

61. L. A. Alekhina, "Arkhivnye materialy M. N. Murav'eva v fondakh otdela rukopisei," *Zapiski otdela rukopisei GBL* 49 (1990): 84–85. Murav'ev refers to his translations from Romans.

62. See William Mills Todd III, "Periodicals in Literary Life of the Early Nineteenth Century," in *Literary Journals in Imperial Russia*, ed. Deborah Martinsen (Cambridge: Cambridge University Press, 1997), 47. A. I. Reitblat cites the smaller but still substantial sum of 2,000 rubles; see his *Ot Bovy k Bal'montu i drugie raboty po istoricheskoi sotsiologii russkoi literatury* (Moscow: Novoe literaturnoe obozrenie, 2009), 88. I. V. Popov (1774–1839) was a minor writer, bookseller, and publisher. In the beginning of the nineteenth century, he leased the Moscow University printing press. It was Popov who conceived, established, and financed *Messenger of Europe*, inviting Karamzin to edit it. See E. D. Kukushkina, "Popov Ivan Vasil'evich," *Akademik: Slovari i entsiklopedii na Akademike*, http://russian_xviii_centure.academic.ru/661/Попов_Иван_Васильевич.

63. Reitblat, *Ot Bovy k Bal'montu*, 88.

64. First published in 1782, *Povest' o prikliuchenii angliiskogo milorda Georga* was reissued about thirty times in the course of the nineteenth century.

65. Karamzin could have known of publications in 1779, 1781, 1791, 1793, and 1794.

66. N. M. Karamzin, "Pis'mo k izdateliu," in his *Izbrannye sochineniia v dvukh tomakh*, ed. G. Makogonenko (Moscow: Khudozhestvennaia literatura, 1964), 2:176.

67. [I. V.] K[ireevskii], "Materialy dlia russkoi istorii i dlia istorii russkoi slovesnosti: Pis'ma N. M. Karamzina k M. N. Murav'evu," *Moskvitianin* 1 (1845): 3–5 (Letter from Karamzin to Murav'ev of November 3, 1803).

68. Andrei Kostin, in his article "Pisatel' na sluzhbe: Sluchai N. I. Strakhova" (*Russian Literature* 75 [2014]: 333–61), examines the curious case of the satirical journalist Strakhov (1768–1843?), who, after a short stint in the military (1780–85) and ten years in retirement when he occupied himself exclusively with literature, returned to the civil service and, as Kostin convincingly demonstrates, used references to his earlier—very successful—career as a satirical writer as well as his writerly abilities in general to advance his service career by substituting "the creation of fanciful proposals for his actual administrative work" (333, quoting from the article's abstract).

Chapter 2. Pushkin as Bureaucrat, Courtier, and Writer

1. See Marcus C. Levitt, *Russian Literary Politics and the Pushkin Celebration of 1880* (Ithaca, NY: Cornell University Press, 1989); Jonathan Brooks Platt, *Greetings, Pushkin! Stalinist Cultural Politics and the Russian National Bard* (Pittsburgh: University of Pittsburgh Press, 2016). It is particularly instructive to observe what Pushkin has to say to the millennial generation of Russian readers: he addresses them as an Orthodox Christian and an ardent Russian patriot, exactly as they would wish.

2. Biographies of Pushkin, such as Iu. M. Lotman's *Aleksandr Sergeevich Pushkin: Biografiia pisatelia* (Leningrad: Prosveshchenie, 1981); T. J. Binyon's *Pushkin: A Biography* (New York: Vintage Books, 2004); and even the comprehensive N. A. Tarkhova's *Zhizn' Aleksandra Sergeevicha Pushkina* (Moscow: Minuvshee, 2009) provide an outline of his service career, without, however, giving it a thorough interpretation in the contemporary context or considering its impact on him as a writer. Tarkhova's chronology of Pushkin's life provides the date of Alexander's decree appointing Pushkin and other graduates of the Lyceum to the College of Foreign Affairs, the date of Pushkin's taking his service oath, and even his service class (tenth), but not his rank; see her *Zhizn' Aleksandra Sergeevicha Pushkina*, 101.

3. *Putevoditel' po Pushkinu* (Moscow: Gos. Izdatel'stvo khudozhestvennoi literatury, 1931).

4. Nikolaev, *Russkie pisateli*, 5:189–216.

5. Victor Terras, ed., *Handbook of Russian Literature* (New Haven, CT: Yale University Press, 1985), 357.

6. See N. E. Miasoedova, *Pushkinskie zamysly: Opyt rekonstruktsii* (St. Petersburg: SpetsLit, 2002), 4, where she notes that the topic "Pushkin the diplomat" "has not been realized to this day, nor has the question even been posed."

7. Notably, Iu. M. Lotman, who in his biography of Pushkin is usually attentive to all details of his life, including his anxiety in the early 1820s over his low standing in the service hierarchy, mentions that Pushkin received access to archives and a yearly salary but does not tell the reader that to gain these favors Pushkin had to return to service. See his *Aleksandr Sergeevich Pushkin*, 86–87 (on anxiety), 196 (on access to archives). Tarkhova, however, includes this information in her chronology; see her *Zhizn' Aleksandra Sergeevicha Pushkina*, 528 and 529.

8. See Lotman, *Aleksandr Sergeevich Pushkin*, 212. It is the only fact concerning Pushkin's service career mentioned in Victor Terras's *A History of Russian Literature* (New Haven, CT: Yale University Press, 1991), 205.

9. V. P. Stark et al., eds., *Aleksandr Sergeevich Pushkin: Dokumenty k biografii; 1799–1829* (St. Petersburg: Iskusstvo-SPB, 2007), 281–82, commentary to document no. 174 (hereafter Stark, *Dokumenty, 1799–1829*). Matiushkin's situation was particularly annoying: he was first on the list of collegiate secretaries.

10. See Lotman, *Aleksandr Sergeevich Pushkin*, 32–33. Pushkin apparently continued to entertain plans to transfer to the military; see S. A. Sobolevskii, "Iz stat'i 'Tainstvennye primety v zhizni Pushkina,'" in *Pushkin v vospominaniiakh sovremennikov v dvukh tomakh*, ed. K. I. Tiun'kin (Moscow: Khudozhestvennaia literatura, 1985), 2:11; A. I. Turgenev, Letter to P. A. Viazemsky of March 12, 1819, in *Ostaf'evskii arkhiv kniazei Viazemskikh*, vol. 1, *Perepiska kniazia P. A. Viazemskogo s A. I. Turgenevym, 1812–1819*, ed. V. I. Saitova (St. Petersburg: Izd. S. D. Sheremeteva, 1899), 202.

11. Stark, *Dokumenty, 1799–1829*, 299–300, document no. 183.

12. See F. F. Vigel', "Iz 'Zapisok,'" in Tiun'kin, *Pushkin v vospominaniiakh sovremennikov*, 1:222; N. I. Turgenev's reproach to Pushkin for his idleness, quoted in A. I. Zaozerskii, "Vtoraia opravdatel'naia zapiska N. I. Turgeneva," in *Pamiati dekabristov: Sbornik materialov* (Leningrad: AN SSSR, 1926), 2:122; Lotman, *Aleksandr Sergeevich Pushkin*, 33. It is noteworthy that the often-quoted letter from E. A. Engel'gardt to A. M. Gorchakov of December 10, 1817, mentioning Pushkin's idleness presents it as an anomaly, the consequence of his illness: "Pushkin does nothing at the College; he doesn't even show up there. I have been told that he is ill now"; see A. E. Engel'gardt, "Pis'mo Gorchakovu A. M., 18 ianvaria 1818 g., Tsarskoe Selo," *Literaturnoe nasledstvo* 52 (1952): 34n2, original in French.

13. See Stark, *Dokumenty, 1799–1829*, 283–84, 294–95, document nos. 177, 181. On Pushkin's classmates' careers, see ibid., 298–99, commentary to document no. 182.

14. See ibid., 295–96, commentary to document no. 181.

15. See V. E. Vatsuro, "Iz razyskanii o Pushkine," *Vremennik Pushkinskoi komissii 1972* (1974): 100 (in Sollogub's text, an anecdote about Paul I follows).

16. Stark, *Dokumenty, 1799–1829*, 343–44, document no. 212.

17. Ibid., 365–66, 383–86, document nos. 226 and 239.

18. See I. P. Medvedev, "Pushkin—perevodchik Kollegii inostrannykh del," *Vremennik Pushkinskoi komissii 1978* (1981): 105–6.

19. In her commentary to the collection of records documenting Pushkin's life from 1811 to 1829, S. V. Berezkina states: "At present, the absence of any business paperwork that came from Pushkin's quill in 1817–1820 can be confirmed"; see Stark, *Dokumenty, 1799–1829*, 301, commentary to document no. 183.

20. See N. K. Piksanov, *Letopis' zhizni i tvorchestva A. S. Griboedova, 1791–1829* (Moscow: Nasledie, 2000), 15, 122, 129.

21. See Mariia Maiofis, *Vozzvanie k Evrope: Literaturnoe obshchestvo "Arzamas" i rossiiskii modernizatsionnyi proekt 1815–1818 godov* (Moscow: Novoe literaturnoe obozrenie, 2008), 24–27 and esp. ch. 5.

22. Ibid., 41–44.

23. Ibid., 44. In her dating of Pushkin's admission, Maiofis follows O. A. Proskurin, "Kogda zhe Pushkin vstupil v Arzamasskoe obshchestvo? (Iz zametok

k teme 'Pushkin i Arzamas')," *Toronto Slavic Quarterly* 15, http://www.utoronto.ca/tsq/14/proskurin14.shtml.

24. Maiofis, *Vozzvanie k Evrope*, 37–38.

25. See Igor' Nemirovskii, "Smyvaia pechal'nye stroki," in his *Tvorchestvo Pushkina i problema publichnogo povedeniia poeta* (St. Petersburg: Giperion, 2003), 22–31. For a rough draft of Pushkin's letter to Alexander, see his *Polnoe sobranie sochinenii v 16-ti tomakh*, 13:227–28.

26. Nemirovskii, "Smyvaia pechal'nye stroki," 30.

27. See L. A. Chereiskii, *Pushkin i ego okruzhenie* (Leningrad: Nauka, 1989), under "Kapodistria Ioann"; Nemirovskii, "Smyvaia pechal'nye stroki," 31; Stark, *Dokumenty, 1799–1829*, 339–40, commentary to document no. 210.

28. Stark, *Dokumenty*, 336–38, document no. 210.

29. Ibid., original in French.

30. Nemirovskii, "Smyvaia pechal'nye stroki," 19–21, 36–37. For Pushkin's presentation of Alexander as Augustus, see Pushkin, "Iz pis'ma k Gnedichu," in his *Polnoe sobranie sochinenii v 16-ti tomakh*, 2:170–71.

31. Stark, *Dokumenty, 1799–1829*, 407–9, commentary to document no. 263.

32. Ibid.

33. Ibid., 416, commentary to document no. 270, original in French.

34. For the quoted letter, see ibid., 421–22, document no. 272. This letter was obviously written in a state of fury, which explains Pushkin's overstating his disengagement from service.

35. Pushkin, *Polnoe sobranie sochinenii v 16-ti tomakh*, 14:77, original in French.

36. Ibid., 14:256.

37. Ibid., emphasis in original.

38. See S. V. Berezkina et al., eds., *Aleksandr Sergeevich Pushkin: Dokumenty k biografii, 1830–1837* (St. Petersburg: Izdatel'stvo Pushkinskii Dom, 2010), 173, document no. 732 and 179–80, document no. 738, respectively (hereafter Berezkina, *Dokumenty, 1830–1837*).

39. Ibid., 349, document no. 914. For a summary of Pushkin's service, see D. Ia[kubovich], "Posluzhnoi spisok Pushkina 1834 g.," in *Pushkin 1834 god*, ed. Innokentii Oksenov (Leningrad: Pushkinskoe obshchestvo, 1934), 141–44.

40. A. S. Pushkin, "Materialy i zametki, sviazannye s izdaniem gazety 'Dnevnik,'" in his *Sobranie sochinenii v 10-ti tomakh*, ed. D. D. Blagoi et al. (Moscow: Izdatel'stvo khudozhestvennoi literatury, 1959–62), 6:373.

41. See Maiofis, *Vozzvanie k Evrope*, 657–59.

42. Filipp Vigel' to Aleksandr Pushkin, 1831, in Pushkin, *Polnoe sobranie sochinenii v 16-ti tomakh*, 14:202, original in French.

43. Maiofis, *Vozzvanie k Evrope*, 658–68.

44. See Pushkin, *Polnoe sobranie sochinenii v 16-ti tomakh*, 14:202.

45. About Pushkin's election to the Academy, see Berezkina, *Dokumenty, 1830–1837*, 284–85, document no. 856.

46. L. S. Pushkin, "Rasskazy L. S. Pushkina v zapisi Ia. P. Polonskogo," in Tiun'kin, *Pushkin v vospominaniiakh sovremennikov*, 1:57.

47. P. V. Nashchokin i V. A. Nashchokina, "Rasskazy o Pushkine, zapisannye P. I. Bartenevym," in Tiun'kin, *Pushkin v vospominaniiakh sovremennikov*, 2:231.

48. Ibid.

49. Ibid.

50. Pushkin, *Polnoe sobranie sochinenii v 16-ti tomakh*, 16:118.

51. Leonid Shepelev, *Tituly, mundiry i ordena Rossiiskoi imperii* (Moscow: Tsentrpoligraf MiM-Del'ta, 2004), 313.

52. S. A. Reiser, "Tri stroki dnevnika Pushkina," *Vremennik Pushkinskoi komissii 1981* (1985): 148.

53. Boris Gasparov rightly points out that there was no malice on Nicholas's part in making this appointment, just "his obsession with laws and rules." See his "Pushkin's Year of Frustration, or How *The Golden Cockerel* Was Made," *Ulbandus Review* 12 (2009/2010): 47.

54. Reiser, "Tri stroki dnevnika Pushkina," 149.

55. Ibid., 150.

56. For the documents pertaining to the episode, see Berezkina, *Dokumenty, 1830–1837*, 428, document no. 982 (Pushkin's letter of resignation); 432–33, document no. 986 (Benkendorf's letter informing Pushkin that his resignation has been accepted by Nicholas but access to archives is denied), and 436–40, document nos. 989, 990, and 991 (Pushkin's letters to Benkendorf withdrawing his resignation). For an analysis of the episode, see Gasparov, "Pushkin's Year of Frustration," 49–50.

57. Gasparov, "Pushkin's Year of Frustration," 41–62.

58. Pushkin, *Polnoe sobranie sochinenii v 16-ti tomakh*, 12:319.

59. "Prilozheniia k pis'mam N. M. Karamzina: 1. Izvlecheniia iz perepiski rodnykh Karamzina v pervoe vremia posle ego smerti," in *Pis'ma k I. I. Dmitrievu*, by Nikolai Karamzin (St. Petersburg: Imperatorskaia Akademiia Nauk, 1866), 439.

60. Pavel Viazemskii, "Aleksandr Sergeevich Pushkin, 1826–1827," in Tiun'kin, *Pushkin v vospominaniiakh sovremennikov*, 2:192.

61. Pushkin, *Polnoe sobranie sochinenii v 16-ti tomakh*, 15:152. "Klunker" is a variant of "kliunker."

62. Gasparov, "Pushkin's Year of Frustration," 53–54.

63. L. S. Pushkin, "Rasskazy L. S. Pushkina," 1:57.

64. N. M. Smirnov, "Iz pamiatnykh zapisok," in Tiun'kin, *Pushkin v vospominaniiakh sovremennikov*, 2:281.

65. Nashchokin i Nashchokina, "Rasskazy o Pushkine," 2:231.

66. V. I. Safonovich, "Vospominaniia," *Russkii arkhiv* 4 (1903): 492.

67. K. P. Bogaevskaia, "Iz zapisok N. M. Smirnova," *Vremennik Pushkinskoi kommissii 1967–1968* (1970): 8.

68. "Kn[iaz'] P. A. Viazemskii to Vel[ikii] kn[iaz] Mikhail Pavlovich, February 14, 1837," *Russkii arkhiv* 1 (1879): 390.

69. Leonid Grossman, "Neizvestnoe izobrazhenie Pushkina," *Literaturnoe nasledstvo* 16–18 (1934): 983.

70. Nashchokin i Nashchokina, "Rasskazy o Pushkine," 2:231.

71. Pushkin, *Polnoe sobranie sochinenii v 16-ti tomakh*, 14:92, original in French.

72. Ibid., 94, original in French, except for one word, "paperwork," which Pushkin transliterates as *boumagui*.

73. F. V. Rostopchin, "Pis'mo grafa F. V. Rostopchina o sostoianii Rossii v kontse ekaterininskogo tsarstvovaniia," *Russkii arkhiv* 1, no. 3 (1878): 294. The translation provided on 297 gives Stackelberg's title as *kammerjunker*, which is thus erroneous. Rostopchin obviously had in mind the younger Stackelberg, not his father, Otto Magnus Stackelberg, also a diplomat, who was made *kammerherr* in 1771, long before the letter was written.

74. Pushkin, *Polnoe sobranie sochinenii v 16-ti tomakh*, 14:202, original in French. Vigel's information about the service requirement is not quite accurate: beginning in 1809, every holder of a court title had to be in the military or civil service; perhaps he meant that for Pushkin such service would have been nominal—as indeed it was after Pushkin returned to service in the fall of 1831.

75. For Uvarov's letter with the translation, see Pushkin, *Polnoe sobranie sochinenii v 16-ti tomakh*, 14:232; for Pushkin's response, see ibid., 236.

76. Reiser, "Tri stroki dnevnika Pushkina," 152.

77. See G. I. Tiraspol'skii, "Opiska ili simvol?," *Voprosy literatury* 5 (2001): 331–35; Anatolii Korolev, "Kamerger dvora ego imperatorskogo velichestva," *Neva* 4 (2006), http://magazines.russ.ru/neva/2006/4/ko17.html. Tiraspol'sky realizes that the opinion is erroneous but sees it as poetic justice. Korolev believes that Nicholas promoted Pushkin after his death.

78. *Duel' Pushkina s Dantesom-Gekkernom: Podlinnoe voenno-sudnoe delo 1837 g.* (1900; repr., Moscow: Rosslit, 1992), 15–115.

79. For Viazemsky's use of Pushkin's title, see ibid., 46.

80. Ibid., 115 and 116.

81. P. A. Efremov, "Aleksandr Sergeevich Pushkin: 1799–1837," *Russkaia starina* 28 (1880): 536–37. Uvarov also wrote to S. G. Stroganov, the trustee of the Moscow School District, instructing him to observe moderation in published responses to Pushkin's death; see Berezkina, *Dokumenty, 1830–1837*, 801–2, document no. 1318. Stroganov, in his turn, forbade the use of black borders around obituaries for the poet; see ibid., 850, document no. 1372.

82. V. A. Nashchokina, "Rasskazy o Pushkine," in Tiun'kin, *Pushkin v vospominaniiakh sovremennikov*, 2:247.

83. O. I. Senkovskii, "Poeticheskoe puteshestvie po belu svetu," in his *Sochineniia barona Brambeusa* (Moscow: Sovetskaia Rossiia, 1989), 38–39.

84. Ibid., 39.

85. Ibid.

86. For an overview of Pushkin's attitude to the insurgency, see Miasoedova, *Pushkinskie zamysly*, 106–16; for the letter, see Pushkin, *Polnoe sobranie sochinenii v 16-ti tomakh*, 13:86.

87. Senkovskii, "Poeticheskoe puteshestvie," 41.

88. Pushkin, *Polnoe sobranie sochinenii v 16-ti tomakh*, 6:202.

89. Senkovskii, "Poeticheskoe puteshestvie," 43.

90. See Pushkin, *Polnoe sobranie sochinenii v 16-ti tomakh*, 15:109–11.

91. Senkovsky, for example, joined other critics in mocking Pushkin for allowing Efim Liutsenko to publish anonymously his partial translation of Christoph Martin Wieland's tale in verse "Pervonte oder die Wünsche" ("Pervonte, or Desire," 1778); Liutsenko published it in 1836 under the title "Vastola, ili zhelaniia" ("Vastola, or Desires"), naming Pushkin as the publisher. For Senkovsky's mockery, see "Raznye izvestiia," *Biblioteka dlia chteniia* 14 (1836), section "Literaturnaia letopis'," 30.

92. Gogol's article, "O dvizhenii zhurnalistskoi literatury v 1834 i 1835 godu," was published anonymously in the first issue of *Sovremennik* (1836). Pushkin's refutation, "Letter to the Editor" ("Pis'mo k izdateliu"), signed A. B., appeared in volume 3.

93. TMFV is A. V. Timofeev (1812–83), a minor writer and, in 1835–39, a frequent contributor to the *Library for Reading*.

94. See Nina Nazarova, "Lzhe-Belkin i psevdo-Senkovskii: Ob istinnom avtore povesti 'Turetskaia tsyganka' i odnom episode iz otnoshenii Senkovskogo s Pushkinym v 1835 godu," in *Pushkinskaia epokha i russkii literaturnyi kanon: K 85-letiiu Larisy Il'inichny Vol'pert*, ed. Roman Leibov, Pushkinskie chteniia v Tartu 5 (Tartu: Tartu Ülikool, 2011), 1:137–38. For an argument that the pseudonym was a hostile gesture toward Pushkin as the editor of the newly launched *Contemporary*, see 142. It is generally agreed that Senkovsky controlled everything published in his journal, and the pseudonym thus had to have been chosen by him.

95. A. Belkin, "Poteriannaia dlia sveta povest'," *Biblioteka dlia chteniia* 10 (1835): 135. For N. I. Mikhailova's analysis of the passage as linked to "The Station Master," see her "Boldinskie povesti Pushkina i parodii Senkovskogo," *Boldinskie chteniia* (1977): 146–47.

96. *Severnaia pchela*, August 27, 1834, quoted in Mikhailova, "Boldinskie povesti," 145.

97. The third tale ascribed by Senkovsky to A. Belkin (and A. B. Timofeev), "Dzhulio," contains some references to Pushkin's works, but not to ranks. For the references to Pushkin's work in "Dzhulio," see Mikhailova, "Boldinskie povesti," 149–51.

98. Pushkin himself wasn't seriously upset by Senkovsky's use of Belkin's name. In his October 1835 letter to P. A. Pletnev, he writes: "I rejoice that Senkovsky is taking advantage [*promyshliaet*] of Belkin's name, but isn't it possible

(to be sure, surreptitiously and quietly [. . .]) to announce that the real Belkin is dead and doesn't take upon himself his namesake's sins? Indeed, this would be nice" (see Pushkin, *Polnoe sobranie sochinenii v 16-ti tomakh*, 16:56). It is noteworthy that Pushkin signed his defense of Senkovsky with the initials "A. B.," perhaps in a playful reference to Senkovsky's A. Belkin.

99. For a detailed discussion of this question, see Irina Reyfman, "*Kammer-junker* in 'Notes of a Madman': Gogol's View of Pushkin," in Reyfman, *Rank and Style*, ch. 6, 91–94.

100. See Edyta Bojanowska, "Equivocal Praise and National-Imperial Conundrums: Gogol's 'A Few Words about Pushkin,'" *Canadian Slavonic Papers/Revue canadienne des slavistes* 51, nos. 2–3 (June–September 2009): 175–201.

101. Nikolai Gogol', "Zapiski sumasshedshego," in his *Peterburgskie povesti*, ed. O. G. Dilaktorskaia, Seriia Literaturnye pamiatniki (St. Petersburg: Nauka, 1995), 113. In the 1835 edition of *Arabeski* the poem quoted was different, but the reference to Pushkin was also present.

102. Gogol', "Neskol'ko slov o Pushkine," in his *Arabeski*, ed. V. D. Denisov, Seriia Literaturnye pamiatniki (St. Petersburg: Nauka, 2009), 84. In his comments to Gogol's article (ibid., 412–13), Denisov asserts that the anonymous poem "First Night" ("Pervaia noch'") was circulated in the early 1830s as a mockery of Pushkin's family life. He cites A. V. Dubrovsky, senior fellow in the Manuscript Division of the Institute of Russian Literature (Pushkin House), as his source. Dubrovsky's sources are not provided. Denisov also suggests that Pushkin himself asked Gogol to include this footnote, in order to protect his good name—an assertion for the veracity of which Denisov alone stands surety.

103. For Tikhonravov's commentary, see Gogol', *Sochineniia*, 10th ed., ed. Nikolai Tikhonravov (Moscow: Nasledniki br. Salaevykh, 1889–96), 5:610.

104. See commentary to "Notes of a Madman," in Gogol', *Polnoe sobranie sochinenii v 14-ti tomakh*, ed. V. L. Komarovich (Moscow: Akademii Nauk SSSR, 1938), 3:697.

105. Neither Tikhonravov nor V. L. Komarovich, the editor of volume 3 of Gogol's *Polnoe sobranie sochinenii v 14-ti tomakh*, comes to such a conclusion; both relate the "O P." title to "A Few Words about Pushkin" alone.

106. Gogol', "Zapiski sumasshedshego," 119.

107. For a succinct and penetrating analysis of "My Genealogy" in the context of the debate about "literary aristocracy," see David M. Bethea, *Realizing Metaphors: Alexander Pushkin and the Life of the Poet* (Madison: University of Wisconsin Press, 1998), 199–201. Of course, "My Genealogy" was not published in Pushkin's lifetime, but, as is evident from his letter to Benkendorf of November 24, 1831, it was broadly disseminated in manuscript, apparently with Pushkin's blessing. See Pushkin, *Polnoe sobranie sochinenii v 16-ti tomakh*, 14:241–42. For discussions of the controversy over "literary aristocracy" (that is, a disagreement between the market-oriented journalists and writers, such as Faddei Bulgarin and Nikolai Grech, and literati who preferred to address their work to

their peers, such as Pushkin, Viazemsky, and Baratynsky), see Todd, *Fiction and Society*, 83–93; Chester M. Rzadkiewicz, "N. A. Polevoi's 'Moscow Telegraph' and the Journal Wars of 1825–1834," in *Literary Journals in Imperial Russia*, ed. Deborah A. Martinsen (Cambridge: Cambridge University Press, 1997), 73–83. For more on this controversy, see the section on Pushkin's prose fiction in this chapter.

108. Todd, *Fiction and Society*, 171.

109. Bojanowska, "Equivocal Praise"; the quotes come from 195 and 196.

110. Gogol', "Neskol'ko slov o Pushkine," 87. The translation is Bojanowska's ("Equivocal Praise," 196).

111. See Bojanowska, "Equivocal Praise," 198.

112. Gogol', "Zapiski sumasshedshego," 119.

113. See Robert A. Maguire, *Exploring Gogol* (Stanford, CA: Stanford University Press, 1994), 111; see also Yuri Druzhnikov, "Hitting It Off with Pushkin," in his *Contemporary Russian Myths: A Skeptical View of the Literary Past*, Studies in Slavic Languages and Literature 14 (Lewiston, NY: Edwin Mellen Press, 1999), 48–49.

114. Alexander Pushkin, *Eugene Onegin*, trans. James E. Falen (Carbondale: Southern Illinois University Press, 1990), 158.

115. Of these, "Kirdzhali," a biography of a brigand subtitled "a tale," can hardly be called a work of fiction. It is a tale (*povest'*) only in the idiosyncratic sense that Pushkin sometimes gives the word to emphasize the narrative's supposedly factual nature.

116. Paul Debreczeny, *The Other Pushkin: A Study of Alexander Pushkin's Prose Fiction* (Stanford, CA: Stanford University Press, 1983), 25–55. Victoria Somoff similarly argues that Pushkin (like some of his other contemporary prose writers) had difficulty finding a convincingly reliable third-person narrative voice; see her *The Imperative of Reliability: Russian Prose on the Eve of the Novel, 1820s–1850s* (Evanston, IL: Northwestern University Press, 2015), 3, 53–54.

117. Monika Greenleaf, *Pushkin and Romantic Fashion: Fragment, Elegy, Orient, Irony* (Stanford, CA: Stanford University Press: 1994), 1–18.

118. Iu. N. Tynianov, "Pushkin," in his *Pushkin i ego sovremenniki* (Moscow: Nauka, 1968), 162.

119. See Svetlana Evdokimova, *Pushkin's Historical Imagination* (New Haven, CT: Yale University Press, 1999), 255n2.

120. See, for example, A. A. Faustov, *Avtorskoe povedenie Pushkina* (Voronezh: Voronezhskii gosudarstvennyi universitet, 2000), 7–8, 164–242; A. L. Ospovat, "Imenovanie geroia 'Kapitanskoi dochki,'" *Lotmanovskii sbornik* 3 (2004): 262–64; Bethea, *Realizing Metaphors*; and Irina Reyfman, "Poetic Justice and Injustice: Autobiographical Echoes in Pushkin's *The Captain's Daughter*," in Reyfman, *Rank and Style*, ch. 5.

121. Catharine Theimer Nepomnyashchy, "The Telltale Black Baby, or Why Pushkin Began *The Blackamoor of Peter the Great* but Didn't Finish It," in *"Under*

the Sky of My Africa": Alexander Pushkin and Blackness, ed. Catharine Theimer Nepomnyashchy, Ludmilla Trigos, and Nicole Svobodny (Evanston, IL: Northwestern University Press, 2006), 150–71. For a similar argument about *Egyptian Nights*, see David Herman, "A Requiem for Aristocratic Art: Pushkin's 'Egyptian Nights,'" *The Russian Review* 55 (1996): 661–80.

122. See Wacław Lednicki, *Pushkin's "Bronze Horseman": The Story of a Masterpiece* (Berkeley: University of California Press, 1955), 58–72; Sam Driver, *Pushkin: Literature and Social Ideas* (New York: Columbia University Press, 1989), 67–76; Catriona Kelly, "Pushkin's Vicarious Grand Tour: A Neo-Sociological Interpretation of 'K vel'mozhe' (1830)," *Slavonic and East European Review* 77 (1999): 1–29.

123. Alexander Pushkin, *Complete Prose Fiction*, trans. Paul Debreczeny (Stanford, CA: Stanford University Press, 1983), 69–70. For the original, see Pushkin, "Vystrel," in his *Polnoe sobranie sochinenii v 16-ti tomakh*, 8:1:69. All future references to both the translation and the original are given parenthetically in the text, with the first number indicating the page of Debreczeny's translation followed by the volume, book, and page numbers of the original.

124. See Pushkin, "Oproverzhenie na kritiki," in his *Polnoe sobranie sochinenii v 16-ti tomakh*, 11:160–62; "Nachalo avtobiografii," ibid., 12:311–13.

125. Mark Altshuller, *Mezhdu dvukh tsarei: Pushkin v 1824–1836 gg.* (St. Petersburg: Akademicheskii proekt, 2003), 186–98.

126. See Reyfman, *Ritualized Violence Russian Style*, 80–84.

127. On the history of Pushkin's work on the story, see commentary to Pushkin, "The Shot," in his *Polnoe sobranie sochinenii v 10-ti tomakh*, ed. B. V. Tomashevskii (Leningrad: Nauka, 1977–79), 6:518–19.

128. Lotman, *Aleksandr Sergeevich Pushkin*, 86–87.

129. Pushkin's honorarium for *The Tales of Belkin* (published in 1831) comprised the substantial sum of 3,900 rubles. By that time, however, he had had to mortgage Kistenevka to provide a dowry for his bride and thus help his future mother-in-law save face.

130. Pushkin, "Stantsionnyi smotritel'," in his *Polnoe sobranie sochinenii v 16-ti tomakh*, 8:1:98. Debreczeny's translation has been slightly altered to emphasize that the narrator of "The Stationmaster" listens more than he talks.

131. Greenleaf, *Pushkin and Romantic Fashion*, 315.

132. Pushkin inserted into the text of the chapter a copy of a real court ruling on a similar case, changing only the dates and names. See commentary in Pushkin's *Polnoe sobranie sochinenii v 16-ti tomakh*, 8:2:1054, and in his *Polnoe sobranie sochinenii v 10-ti tomakh*, 6:527.

133. I. I. Lazhechnikov, "Moe znakomstvo s Pushkinym," in Tiun'kin, *Pushkin v vospominaniiakh sovremennikov*, 2:174.

134. A classic work on this topic is André Meynieux, *Pouchkine, homme de lettres, et la littérature professionelle en Russie* (Paris: Librarie des Cinq continents, 1966). For an excellent overview of Pushkin's experiments with different

models of professionalism throughout his creative life, see Andrew Kahn, *Pushkin's Lyric Intelligence* (Oxford: Oxford University Press, 2008), ch. 6, "Genius and the Commerce of Poetry."

135. Pushkin, *Polnoe sobranie sochinenii v 16-ti tomakh*, 13:96, emphasis in original.

136. On Pushkin's treatment of Trediakovsky, see Irina Reyfman, *Vasilii Trediakovsky: The Fool of the "New" Russian Literature* (Stanford, CA: Stanford University Press, 1990), 196–225.

137. Pushkin, *Polnoe sobranie sochinenii v 16-ti tomakh*, 13:89.

138. Pushkin, "Razgovor knigoprodavtsa s poetom," in his *Polnoe sobranie sochinenii v 16-ti tomakh*, 2:330. For Herman's interpretation of this poem and its relation to *Egyptian Nights*, see his "A Requiem for Aristocratic Art," 669–70.

139. Kahn, *Pushkin's Lyric Intelligence*, 198–99.

140. Pushkin, *Polnoe sobranie sochinenii v 16-ti tomakh*, 15:124. The expression Pushkin uses, *pro sebia*, usually refers to silent reading. Pushkin thus powerfully emphasizes the private nature of his art.

141. Ibid., 180.

142. See Joseph Peschio and Igor' Pil'shchikov, "The Proliferation of Elite Readership and Circle Poetics in Pushkin and Baratynskii (1820s–1830s)," in *The Space of the Book: Print Culture in the Russian Social Imagination*, ed. Miranda Remnek (Toronto: University of Toronto Press, 2011); see also I. A. Pil'shchikov and M. I. Shapir, "The Poet and the Readership in Puškin's Fragment 'Despite the Great Advantages . . .' (Addenda to the Commentary)," *Philologica: Bilingual Journal of Russian and Theoretical Philology* 8, nos. 19–20 (2003/2005): 215–16.

143. Pushkin, *Polnoe sobranie sochinenii v 16-ti tomakh*, 15:124.

144. Todd, *Fiction and Society*, 108.

145. See Herman, "A Requiem for Aristocratic Art," 665 and 666.

146. For an insightful analysis of this process, which was, to a large degree, orchestrated by Pushkin himself, see Peschio and Pil'shchikov, "The Proliferation of Elite Readership," 82–107, esp. 99–101.

147. "What genius! What sacred fire! What am I beside him?" Quoted and translated in Herman, "A Requiem for Aristocratic Art," 665. The discussion of the Italian's obvious similarity to Mickiewicz and the analysis of Pushkin's view of the Polish poet are beyond the topic of this chapter.

148. Pushkin, *Polnoe sobranie sochinenii v 16-ti tomakh*, 16:48.

149. Ibid.

Chapter 3. The Hierarchy of Ranks according to Gogol

1. See Aleksandr Kirpichnikov, "Somneniia i protivorechiia v biografii Gogolia (Kommentarii k biograficheskoi kanve)," *Izvestiia Otdeleniia russkogo iazyka i slovesnosti Imperatorskoi Akademii nauk* 5 (1900): part 2, 591–623; Donald Fanger, *The Creation of Nikolai Gogol* (Cambridge, MA: Belknap Press of Harvard

University Press, 1979), ch. 1, "The Gogol Problem: Perspectives from Absence," 3–23.

2. See V. V. Gippius, pub., "Dokumenty o sluzhbe Gogolia v Departamente gosudarstvennogo khoziaistva i publichnykh zdanii," in *N. V. Gogol': Materialy i issledovaniia*, ed. V. V. Gippius (Moscow: Izd-vo AN SSSR, 1936), 1:288–89.

3. A. I. Reitblat, "Sluzhil li Gogol' v III otdelenii," in his *Kak Pushkin vyshel v genii* (Moscow: Novoe literaturnoe obozrenie, 2001), 261–67. Bulgarin's memoir is quoted in full on 261–62.

4. Ibid., 267.

5. See Gippius, "Dokumenty o sluzhbe Gogolia," 288–89.

6. Gogol later dropped the second part of his last name. The story of the double last name is as complicated and enigmatic as everything else in Gogol's biography, but it is too long to retell it here.

7. See I. Linnichenko, pub., "Posluzhnoi spisok N. V. Gogolia," *Russkaia mysl'* 17 (1896): 5:173.

8. I. G. Iampolskii, pub., "Dokumenty o sluzhbe Gogolia v Departamente udelov," in Gippius, *N. V. Gogol'*, 1:304.

9. See, for example, N. A. Belozerskaia, "Nikolai Vasil'evich Gogol': Sluzhba ego v Patrioticheskom institute, 1831–1835," *Russkaia starina* 56 (1887): 741.

10. Iampolskii, "Dokumenty o sluzhbe Gogolia," 303.

11. Ibid., 296–99 (documents 3, 4, and 6).

12. Ibid., 300–301 (documents 9 and 10).

13. Ibid., 301–2 (document 11). For the certificate (*attestat*) of service that Gogol eventually received from the Department of Domains, see Belozerskaia, "Nikolai Vasil'evich Gogol'," 749.

14. Belozerskaia, "Nikolai Vasil'evich Gogol'," 742.

15. Linnichenko, "Posluzhnoi spisok N. V. Gogolia."

16. See Belozerskaia, "Nikolai Vasil'evich Gogol'," 742; P. A. Kulish, *Zapiski o zhizni Nikolaia Vasil'evicha Gogolia, sostavlennye iz vospominanii ego druzei i znakomykh i iz ego sobstvennykh pisem* (St. Petersburg: V tipografii A. Iakobsona, 1856), 84.

17. N. V. Gogol', *Polnoe sobranie sochinenii v 14-ti tomakh* (Moscow: Izd-vo AN SSSR, 1937–52), 10:18. All future references to this edition are given parenthetically in the text, with the first number indicating the volume and the second, the page.

18. Linnichenko, "Posluzhnoi spisok N. V. Gogolia."

19. See Belozerskaia, "Nikolai Vasil'evich Gogol'," documents 3, 4, and 7 (Wistinghausen's letters), and 5 and 10 (court documents).

20. Shepelev, *Tituly, mundiry i ordena Rossiiskoi imperii*, 155–56.

21. See Belozerskaia, "Nikolai Vasil'evich Gogol'," 753 (document 9, on admission of sisters free of charge) and 754 (document 10, on Her Majesty granting the ring).

22. Before accepting the adjunct position at Saint Petersburg University, Gogol tried to secure for himself a professorship in general history at Kiev (Kyiv) University. Despite the help from Zhukovsky, Sergey Uvarov, and others, the position went to someone else.

23. Linninchenko, "Posluzhnoi spisok N. V. Gogolia."

24. See Belozerskaia, "Nikolai Vasil'evich Gogol'," 747 and 755 (document 14).

25. For an account of Gogol's unsuccessful stint at the university, see V. V. Gippius, *Gogol*, ed. and trans. Robert A. Maguire (Durham, NC: Duke University Press, 1989), 54–57. It was after Gogol left the university that the service record Linnichenko later published was compiled. It is noteworthy that Gogol was not promoted upon retirement, as was customary, which suggests failure.

26. In his biography of Gogol, P. A. Kulish published two samples of Gogol's classwork, unfortunately undated. One of them is on Russian law and can provide some idea of Gogol's competence in this field as assessed by his teacher, whose evaluation is positive but not stellar: "Even though this [report] is not quite thorough, one can see some understanding of the subject." See P. A. Kulish, *Opyt biografii Nikolaia Vasil'evicha Gogolia* (St. Petersburg: V tip. E. Pratsa, 1854), 204.

27. Gogol makes idiosyncratic use of animate, inanimate, collective, and plural forms for "everything" and "everyone" in this passage: "Тишина в нем необыкновенная, никакой дух не блестит в народе, *всё* служащие да должностные, *все* толкуют о своих департаментах да коллегиях, *всё* подавлено, *всё* погрязло в бездельных, ничтожных трудах, в которых бесплодно издерживается жизнь их" (my emphasis).

28. See V. I. Shenrok, *Materialy dlia biografii Gogolia*, 4 vols. (Moscow: Tip. A. I. Mamontova, 1892–97), 1:183–84.

29. For the text of the deed of trust for his property that Gogol signed over to his mother on July 23, 1829, see V. V. Veresaev, *Gogol' v zhizni: Sistematicheskii svod podlinnykh svidetel'stv sovremennikov* (Moscow: Academia, 1933), 82, item 541. For a detailed analysis of this letter, see Vladimir Nabokov, *Nikolai Gogol* (New York: New Directions, 1971), 14–23; Nabokov cites the letter in full on 14–21.

30. See Reitblat, "Sluzhil li Gogol'," 265–66.

31. Gogol started to write the word "ser[vice]" (*slu[zhb]*), but crossed it out and wrote *zaniatii* (activities) instead.

32. For a description of Mariia Gogol's disposition and the analysis of the complicated mother–son relationship, see Nabokov, *Nikolai Gogol*, 13–14.

33. P. V. Annenkov, *Literaturnye vospominaniia* (Moscow: Gosudarstvennoe izdanie khudozhestvennoi literatury, 1960), 79.

34. M. K. Lemke, ed., *M. M. Stasiulevich i ego sovremenniki v ikh perepiske* (St. Petersburg: Tip. M. Stasiulevicha, 1912), 3:327.

35. Veresaev, *Gogol' v zhizni*, 105n.

36. Recall Gogol's words in the letter to his mother of February 2, 1830, "I am going to the office every day again," which presumably means that there was a period of time when he did not go there every day. T. G. Pashchenko, a younger brother of one of Gogol's classmates, who knew him in Saint Petersburg, confirms Gogol's neglect for service in his memoir: "Having neither the calling nor the desire to serve, Gogol perceived service as a burden and therefore often skipped days of attendance, when he occupied himself with literature at home"; see his "Cherty iz zhizni Gogolia," in *N. V. Gogol' v vospominaniiakh sovremennikov*, ed. S. Mashinskii (Moscow: Gosudarstvennoe izdatel'stvo khudozhestvennoi literatury, 1952), 46.

37. For the argument that Gogol had a poor understanding of Ukrainian life, see Gippius, *N. V. Gogol'*, 30. For S. A. Vengerov's calculations of the number of days Gogol spent in provincial Russia, see his "Gogol' sovershenno ne znal real'noi russkoi zhizni," in *Sobranie sochinenii* (St. Petersburg: Prometei, 1913), 2:124, 127–32, and 135. On Gogol's constructing an image of Russian provincial life, see Anne Lounsbery, "'No, This Is Not the Provinces!' Provincialism, Authenticity, and Russianness in Gogol's Day," *Russian Review* 64, no. 2 (2005): 259–80.

38. The only other one of Gogol's works that presents a stable hierarchy of ranks is "The Carriage" ("Koliaska," 1836). It is also exceptional in that all ranks in it are military. The stability of the hierarchy of ranks in this story is constantly emphasized. For example, every time a lower-ranking officer says something, the regimental commander, a general, asks "What?," forcing the officer to repeat his remark and thus acknowledge the general's right to remind him of his inferior position.

39. The stories are listed in the order in which Gogol arranged them in the third volume of his first collected works, in 1842.

40. The color of a uniform depended on the particular type of service and was not always the same across different ministries and departments. Beginning in 1810, the everyday uniform of a Senate bureaucrat was dark green, and evidently Gogol presents Nevsky as dominated by them. However, according to "The Decree on Civil Uniforms," issued on February 27, 1834, almost all civil uniforms, with very few exceptions, were made dark green. "Nevsky Prospect" was written between 1831 and the summer of 1834, and Gogol thus could be incorporating a reference to the new regulation (if not the actual practice, since of necessity the change of the uniforms could not happen overnight), which would make his metaphor a general allusion to civil uniforms. On the color of uniforms, see Shepelev, *Tituly, mundiry i ordena*, 216 (uniforms of the Senate) and 248, 251–52 (on the 1834 decree).

41. See Shepelev, *Tituly, mundiry i ordena*, 143, 148, and 330.

42. See commentary to "The Nose," in Gogol', *Peterburgskie povesti*, 272n11. The author of the commentary, O. G. Dilaktorskaia, does not point out the contradiction between the plumes and Kovalev's conclusion that Nose is a state councilor.

43. See Shepelev, *Tituly, mundiry i ordena*, 216, 234.

44. Quoted in Shepelev, *Tituly, mundiry i ordena*, 159–60. It was Mikhail Speransky—at the time, Minister of Justice and one of Alexander's closest advisers—who initiated these reforms.

45. See Dilaktorskaia's commentary to "Notes of a Madman," in Gogol', *Peterburgskie povesti*, 293n22.

46. Quoted in Shepelev, *Tituly, mundiry i ordena*, 161–62. There was no rank of collegiate councilor; Karamzin apparently meant collegiate secretary, tenth class.

47. For Poprishchin's failure to qualify as a cultured nobleman, see Reyfman, *Rank and Style*, ch. 2, "What Makes a Gentleman? Revisiting Gogol's 'Notes of a Madman.'"

48. V. V. Vinogradov, *Evoliutsiia russkogo naturalizma: Gogol' i Dostoevskii*, in his *Poetika russkoi literatury: Izbrannye trudy* (Moscow: Nauka, 1976), 158n8.

49. Faddei Bulgarin, *Polnoe sobranie sochinenii*, vol. 3, *Zapiski Chukhina i Mazepa* (St. Petersburg: Izd. M. D. Ol'khina, V tipografii K. Zhernakova, 1843), 125.

50. See I. G. Iampolskii, ed., *Poety 1860-kh godov* (Leningrad: Sovetskii pisatel', 1968), 182.

51. Consider Petr Fomenko's stage version of Gogol's story titled "He Was a Titular Councilor" (first performed on September 11, 2004).

Chapter 4. Poets in the Military

1. Denis Davydov, "Ocherk zhizni Denisa Vasil'evicha Davydova," in his *Sochineniia* (St. Petersburg: Izd. A. Smirdina, 1848), xiii.

2. Ibid., xv.

3. Denis Davydov, *Stikhotvoreniia* (Leningrad: Sovetskii pisatel', 1984), 52.

4. Ibid., 53.

5. The ruff is a medium-sized wading bird (*Philomachus pugnax*) known for its aggressive behavior.

6. Davydov, *Stikhotvoreniia*, 54–56.

7. Ibid., 57–58.

8. See V. E. Vatsuro, "Denis Davydov—Poet," in Davydov, *Stikhotvoreniia*, 17–21.

9. Ibid., 19.

10. Denis Davydov, *Stikhotvoreniia*, 75–76.

11. Ibid., 77.

12. Ibid.

13. See Vatsuro, "Denis Davydov—Poet," 14, 28–31, 43.

14. M. V. Iuzefovich, "Pamiati Pushkina," in Tiun'kin, *Pushkin v vospomina-niiakh sovremennikov*, 2:121. For an incisive discussion of Davydov's influence on the young Pushkin, see V. E. Vatsuro, "Pushkin i Denis Davydov v 1818–1819 gg.," in *Istochnikovedenie i kraevedenie v kul'ture Rossii: Sbornik k 50-letiiu*

sluzheniia Sigurda Ottovicha Shmidta Istoriko-arkhivnomu institutu, ed. V. F. Kozlov et al. (Moscow: RGGU, 2000), 150–54.

15. Reportedly, Davydov stopped relying on Naryshkina's help once he learned of her status as Alexander's mistress.

16. A. L. Iurganov, "Materialy o voennoi sluzhbe Denisa Davydova," *Sovetskie arkhivy* 4 (1984): 37. The quotation comes from the document titled "Formuliarnyi spisok o sluzhbe general-leitenanta D. V. Davydova," which was put together on February 25, 1836. It is the most complete and accurate record of Davydov's service career.

17. Davydov, *Stikhotvoreniia*, 100. On Pushkin's participation, see commentary to this poem, ibid., 215.

18. Ibid., 100–101.

19. Ibid., 100. The poet calls himself a Cossack because during his time as a guerilla he often fought alongside Cossack regiments.

20. See A. I. Gertsen, *Byloe i dumy*, in his *Sobranie sochinenii v 30-ti tomakh* (Moscow: Izdatel'stvo Akademii Nauk SSSR, 1956), 8:165–68.

21. On *Sashka* as a literary prank, see Joe Peschio, *The Poetics of Impudence and Intimacy in the Age of Pushkin* (Madison: University of Wisconsin Press, 2012), 3–5. A prank also could be an action, like Burtsov's and Davydov's hussar debauches.

22. V. S. Kiselev-Sergenin, "Bespriiutnyi strannik v mire," in *Stikhotvoreniia i poemy*, by A. I. Polezhaev (Leningrad: Sovetskii pisatel', 1987), 12.

23. Gertsen, *Byloe i dumy*, 166–67.

24. *Russkii biograficheskii slovar'* (St. Petersburg: Tip. I. N. Skorokhodova, 1910), 14:310–11.

25. For the official record of Polezhaev's service in the Caucasus, see P. A. Efremov, "Biograficheskii ocherk," in *Stikhotvoreniia A. I. Polezhaeva*, ed. P. A. Efremov (St. Petersburg: Izd. A. S. Suvorina, 1889), xl–xlii.

26. See the entry on Polezhaev in Nikolaev, *Russkie pisateli*, 5:43.

27. A. V. Druzhinin, "Stikhotvoreniia A. Polezhaeva," in his *Sobranie sochinenii* (St. Petersburg: Tip. Imp. Akademii Nauk, 1865–67), 7:426; for Belinsky's opinion, see his 1842 essay "Stikhotvoreniia Polezhaeva," in his *Polnoe sobranie sochinenii v 13-ti tomakh* (Moscow: Izd. Akademii Nauk SSSR, 1955), 6:127; see also 128, 132, 137.

28. Polezhaev, "Pritesnil moiu svobodu," in his *Stikhotvoreniia i poemy*, 75. Sarcastically referring to the sergeant as a "staff-soldier," Polezhaev ridicules his pretensions to supremacy: staff-officers were officers from the eighth to the sixth classes, that is, officers with relatively high ranks.

29. Ibid.

30. Ibid., 78.

31. Ibid.

32. Ibid., 80.

33. Ibid., 90. Text in brackets is restored by the editor of the collection.

34. Ibid., 136.

35. Polezhaev, *Erpeli*, in his *Stikhotvoreniia i poemy*, 262.

36. Ibid., 264.

37. Polezhaev, "Uznik," in his *Stikhotvoreniia i poemy*, 87. Polezhaev uses abbreviations to encipher his invectives. The kiss refers to Nicholas's allegedly kissing Polezhaev on the forehead at the end of their fateful conversation.

38. Polezhaev, *Erpeli*, 290.

39. Ibid., 293.

40. Ibid., 294.

41. Polezhaev, *Chir-Iurt*, in his *Stikhotvoreniia i poemy*, 311–12.

42. Ibid., 295.

43. Ibid., 296.

44. Ibid., 297.

45. Ibid., 322.

46. Polezhaev, "Otryvok iz poslaniia k A. P. L<ozovskom>u," in his *Stikhotvoreniia i poemy*, 149. A. P. Lozovsky had been Polezhaev's close friend since the time of his incarceration in 1828. While Polezhaev was in the Caucasus, he managed his publications.

47. Polezhaev, "K moemu geniiu," in his *Stikhotvoreniia i poemy*, 202.

48. David Powelstock, *Becoming Mikhail Lermontov: The Ironies of Romantic Individualism in Nicholas I's Russia* (Evanston, IL: Northwestern University Press, 2005), 106.

49. For the letter, see Mikhail Lermontov, *Sochineniia v shesti tomakh* (Moscow: Izdatel'stvo Akademii Nauk SSSR, 1954–57), 6:428. Subsequently, references to this edition will be given parenthetically in the text, with the first number indicating the volume and the second the page.

50. L. N. Nazarova, "Shkola gvardeiskikh praporshchikov i kavaleriiskikh iunkerov," in Manuilov, *Lermontovskaia entsiklopediia*, 626.

51. S. N. Malkov, "Voennaia sluzhba Lermontova," in Manuilov, *Lermontovskaia entsiklopediia*, 87.

52. See Powelstock, *Becoming Mikhail Lermontov*, 106–7.

53. Ibid., 209.

54. Malkov, "Voennaia sluzhba," 88.

55. Ibid.

56. See Peschio, *The Poetics of Impudence*, esp. ch. 1.

57. For the particulars of the duel, see E. G. Gershtein, "Dueli Lermontova," in Manuilov, *Lermontovskaia entsiklopediia*, 149–50; Powelstock, *Becoming Mikhail Lermontov*, 252–53.

58. Quoted in V. A. Manuilov and S. B. Latyshev, "Letopis' zhizni i tvorchestva M. Iu. Lermontova," in Manuilov, *Lermontovskaia entsiklopediia*, 651.

59. See the entry on Lermontov, in Nikolaev, *Russkie pisateli*, 3:331.

60. Powelstock, *Becoming Mikhail Lermontov*, 172; see also 35, 106.

61. Ibid., 107.

62. David Powelstock, "Poet as Officer and Oracle: Mikhail Lermontov's Aesthetic Mythology" (PhD diss., University of California, Berkeley, 1994), 269.

63. Quoted in Manuilov and Latyshev, "Letopis' zhizni i tvorchestva," 651.

64. Powelstock, "Poet as Officer and Oracle," esp. ch. 5; Powelstock, *Becoming Mikhail Lermontov*, 267.

65. Except for one episode that lasted from 1833 to 1835 or 1836, when he had a love affair with E. D. Zolotareva, for whom he wrote a number of love poems.

66. The only comparable incident with a poet in civil service happened to Ivan Aksakov in 1851. After learning that Aksakov had publicly read his narrative poem *Vagabond* (*Brodiaga*), Minister of Internal Affairs L. A. Perovsky, under whom Aksakov served, suggested that he should "stop his writerly work" while in service. Aksakov resigned. The difference, however, is significant: Aksakov was under police surveillance at the time; furthermore, he could and did retire.

Chapter 5. Service Ranks in Dostoevsky's Life and Fiction

1. There were four "conductor" grades in the school, the fourth being the lowest.

2. See N. F. Budanova and G. M. Fridlender, eds., *Letopis' zhizni i tvorchestva F. M. Dostoevskogo: V trekh tomakh, 1821–1881*, vol. 1, *1821–1864* (St. Petersburg: Gumanitarnoe agenstvo Akademicheskii proekt, 1993), 46. See also 47, entry for February 12. All future references to this volume are given parenthetically in the text.

3. In his official service record (*formuliarnyi spisok*) for 1843, Dostoevsky's rank is given as lieutenant (*inzhener-poruchik*, twelfth class); see Budanova and Fridlender, *Letopis' zhizni i tvorchestva*, 84, 86. In other documents, however, his rank is given as second lieutenant (ibid., 90, 92). The imperial order dismissing Dostoevsky from service calls him second lieutenant (ibid., 93). It seems that the *formularnyi spisok* contains an error.

4. Quoted in Budanova and Fridlender, *Letopis' zhizni i tvorchestva*, 89–90. Dots in the angle brackets indicate an omission made by the editors of *Letopis'*.

5. For Chatsky's words, see A. S. Griboedov, *Sochineniia*, ed. S. A. Fomichev (Moscow: Khudozhestvennaia literatura, 1988), 55.

6. A. E. Vrangel's memoir, *Vospominaniia o F. M. Dostoevskom v Sibiri, 1854–1856* (St. Petersburg: A. S. Suvorin, 1912), 19, is cited in Budanova and Fridlender, *Letopis' zhizni i tvorchestva*, 198. For Dostoevsky's complaints about the difficulties of his service, see ibid., 200, 201, 203, 212, 213.

7. F. M. Dostoevskii, *Polnoe sobranie sochinenii v tridtsati tomakh*, ed. V. G. Bazanov (Leningrad: Nauka, 1972–90), 1:240. Further references to Dostoevsky's works will be given parenthetically in the text, with the first number indicating the volume and the second, the page.

8. See G. M. Fridlender, Commentary, in F. M. Dostoevskii, *Sobranie*

sochinenii v piatnadtsati tomakh, ed. G. M. Fridlender (Leningrad: Nauka, 1988–96), 1:456.

9. According to Maks Fasmer's etymological dictionary, *goliada* derives from the name of one of the Baltic tribes, *goliad'*, and changed its meaning because of its phonetic association with the word *golyi*. See Fasmer, *Etimologicheskii slovar'*, 1:434. Fasmer notes the Russian appropriation of the word and its changed meaning. The meaning that was current when Dostoevsky was working on *The Double* is more important than the actual etymology.

10. Gogol', *Polnoe sobranie sochinenii*, 3:142.

11. Deborah Martinsen quotes Olga Meerson's aptly formulated difference between Gogol's and Dostoevsky's petty officials: "subject/person/personhood is non-ontological and crazily absurd in Gogol, yet it is absolute and ontological in Dostoevsky"; Meerson stresses that Dostoevsky "endows his characters with ontology *to begin with*." Deborah Martinsen, "*Lolita* as Petersburg Text," *Nabokov Studies* 13 (2014/15): 95–123, quotation in footnote 10.

12. Carol Apollonio, *Dostoevsky's Secrets: Reading against the Grain* (Evanston, IL: Northwestern University Press, 2009), 14.

13. Ibid.

14. See Mikhail Bakhtin, *Problems of Dostoevsky's Poetics*, ed. and trans. Caryl Emerson, Theory and History of Literature 8 (Minneapolis: University of Minnesota Press, 1984), 211–21.

15. Martinsen, "*Lolita* as Petersburg Text," 102.

16. For Bakhtin's remark, see his *Problems of Dostoevsky's Poetics*, 211.

17. See Fridlender, Commentary, in Dostoevskii, *Sobranie sochinenii v piatnadtsati tomakh*, 1:485.

18. See E. M. Sokol, "'Malen'kii chelovek' v tvorchestve russkikh pisatelei 1840-kh godov v svete khristianskoi traditsii: Ot Gogolia k Dostoevskomu" (Avtoref. diss., Moskovskii gosudarstvennyi oblastnoi universitet, 2003), http://www.dissercat.com/content/malenkii-chelovek-v-tvorchestve-russkikh-pisatelei-1840-kh-godov-v-svete-khristianskoi-tradi. Sokol rightly points out that Belinsky's understanding of "insignificant men" was more nuanced than it became later, in Soviet scholarship; nonetheless, Belinsky believed that insignificant men, including low-ranking clerks, deserved compassion.

19. V. G. Belinskii, "Vzgliad na russkuiu literaturu 1846 goda," in his *Polnoe sobranie sochinenii v 13-ti tomakh*, 10:40; see also 41 for Belinsky's criticism of what he calls the novella's "fantastic color."

20. Ibid., 41–42.

21. Ibid., 42.

22. See Iu. N. Tynianov, "K teorii parodii," in his *Poetika, Istoriia literatury, Kino* (Moscow: Nauka, 1977), 198–226 (first published in 1921). A. A. Kraevsky was the first to point out Foma's similarity to Gogol; see "Pis'ma M. M. Dostoevskogo k F. M. Dostoevskomu," in *F. M. Dostoevskii: Materialy i issledovaniia*, ed. A. S. Dolinin (Leningrad: AN SSSR, 1935), 525.

23. On references to *Dead Souls*, see M. Gus, *Idei i obrazy F. M. Dostoevskogo* (Moscow: Khudozhestvennaia literatura, 1971), 163–64.

24. "His Excellency" is mentioned in "Mr. Prokharchin" as well, but only once (1:244); unlike in Dostoevsky's other two early works, in "Mr. Prokharchin" this character is not developed.

25. For interpretations of *The Village of Stepanchikovo* as a work that was necessary for Dostoevsky to free himself from Gogol's influence, see K. V. Mochul'skii, *Dostoevskii: Zhizn' i tvorchestvo* (1947; repr., Paris: YMCA-Press, 1980), 145, 146; Ronald Hingley, *Dostoevsky: His Life and Work* (New York: Scribner's, 1978), 80; Kristin Vitalich, "*The Village of Stepanchikovo*: Toward a (Lacanian) Theory of Parody," *Slavic and East European Journal* 53, no. 2 (2009): 203–18.

26. It is irrelevant that almost all the ranks mentioned in the novella are military: it is the service hierarchy that is important for Dostoevsky, not the nature of the service itself.

27. The honorific *vashe siiatel'stvo* (lit. "Your Radiancy") was used in addressing princes, counts, dukes, and barons, i.e., high nobility, not high-ranking servitors.

28. There were exceptions. For example, Pushkin, a titular councilor, received a huge sum: 5,000 rubles a year. For the discussion of his anomalous situation, see chapter 2.

29. Officials in the ranks of first to fourth class were to be addressed "Your Excellency"; fifth to eighth, "Your High Ancestry"; ninth to fourteenth, "Your Nobleness." All titles could be used in third person: His/Her Excellency, etc.

30. Vitalich, "*The Village of Stepanchikovo*," 216.

31. For some observations on other references to Gogol's works in Dostoevsky's story, see G. V. Stepanova, "'Skvernyi anekdot' (Dostoevskii i Gogol')," *Dostoevskii: Materialy i issledovaniia* 7 (1987): 166–69; for a more general analysis of the story, including a discussion of its New Testament subtexts, see Roman Leibov, "Zametki o 'Skvernom anekdote,'" *Novoe literaturnoe obozrenie* 8 (1994): 158–73.

32. Nikolay Gogol, "The Overcoat," in his *Diary of a Madman, The Government Inspector, and Selected Stories*, trans. Ronald Wilks, intro. Robert A. Maguire (London: Penguin, 2005), 143; for the original, see Gogol', *Polnoe sobranie sochinenii*, 3:144. Wilks's translation has been slightly modified.

33. Boris Eichenbaum, "How Gogol's 'Overcoat' Is Made," in *Gogol from the Twentieth Century: Eleven Essays*, ed., trans., and intro. Robert A. Maguire (Princeton, NJ: Princeton University Press, 1974), 282.

34. Dostoevsky refers here to the eight days Pralinsky spent at home after the incident at Pseldonimov's wedding party.

35. On Raskolnikov's eventual remorse, see Deborah A. Martinsen, "Getting Away with Murder: Teaching *Crime and Punishment*," in *Teaching Nineteenth-Century Russian Literature*, ed. Deborah Martinsen, Cathy Popkin, and Irina Reyfman (Brighton, MA: Academic Studies Press, 2014), 162–74.

36. The similar inability to repent and change morally is also displayed by Velchaninov, the protagonist of *The Eternal Husband* (*Vechnyi muzh*, 1870). Like the young man who offends Akaky and is supposedly affected for life by his meek response, Velchaninov recalls, among numerous memories of his past unseemly actions, how he offended "one kind old clerk" and how this clerk cried and "covered his face with his hands like a child" (9:8). The memory of this past misdeed does not change him, however: he remains as egotistical and ruthless as before. It seems that Dostoevsky continued to be skeptical about the ability of the likes of Pralinsky and Velchaninov to change through experiencing compassion.

37. See Nancy Workman, "Notes from a Cave: Teaching *Notes from Underground* in a Philosophy Class," in Martinsen et al., *Teaching Nineteenth-Century Russian Literature*, 175–85.

38. See David Herman, *Poverty of the Imagination: Nineteenth-Century Russian Literature about the Poor* (Evanston, IL: Northwestern University Press, 2001), 179, 187. Dostoevsky uses *shinel'* (overcoat) and *shinelishka* (little old overcoat) to describe Myshkin's overcoat.

39. Quoted in Herman, *Poverty of the Imagination*, 181; for the original, see Dostoevsky, Letter to S. A. Ivanova of January 1, 1868, in Dostoevskii, *Polnoe sobranie sochinenii v tridtsati tomakh*, 28: 2:251.

40. For an analysis of General Ivolgin's character and vicissitudes in the novel, including his fateful confrontation with Lebedev, see Deborah A. Martinsen, *Surprised by Shame: Dostoevsky's Liars and Narrative Exposure* (Columbus: Ohio State University Press, 2003), ch. 4. Martinsen documents Dostoevsky's references to Gogol throughout the chapter.

41. The quote is from Kenneth Lantz's translation: Fyodor Dostoevsky, *A Writer's Diary*, vol. 1, *1873–1876*, translated and annotated by Kenneth Lantz, with an introductory study by Gary Saul Morson (Evanston, IL: Northwestern University Press, 1993), 665. Lantz's translation will be cited in parentheses, with the page number of his translation, followed by the volume and page numbers of the original.

42. For a discussion of Dostoevsky's views of honor, see Reyfman, *Ritualized Violence Russian Style*, ch. 6.

43. For the narrator of "Bobok" as Poprishchin's double, see commentary to "Bobok" in Dostoevskii, *Sobranie sochinenii v piatnadtsati tomakh*, 21:402–3.

44. Dostoevsky's original uses the same expression both times: *Net, etogo ia ne mogu dopustit'*; Lantz translates the second instance differently: "No, I cannot accept this" (185). However, the repetition is important here.

45. Gogol', *Polnoe sobranie sochinenii*, 3:206.

46. See Irina Reyfman, "Dishonor by Flogging and Restoration by Dancing: Leskov's Response to Dostoevsky," in Reyfman, *Rank and Style*, 259–66.

47. On Dostoevsky's biters, see Reyfman, *Ritualized Violence Russian Style*, 250 and 340–41n128.

Conclusion

1. See Riasanovsky, *A Parting of Ways*.

2. The term *raznochintsy* (people of various ranks; singular *raznochinets*) had a long history in Russia, from the seventeenth century to the nineteenth; see Elise Kimmerling Wirtschafter, *Structures of Society: Imperial Russia's "People of Various Ranks"* (DeKalb: Northern Illinois University Press, 1994). Around the mid-nineteenth century this term began to be applied to the group of "people of various ranks" (that is, coming from all estates, except nobility) who acquired higher social standing through education and who practiced liberal professions, including journalism. Nineteenth-century radicals, such as Nikolai Chernyshevsky and Nikolai Dobroliubov, were, like Belinsky, quintessential *raznochintsy*.

3. Quoted in Nikolaev, *Russkie pisateli*, 1:207.

4. Ibid., 216. For a thorough and highly original discussion of the strategy Belinsky used to create for himself a reputation as the "organizer" of Russian literature, see Aleksei Vdovin, "Kontsept 'glava literatury' v russkoi kritike 1830–1860-kh godov" (PhD diss., Tartu Ülikooli Kirjastus, Tartu, Estonia, 2011), ch. 1, 21–89.

5. Wikipedia cites the online Russian Federal Informational Address System (Federal'naia informatsionnaia adresnaia sistema), http://fias.nalog.ru/Public/SearchPage.aspx?SearchState=2.

6. His father, Sergei, was a prominent writer, the author of the autobiographical *Family Chronicle* (*Semeinaia khronika*, 1856) and *Childhood Years of Bagrov-the-Grandson* (*Detskie gody Bagrova-vnuka*, 1858); his younger brother Ivan was active in the Slavophile movement and, after the Crimean War, put forth the highly influential doctrine of Pan-Slavism. The noble status of the Aksakov family, although not very high, was of ancient origin.

7. N. G. Chernyshevskii, *Polnoe sobranie sochinenii*, ed. V. Ia. Kirpotin (Moscow: Gosudarstvennoe izdatel'stvo khudozhestvennoi literatury, 1953), 16:664.

8. L. N. Tolstoi, *Polnoe sobranie sochinenii* (Moscow: Gosudarstvennoe izdatel'stvo Khudozhestvennaia literatura, 1937), 47:38.

9. See A. Liatskii, B. L. Modzalevskii, and A. A. Sivers, eds., *Ogni: Istoriia, literatura* (Petrograd, 1916), 1:176. Goncharov's grandfather served in the military and thus was a nobleman; his father, however, chose to become a merchant and therefore lost his noble status. After Goncharov graduated from the university and obtained personal nobility, he was officially "excluded from the merchant estate [*kupecheskoe zvanie*]"; see A. D. Alekseev, *Letopis' zhizni i tvorchestva I. A. Goncharova* (Leningrad: Izdatel'stvo Akademii nauk SSSR, 1960), 19. Information on Goncharov's service comes primarily from this edition.

10. Beginning in 1845, this was the rank that afforded hereditary nobility. There is no information to be found in biographies of Goncharov on the relevance of this promotion to Goncharov's status as a nobleman.

11. Leaving aside the question of how typical it was in the 1830s or 1840s for a nobleman in service to own factories that were not located on his estate, it is significant to point out that Goncharov (perhaps due to his merchant origins) was consistently interested in the figure of a nobleman engaged in business. Andrei Shtolts of *Oblomov* and Ivan Tushin of *The Precipice* (*Obryv*, 1869) are both businessmen.

12. I. A. Goncharov, *Obyknovennaia istoriia*, in his *Polnoe sobranie sochinenii i pisem v dvadtsati tomakh* (St. Petersburg: Nauka, 1997), 1:335.

13. Quoted in K. Tiun'kin, *Saltykov-Shchedrin* (Moscow: Molodaia gvardiia, 1989), http://az.lib.ru/s/saltykow_m_e/text_0230.shtml.

14. All Saltykov-Shchedrin biographers cite his dependence on service for his financial well-being. While there is no doubt that this was a factor in his staying in and, especially, returning to the service, the matter is complicated and requires a special investigation, for which there is no room here.

15. V. V. Prozorov, entry on Saltykov-Shchedrin, in *Russkie pisateli: Biobibliograficheskii slovar'*, ed. P. A. Nikolaev (Moscow: Prosveshchenie, 1990), 2:212.

16. M. I. Semevskii, "Mikhail Evgrafovich Saltykov (6 fevralia 1882 g.)," in *M. E. Saltykov-Shchedrin v vospominaniiakh sovremennikov*, 2nd ed., ed. S. A. Makashin (Moscow: Khudozhestvennaia literatura, 1975), 1:184.

17. M. I. Semevskii, *Znakomye, Vospominaniia, Stikhotvoreniia, Epigrammy, Shutki, Podpisi: Al'bom M. I. Semevskogo, izdatelia redaktora istoricheskogo zhurnala "Russkaia starina"; Kniga avtobiograficheskikh sobstvennoruchnykh zametok 850 lits, 1867–1888* (St. Petersburg: Tip. Balasheva, 1888), 208.

18. Quoted in A. Zorin, *Glagol vremen: Izdaniia G. R. Derzhavina i russkie chitateli*, in *Svoi podvig svershiv. . . .*, ed. A. Zorin et al. (Moscow: Kniga, 1987), 26. The omission in angle brackets is Zorin's.

19. For the history of this playful endeavor, see P. N. Berkov, *Koz'ma Prutkov—direktor Probirnoi palatki i poet* (Moscow: Izdatel'stvo Akademii Nauk SSSR, 1933); A. Smirnov, *Koz'ma Prutkov* (Moscow: Molodaia gvardiia, 2011).

20. *Sochineniia Koz'my Prutkova* (Moscow: Khudozhestvennaia literatura, 1974), 332, emphasis in the original.

21. Ibid., 333.

22. Ibid.

23. Ibid., 334. This schedule reflects the times when the creators of Kozma Prutkov's persona produced and published his writings.

24. A. K. Tolstoi, *Sobranie sochinenii: V chetyrekh tomakh* (Moscow: Izdatel'stvo Pravda, 1969), 4:311, original in French, Tolstoy's emphasis.

25. Quoted in Nikolaev, *Russkie pisateli*, 2:267.

26. Letter to K. R. of August 24, 1890, quoted in B. Ia. Bukhshtab, *A. A. Fet: Ocherk zhizni i tvorchestva*, 2nd ed. (Leningrad: Nauka, 1990), 55–56n142. By a morbid coincidence, Fet's family suffered from hereditary madness; six of his close relatives were mentally ill: his mother, two sisters, two brothers, and a nephew. Whether his extreme views in the late years of his life were caused by

mental instability (as Turgenev suggested in his 1872 letter to Iakov Polonsky [see ibid., 14]) is hard to ascertain.

27. See I. A. Kuz'mina, "Materialy k biografii Feta," *Russkaia literatura* 1 (2003): 122–42.

28. For the complicated circumstances of Fet's birth and the story of his eventual discovery of his true parentage, see G. P. Blok, *Letopis' zhizni A. A. Feta*, in *A. A. Fet: Traditsii i problemy izucheniia; Sbornik nauchnykh trudov*, ed. Nikolai Nikolaevich Skatov (Kursk: KGPI, 1985); the publication is available online at http://www.afanasiyfet.org.ru/lib/ar/author/132; Bukhshtab, *A. A. Fet*, 5–9; Kuz'mina, "Materialy k biografii Feta." Fet chose the variant spelling (or accepted a typesetter's misspelling) of his surname when he first began publishing.

29. See Blok, *Letopis'*; Bukhshtab, *A. A. Fet*, 35.

30. Bukhshtab, *A. A. Fet*, 41–42.

31. Blok, *Letopis'*.

32. Quoted in Bukhshtab, *A. A. Fet*, 50.

33. While marking literary jubilees by awarding high ranks was a novelty, one should remember that Maikov served all his life and at the time of the jubilee was in the rank of actual state councilor (fourth class).

34. Quoted in Bukhshtab, *A. A. Fet*, 55.

35. P. A. Kozlov, "Na A. A. Feta," in *Russkaia epigramma (XVIII–nachalo XX veka)*, ed. Iu. A. Andreev (Leningrad: Sovetskii pisatel', 1988), 454. In Russian, "key" and "clue" are homonyms. The key was part of the *kammerherr*'s uniform. It could also be a hint at K. R.'s secret homosexuality.

36. Blok, *Letopis'*; Bukhshtab, *A. A. Fet*, 57–58.

Index

Publications of the Wisconsin Center for Pushkin Studies

Realizing Metaphors: Alexander Pushkin and the Life of the Poet
David M. Bethea

The Pushkin Handbook
Edited by David M. Bethea

The Uncensored "Boris Godunov": The Case for Pushkin's Original "Comedy," with Annotated Text and Translation
Chester Dunning with Caryl Emerson, Sergei Fomichev, Lidiia Lotman, and Antony Wood

Alexander Pushkin's "Little Tragedies": The Poetics of Brevity
Edited by Svetlana Evdokimova

Taboo Pushkin: Topics, Texts, Interpretations
Edited by Alyssa Dinega Gillespie

Pushkin's Tatiana
Olga Hasty

Derzhavin: A Biography
Vladislav Khodasevich; Translated and with an introduction by Angela Brintlinger

The Poetics of Impudence and Intimacy in the Age of Pushkin
Joe Peschio

The Imperial Sublime: A Russian Poetics of Empire
Harsha Ram

How Russia Learned to Write: Literature and the Imperial Table of Ranks
Irina Reyfman

Challenging the Bard: Dostoevsky and Pushkin, a Study of Literary Relationship
Gary Rosenshield

Pushkin and the Genres of Madness: The Masterpieces of 1833
Gary Rosenshield

Pushkin's Rhyming: A Comparative Study
J. Thomas Shaw

A Commentary to Pushkin's Lyric Poetry, 1826–1836
Michael Wachtel